school-community relations
a new approach

ADMINISTRATION IN EDUCATION
HARLAN HAGMAN *Consulting Editor*

school-
community
relations
a new approach

Merle R. Sumption
University of Illinois

Yvonne Engstrom
Consultant in Public Relations

McGraw-Hill Book Company

New York   St. Louis   San Francisco
Toronto   London   Sydney

School-Community Relations: A New Approach

62288

34567890   MP   73210698

The nature of the community largely determines what goes on in the school. Therefore to attempt to divorce the school from the community is to engage in unrealistic thinking, which might lead to policies that could wreak havoc with the school and the lives of children. The community and the school are inseparable.

James B. Conant

preface

This book presents a view of school-community relations which is based on the concept of the changing school in the changing community. The authors take the position that the modern American community is in a continuous state of emergence. It is driven by the forces of social and economic change and either in some measure recognizes, adapts to, and utilizes these changes or is submerged by them. The school will in a large measure help to determine which course the community will take. A school unaware of the elements of change among the people it should serve fails in its basic responsibility. A school unresponsive to changing educational needs fails in its unique function.

John Stuart Mill said,

> Great economic and social forces flow like a tide over half-conscious people. The wise are those who foresee the coming event and seek to shape their institutions and mold the thinking of the people in accordance with the most constructive change. The unwise are those who add nothing constructive to the process, either because of ignorance on the one hand or ignorant opposition on the other.

The role of the school in the American community is vital and challenging. If it is to exercise intellectual leadership, if it is to recognize and provide for educational needs, it must develop and maintain a close relationship with the community. This relationship must not be a superficial one, but rather a deep and meaningful one. It must not be occasional or temporary, but continuous and lasting.

In order to develop and maintain a desirable and adequate relationship between school and community, four essential principles must be operative. They are, first, a *recognition of the school as a public enterprise.* The school belongs to the public, is supported by the public, and is responsible to the public. No school is a law unto itself. It exists to serve the public. In the best sense of the word, a school is an enterprise. Webster's Third New International Dictionary defines an enterprise as "a project which involves activity, courage, energy; a bold, arduous or hazardous attempt; an important venture." [1] Such a concept of the school permits no resting on the laurels of the past. It insists on looking to the future. Ever-changing educational needs are a challenge to which the school should respond actively, boldly, and courageously. The spirit of adventure, ambition, and achievement characterizes such a school. It is not only aware of educational needs; it anticipates them. It is not only responsive to educational needs; it exploits them.

Second, that truth, in the pragmatic sense, is the only valid and legitimate guide to action among free men and that *the public school in the United States has the unique function and moral responsibility to seek out truth, whatever or wherever it may be, and teach people to live by it.* Our democratic society requires this and provides the framework and the safeguards within which this may be done. It is essential that the public school accept this responsibility from kindergarten to graduate school in all the areas of learning. For the school to fail to do so would be to

---

[1] By permission. From Webster's Third New International Dictionary, copyright 1966 by G. & C. Merriam Company, Publishers of the Merriam-Webster Dictionaries.

fail in its essential purpose of maintaining and developing our free society.

Third, *there must be a structured, systematic, and active participation on the part of the people of the community in the educational planning, policy making, problem solving, and evaluation of the school.* A lay board of education, typical of the American school system, is not enough. The knowledgeable participation of hundreds of people is required if the school is to make adequate use of the talents and abilities of those it serves. Only through the studied, thoughtful, and informed participation of the community can the school achieve its full potential as a social institution and an integral part of the community.

Fourth, there must be *a clear and effective two-way system of communication between school and community.* Communication which limits itself to telling the people about the school is doing only one-half the job. Equally important is telling the school about the people who support it and are served by it. It is important that the community knows what the school is doing, but it is equally important that the school knows what the people are doing. In brief, the community should know its school, and the school should know its community.

It is the firm belief of the authors that when the school is fully recognized as a public enterprise, and when it continuously seeks for truth, enjoys widespread community participation, and maintains clear two-way communication with the people it serves, it will inevitably be sensitive to change. This sensitivity is the essential element of the school which effectively meets the challenge presented to a social institution in an age of controversy.

Merle R. Sumption
Yvonne Engstrom

contents

the public school in the modern community

1

The dramatic changes which have taken place in the role of the school in modern American society call for a new concept of the relation of the school to the community it serves.

The expanded role of the school is apparent in broader curricula which include driver training, space science, and electronics as well as many other subjects. Furthermore, the clientele of the school has been vastly increased by the inclusion in the public school system of nursery schools, kindergartens, community colleges, and adult education programs. Education, particularly education in the sciences, has in the past decade become a national concern with direct implications for national defense, even for national survival. Finally, the increased costs which characterize expanding educational programs serve to generate a real concern and widespread interest in the educational process and its results.

These factors have encouraged not only greater interest in the schools but also increased participation by lay people in determining the purposes of the school, developing school policies, evaluating school buildings, and engaging in general educational planning. The popularity of citizens advisory committees, citizens educational councils, and similar groups is ample evidence of the fact.

In view of these developments, the educational venture is no longer a "closed corporation" run by the professionals. The public is becoming increasingly aware of its stake in education and is insisting on a more complete knowledge of the enterprise which so directly affects it. This awakening of public interest and the recognition of ownership by the public can become a valuable asset to professional educators and to education itself. However, it can be of greatest value if it is understood and utilized instead of misunderstood and mistrusted by the professional administrator. The traditional public relations program of the school consisting, as it does, of "telling and selling" the community on education is outmoded. The lay people of the community are becoming interested participants in the educational enterprise and are becoming cognizant of the important role which they can and should play in modern education.

These developments call for a new and more vital concept of school-community relations. The authors in this book present a concept of school-community relations which not only takes into account the marked changes which have asserted themselves in the community as well as in education, but actually utilizes these changes in the interest of better education.

The concept, in brief, is that of shared ownership of the educational enterprise. It regards each individual in the school community as a part owner of an educational venture. He is a shareholder by virtue of the fact that he pays taxes to support education in his community. He receives dividends directly in the form of education for himself and his children and indirectly in local, state, and national benefits. His community is a better place to live because of the school. The state and nation benefit by the advances in science, medicine, industry, art, and culture to which the school contributes.

The parallel with a publicly owned industrial corporation is striking. Both the school system and the corporation are striving to produce the best possible product. In the case of the school it is a better-qualified graduate; in the case of the corporation, a better automobile, refrigerator, or breakfast food. Granted the product of the school is of greater value, the goal toward which each directs its efforts is the same, a superior product.

Both the public school system and the public corporation function within a legal framework established by legislation. The school system has a board of education or similar group whose function is quite comparable with that of the board of directors of a corporation. The administrative head of a school system closely parallels the president of a corporation in his duties.

The typical public corporation, while its offices and plants may be located in one community, turns out a product which serves not only the community in which it is located but the state, the nation, and even the world at large. For example, General Electric products are found not only in the United States but throughout the world. Similarly the products of the local school, its graduates, in many cases go far beyond the confines of the community to serve the state, nation, and world.

The board of education is responsible to the people as is the board of directors to its shareholders. The superintendent is responsible to the board of education in much the same way as a corporation president is responsible to his board of directors. Both the school system and the corporation employ many types of workers. In the case of the school, the employees include teachers, typists, engineers, and maintenance workers. In the case of the corporation, employees may be lathe operators, chemists, salesmen, and computer operators. The problems of personnel are much the same. Employment practices, morale problems, employee efficiency, and remuneration plans are quite comparable.

In any expansion of program or physical facilities, the school usually must go to the community to obtain the financial support necessary. It is a most common practice for the corporation to go to its shareowners for expansion funds through a new issue of stock or debenture or other type of bonds. In both cases the shareowner must be convinced of the soundness of the enterprise and the need for, and value of, the expansion before he gives it his financial support.

The broader communities, the state and the nation, are also shareholders in the community enterprise. They "but into" the corporation by extending financial aid. They, in effect, are minority stockholders who leave the decisions of school operation largely up to the local stockholders as long as those decisions are consistent with state and national policy. Thus the business executive in Cleveland, the factory worker in Akron, and the doctor in Cincinnati all have a financial stake in as well as a valid concern regarding what is happening in the schools of Columbus and Shadesville, Ohio. The lawyer in San Francisco, the housewife in Chicago, and the farmer in Kansas not only have an interest in the school system of Jackson, Mississippi; they, by virtue of Federal aid, are stock-holders.

In this and other situations, the "image" which the school or corporation presents to its shareowners is of paramount importance. Good public relations, policies, and programs are essential in both cases.

The analogy is, of course, not perfect. There are major differences between a school system and a corporation, not the least of which is that school systems count their profits not in dollars and cents, but rather in the development of human resources.

Nevertheless, a basic similarity exists which is sufficient to warrant an approach to school-community relations which takes cognizance of the corporation concept of public relations and adopts those of its practices which seem appropriate and desirable. Such an approach provides many innovations for the typical school and is based on the firm foundation of public ownership of public schools.

Such a concept further emphasizes the educational principle that the school should be an integral part of the community it serves. The functions it performs are closely related to the functions of other community agencies, and a coordinated program of services benefits the total community.

The shareowners in the school are also shareowners in the public library, parks, and museum, and many of them own shares in business corporations located in the community. There is a common interest which, if developed, should bring the school into closer alignment with the rest of the community.

The old concept of the school as a thing apart, transmitting the culture but standing aloof from the local community is no longer valid if indeed it ever was, even in colonial days. Even the concept of the school as an agency to combat "Satan, the Old Deluder" is rooted to some extent in the welfare of the community as well as in the welfare of the pupil's soul.

The proposal espoused by some educators that the goals and standards of the public schools of the nation be established by a committee of eminent scholars is foreign to the democratic traditions of the country. It is contrary to the trend toward greater lay participation in the educational enterprise. It tends to remove the school farther from the community and obscure its identification with the people it serves. Finally, no committee of scholars or any other group can formulate a common set of goals and standards which reflect all the educational needs of all the communities in the nation or even the state.

the modern community

The public school is an integral part of almost every community in the United States. It has a unique function to perform, but one which is closely allied to the activities of all the community. If the school is to serve most effectively, it must be conscious of the social and economic developments which are taking place in the community and which in many instances are but reflections of state and national trends.

There is certainly strong evidence that modern communication and transportation have tended to make communities more and more alike in many ways. Nationwide television networks, for example, contribute significantly to this trend. Automobiles, airplanes, and streamlined trains combined with superhighways, giant airports, and high-speed rail trackage have made travel more extensive. These combined with widespread diversified occupational opportunities have made mobility a characteristic of our population.

However, there are at least six factors which are operative in making communities differ one from the other. They are (1) tradition and nationality background, (2) sets of values which the community holds, (3) economic bases, (4) geographic features, (5) social structure, and (6) political structure. It would indeed be difficult to find two communities in which all six factors were identical.

In brief, although communities share many characteristics, they also have many distinct differences. Influences of history and tradition are plainly visible as one moves from New England through the Dutch settlements of Pennsylvania and on through the Deep South to the California coast. The different values which communities hold are scarcely less evident on such a trip. Geography and the availability of natural resources often dictate the economic development of a community, and these differ widely. Last, but not least, the nature and organization of human resources differ greatly and have far-reaching influence on the community and its development.

As a result of huge building developments, new communities spring up within a very short period of time. Almost overnight small neighborhoods become populous communities. The location of a new industrial complex often changes not only the size but the nature of a community. The location of a new superhighway may change the whole course of development in a community. On the other hand, communities sometimes face dissolution when their economic bases are adversely affected.

The concept of the modern community suggested here is that of a constantly emerging social entity of which the school is a key institution. Its relationship to the state, the nation, and society as a whole will be discussed in a later section of this chapter.

Characteristics of the modern community

Some of the characteristics of the modern community which are of considerable significance to the concept of school-community relations presented here are briefly discussed in this section.

A community is changing. In today's complex world, change is in many cases swift, in others slow, but in all inevitable. Because of the extreme mobility of population, there are some communities in which fewer than fifty percent of the residents have lived in the community ten years or more. New technologies may cause severe unemployment problems in one community and produce a wealth of job opportunities in another. The exhaustion of natural resources may change a thriving community into a ghost town. The establishment of a military or space installation may change a sedate village into a booming community. No observant person who has lived in the United States during the last decade can be unaware of the vast panorama of change which has blanketed the nation. Science alone has contributed immeasurably to change in both individual and community life. The social agency which would live up to its responsibilities in the modern community must change also if it is to keep pace with those it serves. The public school is no exception.

A community is diverse. People of a community have a wide variety of interests, hold many different kinds of jobs, subscribe to varied political views, embrace radically different religious beliefs, represent diverse racial and nationality backgrounds, and have conflicting views of what the schools should be doing. Different standards of social behavior produce serious conflicts. Differing goals produce clashing lines of action. The varying roles which people play in community life often lead to conflict. The larger the community, the greater the diversity is likely to be. The school must serve all the people no matter how diverse their interests may be.

A community is structured. A close study of any community will reveal a series of structures which characterize community life. There is the economic structure upon which the inhabitants depend for a livelihood. There is the social structure which regulates to some extent the social life of the community. There is the political structure which to a large degree dictates the government of the community. Behind the scenes is the power structure which may make the major decisions affecting community development. Only the naïve would believe that any or all of these structures and the many others in a community operate for the public good at all times. It is imperative that the school know these structures for what they are, know how they operate and how to work with them selectively in promoting the educational welfare of the community.

A community is organized. The existence of many organizations in a community is a characteristic of a democratic society. Our type of government not only permits but encourages the formation of organizations to promote common interests and achieve desired ends. Many associations are created by ethnic groups striving for recognition or better understanding of their problems. Other organizations promote the interests of professional or other types of occupational groups. Teachers, lawyers, doctors, architects, bricklayers, ironworkers, and longshoremen all have their associations or unions. Others are interested in tax reduction, wildlife conservation, better government, and similar objectives.

In our modern society the traditional groupings of family, church, and local government are no longer sufficient to meet expanded needs. The association, society, club, or union are devices to meet such needs. It is only natural that many of these organizations apply pressure to attain their objectives. In such cases they assume the role of pressure groups. Such groups bring pressure to bear on many different public agencies but principally upon government and public schools. This is predictable since these institutions are at the service of all the people. Other pressure groups, such as labor unions, direct their efforts toward private agencies also.

The community school cannot avoid dealing with such organizations even if it wishes to do so. They are an integral part of the democratic society and present a genuine challenge to the school. This challenge must be met objectively and constructively.

A community makes decisions. A community is consciously or unconsciously constantly making decisions which affect its future. Some of these decisions, such as whether or not bonds are to be issued to improve streets, are widely publicized. Others, such as whether or not slum areas are to be allowed to develop, go by default. Some community decisions are based on facts; others on fiction. The community as a whole is unaware of many decisions which affect it. This may be due to lack of interest or lack of information.

The school itself is involved in many community decisions and has a definite responsibility in connection with most others. Finally, it will be affected by community decisions whether it affects them or not.

the school and the larger community

Every community in our country is part of a larger community, the state; and every state is a part of a still larger community, the nation. Carrying this concept to its logical conclusion, each nation is a part of the world community—a fact recognized in the creation of the United Nations as a world association. No community exists in isolation, although some in mountain valleys and caves may seem to do so. Every community lives within a framework of state and national government. Each community looks to the larger community for services and benefits. Each community in turn has obligations and responsibilities in its relationship with the larger community.

The term "community" in the local sense is used here in its broad context with full recognition of its close interrelationship with the larger community of which it is a part. The implications of this concept for the school are quite significant. It places certain responsibilities and duties, as well as limitations, on the community school. It denies the proposition that the school exists solely for, and serves only, the local community. The fact that the local community is an integral part of the larger community obligates the school to look, plan, and work beyond local horizons. The needs of the nation and the obligations of the state are part and parcel of community life. Perhaps nowhere is this better illustrated than in our tax structure. By far the greater proportion of the taxes levied in the local community are state and national levies.

To serve well, the school must help the community to contribute its full share to the larger community of which it is a part. It may in some cases be in the position of pointing out to the community the nature, extent, and rationale of its obligations to the larger community. This is in itself a responsibility of the school. In serving the community, the school may find itself in direct opposition to a major segment of the community. For example, its responsibility is to uphold the democratic traditions of the larger community even when they conflict with those of the local community. The worth of the individual irrespective of race, religion, or socioeconomic status, equal opportunity, and equal rights are tenets of American democracy which the school is morally obligated to uphold no matter in what community it is located. This does not mean that the school is against the community, but rather that it recognizes the social responsibility of the community in its larger context. It is in reality serving the local community in the best sense of the word.

It is fair to say in conclusion that the school which serves its community best is the school which best serves its state and nation. The welfare of all three is inextricably woven together in the fabric of our democratic society. The community exists only as a part of the nation, and the nation only as an aggregate of thousands of communities bound together by common ties of democratic ideals that are formulated into government.

additional reading

American Association of School Administrators: "Educational Administration in a Changing Community," pp. 35–68, in *Thirty-seventh Yearbook*, National Education Association, Washington, D.C., 1959.

Bernard, Jessie: *American Community Behavior*, Holt, Rinehart and Winston, Inc., New York, 1952.

Graham, Grace: *The Public School in the American Community*, Harper & Row, Publishers, Incorporated, New York, 1963.

Kinneman, John: *The Community in American Society*, Appleton-Century-Crofts, Inc., New York, 1947.

Melby, Ernest: *Administering Community Education*, pp. 36–57, Prentice-Hall, Inc., Englewood Cliffs, N.J., 1955.

Olsen, Edward: *School and Community*, Prentice-Hall, Inc., Englewood Cliffs, N.J., 1954.

Pierce, Truman, Edward Merrill, Jr., Craig Wilson, and Ralph Kimbrough: *Community Leadership for Public Education*, pp. 3–38, Prentice-Hall, Inc., Englewood Cliffs, N.J., 1955.

Stearns, Harry: *Community Relations and the Public Schools*, pp. 1–14, 343–354, Prentice-Hall, Inc., Englewood Cliffs, N.J., 1955.

the school
and the
community
power structure

2 Much has been written in recent years about the power structure. Various definitions have been presented. The common element in all of them is the goal ascribed to the power structure, namely, decision making. In the broadest sense, every institution and every organization has a power structure as a necessity for operation. If an institution or organization is to function, there must be decisions made. Those who make these decisions form the power structure. As long as the power structure is formed and operated as a recognized, official group selected by and accountable to organization members or those whom it serves, one can have no quarrel with it. When the power structure is identical with the duly constituted authority structure, we have representative democracy.

In almost every facet of our society we find some elements of power structure. The family, for example, usually has a rudimentary power structure. Church congregations, university faculties, farm organizations, labor unions, associations of commerce all have power structures of one order or another. In some cases the power structure coincides with the authority structure; in some cases they overlap; and in others they are almost completely separate and discrete.

It is the community power structure, however, with which we are primarily concerned. Sociologists have recognized for many years the powerful influence exercised by a small and atypical proportion of the citizenry of a community who have only an incidental relationship with the official government structure of the community. These persons form in some communities an "invisible government" which is accountable to no one except its leaders. A number of social scientists such as Lynd,[1] Hunter,[2] and Dahl [3] have sought to probe behind the formal governmental structure to determine the nature of the shadowy alignment which wields power without social responsibility. In such a context the term "power structure" by definition is iniquitous and constitutes a serious threat to representative democracy. If this concept of the community power structure is adopted, it then may be defined as an *interrelationship of vested interests exercising power without social responsibility*. It may be highly organized, embracing a hierarchy of power levels, or it may be operating quite simply on a single level. It may be monolithic in nature as conceived by Hunter or pluralistic in nature as described by Dahl. It may be more shadow than substance, or it may be practically omnipotent in the community.

Whatever its organization, extent, and power, it is this concept of power structure with which we are concerned. The significance of the power structure as here defined for the school system is difficult to overestimate. In some instances its impingement on the school may be slight but invidious; in others, overwhelming and disastrous.

A public enterprise of such broad extent and so all-inclusive as the school is bound to be of concern at some time or place to the community power structure. Decisions which are vital to the school are quite frequently of considerable concern to the power structure. Such decisions as the selection or dismissal of a superintendent, the location of a new

[1] Robert S. Lynd, "Power in American Society as Resource and Problem," in Arthur Kornhauser (ed.), *Problems of Power in American Democracy*, Wayne State University Press, Detroit, Mich., 1956.

[2] Floyd Hunter, *Community Power Structure: A Study of Decision Makers*, University of North Carolina Press, Chapel Hill, N.C., 1954.

[3] Robert Dahl, *Who Governs?*, Yale University Press, New Haven, Conn., 1961.

school, the business firm from which school supplies are to be purchased, or the issuance of school bonds often are of primary concern to the community power structure. These and many other decisions which have considerable significance for the school involve money, status, or prestige and consequently invite the attention of the power structure. It follows, therefore, that any insightful treatment of school-community relations must include an analysis of the nature and characteristics of the power structure and some guides for coping with it.

nature and characteristics of the power structure

The nature of the community power structure as defined earlier in the chapter varies widely from one community to another. However, it has many common characteristics which help to identify it in small hamlets and in huge cities.

A major characteristic, as evidenced by the name, is power and the wielding of that power for selfish ends. Power is usually of an economic, political, or social nature, although, in some cases it is actually physical in form. The influence of money on human behavior is a familiar story. The man or woman who marries for money, the bank clerk who embezzles, and the business man who compromises himself to secure additional capital to ensure the survival of his company are examples of this phenomenon. Society is replete with examples of individuals sacrificing love, friendship, respect, and personal integrity to achieve social status and prestige. Criminal elements as represented by syndicates and the Cosa Nostra type of organization do not hesitate to use physical force and even impose death sentences in the exercise of power.

The community power structure wields its power largely in attempting to influence the community to make decisions that coincide with its own selfish ends. This is the area with which we are primarily concerned. However, it should be noted that power policies may be directed at individuals to ensure that they do not interfere with power structure operations or to wreak vengeance on them if they have. The net result sought is to preserve and enhance the power structure so that it may be more influential in decision making.

Another common characteristic of the power structure is its secrecy. It prefers to operate behind the scenes. It shuns the light of publicity. This is understandable in view of its methods and objectives. Social scientists have encountered all kinds of obstacles in their attempts to observe the machinations of the power structure. In communities where the power structure is well entrenched, many decisions affecting the welfare of thousands of people are made by half a dozen men sitting around a table in a smoke-filled room or by one man of the Boss Crump type sitting behind his office desk with reports from his lieutenants spread out before him.

Although members of the community power structure are commonly more or less active in one or the other of the major political parties, their first allegiance is to the power structure. The political parties are used to whatever extent possible by the power structure. Political candidates and political platforms are of concern to the structure only as they impinge on decision making. It is common practice for the power structure to align itself with the party in power, not because of any political principles but rather because of the greater opportunities to influence decisions. It makes no difference which party is in office. The power structure is "above partisan politics." For example, in one Midwestern state the local community power structure forced its Republican representative to vote Democratic in organizing the state legislative body for its annual session. In another case a Democratic representative was forced by the power structure to vote against a bill he himself had introduced in the legislature without consulting the structure. Both political parties and politicians are to the power structure merely pawns in the game of power politics.

The power structure is impersonal. Whoever will or can be made to be helpful to it is used by it or even absorbed into it; whoever will not or cannot be used and stands in the way may be ruthlessly crushed. An individual's record of service to the community or contributions to the general welfare are of no consequence. If he thwarts the power structure, he can expect no special consideration because of his record, reputation, or good works.

Hidden persuaders

What are the weapons which the community power structure uses to force men to do its will? Ordinarily they are not weapons of violence such as guns, knives, and dynamite, although these weapons are sometimes employed when the structure falls into the hands of violent men. Crime syndicates and hoodlum organizations use them freely and with telling effect. Occasionally the criminal element is allied in an informal way with the community power structure. In such cases violence may be employed with the tacit approval of the structure, but seldom if ever are the "higher-ups" involved in any direct way.

Probably the principal weapon of the typical structure is the rewards offered for compliance. Often these rewards are financial, ordinarily not in cash but rather in opportunities to make money. Such opportunities are typically legitimate or at worst extralegal, although in some cases the avaricious are offered illegal opportunities. Positions in government and private industry as well as posts of honor and influence are also benefits well within the power of the structure to award.

Examples of the type of rewards which are sometimes preferred by the power structure include land options, stock options, shares in oil drilling operations or similar ventures, franchises, and advance information on public contracts, building sites, and freeway interchange locations. In the political arena various party assignments as well as political nominations are common rewards. Even more common is the political job, a sinecure, which permits the jobholder to draw on the public treasury and at the same time maintain his private source of income. In the social world the structure often is able to reward not only the man but also his wife with prestigious positions in society as well as open doors to exclusive clubs and private organizations.

If rewards are not sufficiently attractive or are spurned, the structure frequently resorts to punishment. Men who are not interested in the rewards which the structure may offer can often be brought into line by punishment or the threat of punishment. Such punishment is ordinarily not physical in nature but rather asserts itself in the form of social, political, or economic deprivation. An individual may be warned that failure to comply with the wishes of the power structure may deprive him of his chance to become the president of the Rotary Club or the Republican nominee for state attorney. A school principal may find that his chances to become superintendent will be largely determined on what stand he takes regarding the use of school buildings by certain community organizations. The local school superintendent may learn that his chances for reemployment are likely to be determined by his choice of a site for the new high school. An enterprising business man may learn that a much-needed renewal of his loan at the local bank will depend on his attitude toward a local issue which is of vital concern to the power structure.

Threats of a social, political, or economic nature are seldom made directly. They usually arrive circuitously and are clothed in the niceties of social convention. Occasionally they are so well hidden that the naïve individual does not recognize them as threats or, if he does, fails to take them seriously.

For example, a superintendent of schools in a Midwestern city with a population of over two hundred thousand learned to his surprise that his contract would not be renewed. He had maintained excellent professional relations with his board of education and felt his position was secure. Suggestions that he recommend the promotion of certain local teachers to administrative posts in the school system had been taken at face value—merely as suggestions. The source of these suggestions meant nothing to him since he was unaware of the power structure of the community and unacquainted with its emissaries. He labored under the delusion that his board of education would decide independently on his contract renewal. He was completely oblivious to the community power structure and how it worked, although he knew personally most of the people who composed it. He met and exchanged greetings with them at school functions, at church, and at meetings of community organizations. He was accepted socially by some of them in their homes and in their clubs. His wife joined their wives in promoting church bazaars and raising funds for the needy and poor of the community.

As a person the superintendent was well liked by his teaching staff and fellow administrators. He was reasonably well accepted by lay people in the community. His personal relations with members of the board of education during his three years of tenure covered by the contract had, with minor exceptions, been good. Although nothing had been said, he confidently expected a contract renewal with a substantial increase in salary. The announcement by the board that he would not be re-employed was, to put it mildly, an unpleasant surprise. The reason advanced by the board was simply, "for the good of the school system." It was emphasized that he was not being discharged. He had fulfilled his contract and would be given a good recommendation in case he sought a position elsewhere. No animosity was shown. It was simply the consensus of the majority of the board that a change of educational leadership was desirable. It was intimated that the superintendent did not "fit in" well with the community. The local teachers' organization and several community groups made feeble protests, but with the employment of a new superintendent who presumably "fitted in" with the community, these groups were faced with an accomplished fact and grumblingly accepted the situation. After all, nothing could be done since the local board of education had the legal power to act as it did. The motivation of some members might be questioned, but each had the right, conferred by the electorate, to vote as his interests dictated.

In this case, the power structure moved impersonally to remove from the scene a professional worker who was "uncooperative" and replace him with a man who would not only understand the significance of "suggestions" but would carry them out. The majority of board members evidently felt the rewards or punishments which the structure had at its disposal were decisive. It was easy to rationalize that perhaps a change would be beneficial.

In dealing with the population of the community in general, the chief weapon of the power structure is propaganda. Seldom, however, can such propaganda be traced directly to the structure. It is often disseminated by those whom the structure controls or by those who are vulnerable to its influence in particular areas of community life. In some cases the propaganda barrage represents only strong emphasis on the favorable aspects of an issue which is favored; in others, false propaganda is used. A favorite method used to defeat an issue is to circulate rumors which serve to create doubt, confusion, or even fear among the citizenry.

In some communities the structure is not above disseminating misinformation and even deliberate falsehoods. Not a few school administrators can trace the loss of bond issues for new buildings to false and misleading propaganda issuing indirectly from the power structure which opposed an increase in taxes.

Absence of social responsibility

Another major characteristic of the power structure and one which is most significant is its lack of social responsibility. It frequently, in effect, makes community decisions for which others must assume the responsibility. It may direct the course of major events in a community without assuming responsibility in a single instance. There is no accounting to the people who are vitally affected by structure decisions.

In the case of the representative authority structure, the citizens of the community have the power to recall or vote down an official whose acts are imprudent, unwise, or motivated by self-interest. Such is not the case when decisions of the power structure turn out badly for the community. Although those who are legally responsible in the case of a bad decision may be vulnerable, the structure itself is not. Its operations are such as to place it beyond the reach of the voters of the community.

The lack of social responsibility and legal accountability represents a severe indictment of the power structure of the community. The average citizen has little or no recourse against the unseen influence which operates behind the scenes. When representatives of the people are persuaded, threatened, or cajoled into making community decisions against their better judgment, they are corrupted and the community suffers untold loss. When through misinformation, false propaganda, rumors, and other forms of deceit the power structure engineers the defeat of a worthwhile community project, not only the community, the state, and the nation, but democracy itself is the loser.

The structure is free to go to extremes in deceit simply because no one can call it to account. Lack of accountability is not only a dominant characteristic of the structure; it is a prerequisite to its successful operation.

Maintenance of the status quo

Another noteworthy characteristic of the typical community power structure is its frequent opposition to public projects involving changes of any magnitude. Reorganization of governmental units and the revision of public programs are usually vigorously opposed. School district reorganization, plans for city manager types of municipal government, and proposals for enlarging civil service to cover greater numbers of public employees are almost uniformly vigorously opposed by the local power structure. Efforts to make public administrative offices appointive are opposed on the grounds that the power of selection is being taken from the people while the real reason is that political patronage opportunities will be lost.

The reason for the generally negative attitude of the power structure on such issues is obvious. It wishes to maintain the *status quo* since under existing conditions members of the power structure have a measure of control. Change might well deprive them of their power. Vested interests inherently are generally opposed to change, and the community power structure is no exception.

Bases of power

While the typical community power structure is based upon closely interwoven economic, political, and social factors, its emphasis varies from one community to another. In some communities where one or two industries dominate the economy, it is not uncommon for the power structure to be based largely on economic factors. In some Western states, dominant mining interests provide the economic basis for the power structure.

In some large cities where one or the other of the major political parties has built huge party machines and opened the floodgates of patronage, political factors are paramount in the operation of the power structure. Only in rare instances, usually in wealthy suburban communities, is the social factor the dominant one. Although almost always a factor, social considerations are secondary to economic and political factors in the vast majority of communities.

Goals of the power structure

From the discussion of the nature and characteristics of the community power structure one might get the impression that it perversely seeks to harm or destroy the community. Nothing could be further from the truth. The typical power structure wants the community to grow and prosper economically. The community is its arena of operation, and the more thriving the community, the more fertile the field of operations. It is not unusual for the power structure to use its influence with the state highway department to have a freeway routed past the community or to induce the general assembly to authorize the building of a state institution in or near the local community. In some cases the power structure will pave the way for an increase in school taxes or an expansion of the school plant. In fact, a number of communities owe their growth and prosperity to a highly organized and broadly effective community power structure.

Why then should anyone condemn the power structure? The answer is quite obvious. As defined earlier, the power structure exerts its influence for its own selfish ends; the welfare of the community is incidental. When the welfare of the people of the community coincides with that of the power structure on any issue, all is well and good. However, when their interests diverge, the welfare of the structure will be served. The power structure is of primary importance to its members; the community is secondary. The power structure will first of all preserve, promote, and perpetuate itself so that it may serve its members. Second, it will do the same for the community when such efforts do not conflict with its primary interest.

In this context it should be recognized that the power structure provides no advantages to society that cannot be provided by the authority structure. There is no benefit which the power structure can confer that is not obtainable through duly constituted government. On the other hand, there is much to be lost when improper, immoral, unethical, and even illegal practices enable the power structure to dictate the course of events in a community.

organization of the power structure

The organization of the community power structure is usually depicted as a pyramid whose base represents the lower echelons of the structure and whose apex is the one or several individuals who represent the ultimate in power. Another common and closely related depiction shows the power structure as a hierarchy of power cells with the greatest number at the lowest level and the number of cells decreasing as the levels are ascended until the highest level embraces only one power cell with one or several components. In both cases, power is exercised at various levels but decisions on major issues come from the top. Self-interest is the cement which binds the structure together, and reward and punishment are used to keep members in line as well as to influence those who are outside the structure.

Communication among the membership is usually informal but nevertheless clear and direct. Information, questions, concerns, requests, suggestions, proposals, and even tentative decisions flow upward. From the apex, flowing downward, come information, answers, affirmations, denials, rewards, punishments, orders, and final decisions. In some cases, minor decisions are made at lower levels of the structure with only the major issues reaching the top. Informal meetings are often held at restaurants, in private clubs, or in business offices. Decisions are usually made only after consultation with all top-level members and ordinarily a good many of those at lower levels. Only where the top-level members are firmly entrenched are decisions handed down without prior consultations with some members at the lower levels.

The design of the power structure organization varies from community to community. The size of the community, its economic basis, its political alignment, and its social life are all variables which affect organizational design. However, the basic organizational scheme is only modified by these factors, never revolutionized.

Social scientists are presently debating whether or not power structures are monolithic or pluralistic in form. Investigations in some communities have revealed a single power structure which takes cognizance of all issues and wields power as a single unit. In other communities sociologists have found that while membership is often interlocking, different groups make decisions in different issue areas. That is, the power structure is pluralistic in nature with, for example, one group making decisions on economic development and another on educational matters. In most cases, members of the power structure operate in several groups. This pluralistic design provides no way for the resolution of conflicting decisions among the several groups in the structure. For example, if the economic development group decides that, as an inducement to industry, no new taxes should be levied, and the group operating in the educational field decides a large school building program is to be supported, a conflict immediately arises. One possible inference is that the pressures thus created tend to push the pluralistic structure into the monolithic shape. Add to this the fact that the membership of the power structure is naturally ambitious and each member seizes every opportunity to gain stature and add to his power and we have the basis for a reasonable hypothesis that the pluralistic structure is a stage in the evolution of the power structure toward the monolithic design. Certainly administrative efficiency and general effectiveness would increase as the structure group became more closely knit.

Observations of power structures in newly established communities tend to confirm the above hypothesis. In the early years of the second half of the century, large developers engineered residential building programs which created communities almost overnight. The location of a huge industrial complex in a semirural area has in many instances radically changed community boundaries and in effect created new communities. In such communities it is only natural for various groups and individuals to vie for power and status. Leadership is untested, and the people in general are unfamiliar with those who would lead. The new community lacks stability and affords little opportunity for the development of a solid structure of influence or power. Membership of the formal governmental bodies is likely to be shifting. School board members, particularly, are replaced as rapidly as elections occur. Private and informal organizations of the community are in a state of constant flux as people try out one and then another. New industries bring new power figures to the community as well as new directions to the economy.

In such a sociological environment it is reasonable to assume that there will be a number of individuals who will align themselves with those of similar aspirations to form power cells or groups. It is only natural that the groups formed would have a primary interest in one or two issue areas with only a secondary interest in others. Furthermore, each group would tend to be limited in scope by the restrictions placed on influence at its command by an unstructured community with a largely unassimilated population.

Thus, we can visualize the newly established community in its early development as a sociological unit with only a rudimentary power structure consisting of several or many groups each operating independently in one or two or possibly three or four issue areas. As a result of tests of strength during the early developmental period, the number of issue areas for each group is likely to be reduced to a single one—the one in which the group demonstrates superior power. In the process, weaker groups will consolidate with the stronger ones until a typical pluralistic structure develops with most, if not all, issue areas represented by power structures of their own with varying degrees of power.

Then as the community began to gain maturity, as indicated previously, pressures would tend to develop to force the power structure into a single unit. The necessity for resolution of conflict between issue area groups, the greater power and hence effectiveness of a combination of groups, the administrative efficiency of a single operating unit, and the personal and group ambitions of the membership are all persuasive factors. As time elapses, it seems likely that the number of power groups would tend to decrease until complete consolidation is accomplished and one or several individuals attain the apex position in a single unit of power which includes a number of lower levels of operation. The stabilization which the community achieves over the years would thus be reflected in the nature of the power structure.

In brief, in new, growing, and developing communities and those with great population mobility, we might expect to find a rather rudimentary pluralistic structure of power. The second stage of development would be characterized by rather specialized power structures in each of a number of issue areas. The third stage of development would be found in the older, more stabilized communities where the power groups would tend to be fused into a single unit. How well integrated this unit would be would depend on a number of factors related to the community. Included in the factors affecting the extent of power concentration would be the balance or imbalance of the political parties, the presence or absence of large-scale organized crime, the strength or weakness of legitimate organizations such as associations of commerce and labor unions, and the diversity or lack of diversity in economic production.

A fourth and final stage completing the cycle of the life of the power structure would be its breakdown and subsequent fragmentation brought about by an aroused citizenry revolting against a blatantly corrupt situation. Such a "housecleaning" seldom comes until the invisible government has become so powerful that it is disdainful of the general population and overextends itself. Usually within a short period of time after the community uprising, the ranks of the power structure begin to re-form in independent groups and the cycle begins again. Characteristically, indignation tends to die down, and a more or less lethargic attitude is assumed by the community, allowing the cautious but insistent re-formation of the power structure.

In this respect, as well as others, the structure resembles a parasite which feeds upon the body politic of democracy. When one form is shattered, the structure reappears in another, attaching itself as firmly as before upon its host, the community.

Regardless of whether the preceding hypothesis proves correct, current research indicates that, while the power structure has a standard form of organization, it is subject to various modifications in different communities and at different times in the same community. In some communities only the most rudimentary power structure exists. Little influence is exerted on community decisions since most of the time and energy of the membership is devoted to internal development. In other communities the structure may be highly developed, complex in operation, and all-powerful in community affairs. In some of the larger communities or cities it is closely allied with the political machine of the party in power. It is not above establishing tenuous but effective relationships with the criminal elements in a community. Particularly is this true when those in the gambling, narcotics, prostitution, or "juice" loan rackets are themselves well organized. Deals between the community power structure and the crime syndicate are no doubt common but are seldom, if ever, exposed. They are tacit agreements never put in writing and often arrived at through the office of a third party who may be a political boss or patronage dispenser of the party machine in power.

It is not to be inferred, however, that all community power structures are at one time or another linked with organized crime. Many communities, particularly small ones, are relatively free of syndicated crime. However, conditions which are favorable for the development of an effective power structure are usually favorable for the entry of organized crime. Thus, it is natural for a link to exist between them. In some situations there is reason to believe that a cooperative power structure may be almost exclusively financed by some of the ill-gotten gains accruing to local racketeers. Other communities which are located within the sphere of influence of large city crime syndicates are sources of wealth to foreign vice lords who arrange, for a price, with the local power structure to operate in the community.

Who are the members of the power structure? There are no hard and fast rules for discovering them. They may or may not be public figures. They may or may not hold public office. They may be members of civic or professional organizations or they may not. They may be lawyers, doctors, businessmen, labor leaders, bankers, engineers, newspaper owners, or industrialists. They may represent almost any occupation or profession. They may have no profession at all.

Most of them, however, will be found in the upper regions of the socioeconomic scale. Many are quite wealthy, although they may not appear to be. Some powerful figures of considerable wealth live simply and make no display of their fortunes. Some, on the other hand, are ostentatious and seek to impress others with their wealth. All, or almost all, are for one reason or another keenly interested in public affairs and public figures. This is readily understandable in view of the objectives of the community power structure.

They are people driven by the desire for power or wealth or status or any combination of these. To put it another way, they are people who are afraid—afraid of being powerless or poor or without social status. They are people with leadership ability of one kind or another. They are, on the whole, considerably above average in intelligence, sometimes even approaching genius. They are given to rationalization and are often able to convince themselves that despite contrary facts, a selfish decision benefiting them will, in some distant future and in some unforeseen way, also benefit the community. They are persons who put personal interests above principle, political party, and public welfare. Their attitude is epitomized in the oft-repeated and callous slogan, "If you can't lick 'em, join 'em." No consideration is given to ethics, morality, or integrity—just unequivocal submission to power. In short, members of the power structure are power worshippers.

the school and the power structure

As has been pointed out earlier in this chapter, the interests, concerns, and actions of the community power structure wherever it exists even in rudimentary form will inevitably impinge upon the school and its operation. The school is, or should be, a vital public institution with far-reaching influence in the community. It will pose issues which are of deep concern to the power structure. It will affect the lives of many people in the course of the years. Its basic commitment to truth and to public service may at times place it in direct opposition to the power structure.

How can the school under its professional leadership cope with the power structure? Is it obliged to make deals with the structure to get its support for school issues? What is the role of educational leadership in dealing with the power structure? Is there justification for joining it? for disregarding it? for openly opposing it?

Whether he likes it or not, the school administrator cannot escape the implications of the power structure for the operation of the school and for the issues which arise in the school community.

Identifying the power structure

Perhaps as a first step in meeting the situation, the school administrator should examine the traditional concept of power in relation to his community. What is the evidence with regard to the basic assumptions of formal institutional government? Do those elected to public office hold actual power? Does the dominant power in public policy rest with institutional government? Are basic policy decisions made in formal meetings of legislative groups, boards, and agencies which are clothed with proper authority?

Most educators, even those who hold advanced academic degrees, believe without serious reservations that the primary source of power in public policy is institutional government, and thus the use of power is observable and controlled by free citizens. Accordingly, they readily accept the concept of formal interest groups such as teachers associations, labor unions, associations of commerce, veterans organizations, and many others which openly exert influence upon legislative bodies. Presumably the influence exerted is generated by facts presented to show that the policy action sought is not only beneficial to the interest group, but conducive to the public welfare also. The amount of influence which any formal group could exert would in a large measure be dependent on the justice of its cause as reflected in public opinion. Thus any interest group, to be successful in influencing public policy, would necessarily give as wide publicity as possible to its cause and the facts supporting it. Favorable public opinion is essential to success in reaching group goals; hence the wide use of communications media to present the interest group's cause to the public. Those organizations which are intensely active politically are known as pressure groups.

The astute educator must study his community carefully to determine whether or not this conceptualization of policy making is fully operative in his community. He must determine to what extent, if any, it acts as a facade behind which some, many, or most community decisions are made.

Once it is established that the formal institutional concept of power breaks down at one or more places, it behooves the educator to look behind the scenes. Why does it break down? Who is benefited? How? The answers to these and other questions may suggest the outlines of a community power structure. Further explorations may reveal key figures who can be identified with the power structure.

Therefore, as a corollary to or perhaps as an aspect of knowing the community, the educator must identify the power structure if one exists. Furthermore, he must know in what areas it operates and roughly the extent of its influence in community decision making, particularly in making those decisions which affect the school. Such knowledge will not come easily. Discreet inquiries, casual conversations, study of past policy decisions, and, above all, careful observation are essential. The delineation of a community power structure is somewhat like solving a crossword puzzle; each step toward the solution makes the subsequent step easier.

The identification of key figures in the structure is likely to prove most difficult, particularly if there exists an alliance with crime. Sociologists have employed what is known as the reputational technique of identifying power figures. This, essentially, is asking well-informed persons who, in their opinion, are the most influential people in the community and in what areas they exert their influence. This method, however, will sometimes overlook the really influential figures who operate from relatively unknown power posts.

Another approach is to make a listing of proponents of successful issues and opponents of defeated ones. The consistent appearance of certain names on these lists over a period of years indicates they are influential people. A further examination of these lists to determine if a pattern of names exists as related to the various issues is also of value. For example, the names A, B, and C may appear consistently on the winning side of most if not all issues. Combined with them on educational issues might be D, E, and F, while on economic issues the pattern would be A, B, C, G, H, and J. Although this method is valuable, it is by no means infallible since some power figures never make public declarations. They speak through those they control. In fact, some of the most comprehensive and powerful structures have as their key figures men who themselves seldom take public positions on any issue. It is probably true that the more effective a power structure is, the more difficult it will be to identify those occupying the top levels.

To be able to cope with the power structure, the educational administrator must have his own house in order. He must be committed to a code of ethics which will ensure that he places the public welfare above personal interest. As an educational leader of the community, he should never forget that the school serves *all the people* and he is responsible to *all the people*.

In most states provision has been made to keep the schools fiscally independent and politically nonpartisan. It is essential that this be so if they are to seek the truth and teach people to live by it. It is a sacred trust for professional leadership and should never be taken lightly by the school administrator. Although compromise is almost a way of life in the field of administration, he cannot compromise on the principle of truth. It is the keystone of the educational structure. Once it is subverted the educational system can become the tool of power structures, pressure groups, propagandizers, economic interests, and ultimately, as history shows, of total dictatorship. The educator above all others must take a firm and unequivocal stand against any compromise of the major principle to which the school is dedicated.

If those who are responsible for educational leadership have clearly thought through their moral obligations to the profession of which they are a part, the people they serve, and the democracy in which they live, and if they have adopted a code of professional ethics *before* the community pressures besiege them, they will be in a much better position to discharge their responsibilities successfully. It will not only serve as a guide but also help to ensure a consistency in actions which will merit the confidence and respect of the public in general and the community leaders in particular.

The full disclosure policy

The school as a public enterprise should supply full information to the public. There is no place for secrecy, concealment, intrigue, or half-truths in the operation of the community school. Edward M. Tuttle, first executive secretary of the National School Boards Association, says, "When all the people have all the facts all the time concerning their schools, crises are anticipated and resolved before they occur." [4]

In the relationship of the school to the power structure of a community, there is no better shield against the pressures which may be imposed than a policy of full, free, and uncompromising publicity. A public relations program which makes it standard procedure to disclose the facts of school operation will, in many cases, forestall attempts by the power structure or other types of pressure groups to influence school decisions for selfish purposes. In fact, full disclosure and wide publicity in connection with school policies and programs are the best safeguards against any exertion of power or influence of a selfish nature on the school. Those who would use the school or its program for the advancement of their own ends usually shun publicity like the plague. Particularly is this true if questionable methods are being

[4] Edward M. Tuttle, *School Board Leadership in America*, p. 132, Interstate Printers and Publishers, Inc., Danville, Ill., 1963.

employed to influence decisions of the school board or professional administrators.

There is little if any basis upon which to criticize an open disclosure policy on the part of the public school. On the other hand, there is valid basis for condemnation of a policy which encourages secrecy and concealment in an educational institution supported by the public. The school administrator is on sound ground when he insists that the people are entitled to know all the facts all the time where the schools are concerned. The only exceptions are in the areas of personnel and, in some cases, the purchase of school sites.

Recognizing that full disclosure is his first line of defense against the community power structure which seeks to use the school for its own purposes, the wise superintendent will make every effort to see that there is clear and effective communication between the school and the community. It is only through such communication that rumors, half-truths, and even deliberate falsehoods may be combated and the facts made known to the people. The importance of a well-established two-way communication structure which will bring propaganda to the immediate attention of school authorities and permit a quick and effective response can hardly be overestimated. If a rumor can be scotched at its inception by a simple statement of the truth, it will die quickly and may even reflect unfavorably upon its originator. A barrage of propaganda may be rendered relatively ineffective by a clear, concise statement of the facts with unassailable documentation. Truth is the sword which goes hand in hand with the shield of full publicity. Quickly and effectively used, it cuts to the heart of false rumor and lays the fabrication wide open to public view.

The vital importance, in this context, of a well-established two-way communication structure serves to emphasize the value of the citizens advisory committee. Such a group provides an ideal means of communication between school and community and will ordinarily, if properly selected, carry sufficient prestige to ensure a fair hearing by people of the community. Statements emanating from the committee invariably will carry more weight than similar ones from professional educators who may be accused of prejudice or partiality. Nor should the fact be overlooked that committee members are much more likely to hear of rumors and propaganda about the school at their inception than are school officials. As a result, action may be taken early, an important factor for success.

The presence of an active, dedicated citizens advisory committee is in itself a deterrent to the ambitions of selfish pressure groups. This is true not only because of the communication factor but also because of the fact that fifteen or more citizens of the community have an intimate knowledge of the school and its operation. Any decision made by the board or the professional administrator would be subject to the scrutiny of a number of people who were knowledgeable about the school and in a position to raise questions regarding any policy decisions which were of a dubious nature.

School personnel and the power structure

In every community with a well-developed power structure, the educational administrator, particularly the superintendent and in some cases principals and supervisors, will at one time or another have direct contact with the power structure. Influential teachers, especially those who are leaders of professional groups, will often be approached. In small communities where the teacher is recognized as a person of considerable status, members of the teaching staff as well as the administrators may be the object of direct overtures. However, the vast majority of teachers and many administrators at the lower levels of administration will never be contacted personally since they do not possess the degree of influence or power which would make them of use to the power structure.

The original direct approach to school personnel usually has one or both of two objectives. They are (1) to secure aid in influencing decision making, and (2) to incorporate the individual in the power structure. More often it is the first objective, but occasionally a high level administrator is given the opportunity to align himself with those who wield extralegal power. Usually the benefits offered include a practical guarantee of tenure in a top-level position or promise of promotion. Additional advantages offered include promises of support for school bond issues, school tax increases, physical plant expansion, and similar school-initiated proposals which enhance the prestige of the administrator as well as improve and enlarge the school system. These are quite tempting to an ambitious superintendent, particularly if he is not fully aware of the obligations to the power structure which he will inevitably assume. It is easy for him to rationalize that he can be more effective as an administrator and secure greater benefits for the school if he joins the informal group of citizens who are powerful and influential. He may not readily recognize that favors conferred create obligations which may place him in a very difficult position later on. And once he has involved himself in a deal which reflects on his honesty or integrity, he is at the mercy of the structure. Disclosure would mean the loss of his position and quite possibly ruin his professional career. He becomes in a real sense a tool of the power group, and he must place his full trust in it. His only escape is to secure a job elsewhere, and then he may not be completely free if he can be of use to his old friends of the local power structure. If it is especially advantageous for the power structure that he remain, he may be forced by threats of exposure to spend the remainder of his professional life as a prisoner of his own indiscretion.

A case in point may be cited here. In a small Midwestern community the superintendent of schools, after an extensive courtship by the local power group, was persuaded to allow a private citizen to exercise the privilege of the school to purchase government surplus materials at a discount. This citizen subsequently reaped a large profit from a series of transactions. Seeing his mistake, the superintendent tried to move but was told that such action would result in exposure. He stayed until government officials closed in on the case. Although two board members resigned, the major portion of the blame was placed on the superintendent, and he was discharged and forced to stand trial for embezzlement even though he profited not one cent from the transactions. Those who had profited were legally untouchable although morally as guilty as the superintendent. Once he had approved the first small transaction, he was committed for the remainder of his professional life, which in this case was not long.

An invitation to join the power structure is seldom, if ever, in a form which is unfamiliar to the social world. It is often cloaked in an atmosphere of concern for the welfare and progress of the school. It may be proposed as a way to secure help in promoting a school bond issue or to obtain a desirable school site. An informal party, a steak fry, a gathering at the sportsmen's lodge or the country club may be the occasion for the first overtures. Often the superintendent is flattered to be invited, and if he is new in the community it represents a valuable opportunity to get acquainted. His first visit with power people may convince him that their interests are legitimate, as many of them are, and that he may enhance his own prestige by "going along" on some project or lending his support to a community political or economic proposal initiated or sponsored by the power group. He wants to be known as a "good fellow" rather than a retiring academician. He sometimes loses sight of the fact that as the educational leader of the school system he serves *all* the people and is responsible to all of them.

Once the administrator allows himself to become obligated in any way he is in a precarious position. The first deal may be innocent on the surface. The bargain, for example, may be the support of the power group for an expansion of school facilities in exchange for the administrator's endorsement of a community project which is being sponsored, usually indirectly, by the power structure. There may be no thought in the mind of the administrator that he is joining the group. Indeed, the structure may not want him as a member but rather as a useful tool which can be used as needed. If he is compliant, he may be retained indefinitely in that role and never allowed to achieve membership in the power circle. This is probably the typical situation with only the more aggressive and influential school administrator ever attaining full membership.

However, the superintendent who allows the structure to talk him into "deals," that is, exchanges of influence, may find himself in a worse position than if he had attained membership. As a tool he scarcely merits the protection of the power group and will be cast adrift once his usefulness is over.

One city superintendent a few years ago learned this fact to his sorrow. He had suspended the rules for promotion established by his personnel director and ratified by the board of education in order to promote a favorite of a power figure in return for support of a broad curriculum revision. The curriculum change was badly needed, and the superintendent thought the unorthodox promotion of one person was a small price to pay for a substantial improvement in the school system. The expected gain so far overshadowed the fact that a number of school personnel were better qualified for the position—and one had been strongly recommended for the promotion by the personnel director—that the superintendent felt justified in suspending the regular promotional procedure.

A few months later, when the superintendent faced discharge at a board hearing, the most damaging and perhaps the only legitimate charge against him was the violation of the procedures for promotion established by the board. The personnel director, a close friend, was his most damaging witness as he testified that the promotional policies had been suspended over his strong objections and solely on the superintendent's responsibility. The board dismissed the superintendent, a highly competent administrator and dedicated educator. One deal was enough to make him vulnerable, and the power structure was quick to seize the opportunity to toss him overboard. In fact, there was some evidence to the effect that the deal was a carefully laid trap for the specific purpose of providing grounds for the dismissal of the superintendent.

Regardless of whether this was or was not the case, the result was the same.

How can the professional educator best meet situations in which he is approached by the power structure in efforts to secure his influence or attract him to membership? The answer to such a question is not as easy as it may seem at first glance. The power group moves in devious ways; it often wears the cloak of respectability; it has attractive inducements to offer.

However, there are guidelines for his personal conduct which will stand the administrator in good stead in meeting this problem. Assuming that he is cognizant of the power structure in his community, that he is committed to a code of ethics which stresses his responsibility to his profession and to *all* the people as opposed to any single group, and that he accepts the concept of the school's unique responsibility to seek truth, he can avoid entangling alliances by observing several basic rules.

First, he will maintain a complete independence and freedom of action. This means he will make no deals and accept no favors which are predicated on a return in kind. To do this he need not isolate himself. He can, and should, be active in community affairs. He has the privilege of every citizen of supporting or opposing economic and political policies.

Second, he will judge each issue on its merits and act accordingly. Insofar as possible, he will avoid personalities and give battle only on the issues.

Third, he will never align himself with any group which is self-serving at the expense of the people he serves. His responsibility as an educational leader precludes such action.

Fourth, he will conduct himself in such a manner as to develop a reputation for fairness, consistency, and impartiality in his relations with all groups in the community. Even members of the power group respect a man who will not yield to influence from any quarter and, as long as he treats all groups alike, are more or less content to leave him alone most of the time.

Finally, he will recognize that losing his job is not as bad as losing his integrity. There are other and better positions for a man of integrity; the only position left for the man that loses his is a kneeling one. Fortunately, such a choice is not often faced by the knowledgeable administrator; but occasionally it is, and when it is, he should have the moral courage to place his personal and professional integrity above his desire to keep his job.

The position of the school in relation to the power structure

The school must maintain complete independence from the power structure or any other pressure group. It has an obligation to support true democratic government. The public school has the responsibility of serving all the people without fear or favoritism. Both lay and professional efforts are necessary to maintain the school as an independent institution, free to perform its essential function. Only through joint effort can this concept of the school be realized. One of the goals of the public school is to make democracy work. Boys and girls are taught the values of representative government as a part of our culture. The very freedoms which we cherish are dependent on representative government based on justice, fairness, and the rule of law. To ally itself in any way with a pseudo-government which subverts the essence of democracy is unthinkable on the part of the public school.

On the other hand, it must be recognized that the power structure is very likely to outlast any given administration in the school system. In other words while the school as an institution may well have a longer life than the power structure, the administration is at best short-lived in the overall picture. Members of the power structure likewise have their day and are replaced. Therefore, to view the problem in its total perspective is to recognize that the individuals concerned appear on the stage for only relatively short periods while the structure and the institution are long-range operations. This fact should dissuade the school administrator from launching a frontal attack upon a shadowy adversary, an action which would not only incur the wrath of the structure but also leave him little time to devote to the job of educational administration.

His basic task is to see that the school is effectively fulfilling its purpose. As he does this, he may find himself at odds with the power structure. It is at this point that as a responsible professional educator he must take his stand. The same can be said in the case of other pressure groups which operate more or less openly in attempts to influence the school. In every case his attitude should be a constructive one. His role is not that of an evangelist but an administrator. He must recognize that political forces will impinge on the school and he must deal with them, wisely and firmly it is to be hoped.

However, in so doing he must keep in mind the fundamental purpose of the school and his professional obligation to maintain its integrity.

This, in effect, means that there are some matters which are not negotiable and these should be clearly understood by all. They include scientific truth, the inalienable rights of the individual in a democratic society, the rule of law, and accepted moral and ethical standards such as truthfulness, honesty, justice, and equality. In fact, these constitute the solid foundation upon which not only good public relations but the total school operation should rest.

The maintenance of this foundation not only is the inherent responsibility of the school as a democratic institution, but is essential to community support and public confidence. Once this foundation is established, the school, like any other institution, is free to and must operate in the complex political arena of our society. Fortunately or unfortunately, depending on one's point of view, the school is seldom if ever called on to deal with the power structure officially or directly. As has been pointed out earlier, the structure by definition is unofficial and seldom uses a direct approach. Its emissaries ostensibly represent formal organizations in which they have membership. Thus, the school negotiates formally with the substance even though the shadow, powerful as it may be, takes its position in the background. Thus, on some occasions it may be a labor leader who, ostensibly in the cause of labor, urges a course of action on the school administrator; on others it may be the president of the association of commerce who advertently or inadvertently espouses the cause of the power structure.

In an important respect this situation is particularly advantageous for the school since it can negotiate openly on the merits of the issue and enlist public support for its position and thereby completely disregard the ulterior motives represented by the power structure designs. For example, if the power structure seeks to channel the growth of a city in a direction which would enhance the value of lands and building owned by its leaders, the structure will be vitally concerned with the location of new school buildings. A new school building is a significant inducement for the development of residential subdivisions which in turn increase land values. However, in such a case the school administration is free to go to the public on the merits of the issue. Even if a local PTA leader is the innocent spokesman for the power structure, the administration can make a free choice consistent with the best interests of the total school community as it sees them and support its position with the evidence. Thus if the administration is to do battle with the power structure, it will be openly and on the administration's own grounds.

Operation in the political milieu of our society requires compromise on the part of the school as well as other social institutions and organizations. For example, the matter of the amount of a proposed tax increase or plant expansion on the part of the school may have to be reduced in the light of other community demands on the taxpayers' purse. In some cases calls on the public treasury may have to be delayed so as not to conflict with similar requests from the sanitary district or fire and police departments. The school administration by reducing or deferring a financial request is not thereby admitting that it originally wanted too much too soon, but rather that it seeks to cooperate with other community institutions for the welfare of all.

The purchasing of school supplies, the awarding of building or transportation contracts, and the handling of school funds are matters which often are of concern to the power structure in both large and small communities. The awarding of a contract for textbooks or transportation of pupils involves hundreds of thousands of dollars in many school communities. Therefore, it is to be expected that many parties and interests will be concerned. The preferred practice of subjecting these awards to open public bidding does much to thwart unfair competition. No administration should let itself be talked into presenting specifications designed to give an advantage to one bidder over another. Rather specifications should be written in the best interests of the school and the award given to the lowest bidder on the basis of those specifications.

In short, a sound course for the school administration is one of a constructive offense in the interests of the school rather than of a static defense against pressure groups or individuals who represent the power structure.

In dealing with the power structure, the large metropolitan school districts present a vastly more complex problem than do the small communities. But the elements of power, the principles of operation, and the selfish greed of men are essentially the same in the sprawling metropolis and the country village; only the names are changed. In the large city complex face-to-face or word-of-mouth communication, while significant, is inadequate. Individuals assume, in general, less importance and organizations more. The diversity of social groups is usually greater. Often the range of economic well-being is greater, stretching from abject poverty to vast wealth. These factors and many others add to the complexity of the problem but in no way decrease the importance of establishing a foundation of public confidence, of maintaining clear and effective channels of communication, of involving, in the educational process, representatives of the public in an organized constructive fashion, and, finally, of openly working for the school's best interests on the basis of all the available evidence.

additional reading

Bloomberg, Werner, Jr., and others: *Suburban Power Structures and Public Education,* Syracuse University Press, Syracuse, N.Y., 1963.

Cahill, Robert, and Stephen Hencley (eds.): *The Politics of Education in the Local Community,* Interstate Printers and Publishers, Inc., Danville, Ill., 1964.

Dahl, Robert: *Who Governs?,* Yale University Press, New Haven, Conn., 1961.

Hunter, Floyd: *Community Power Structure,* University of North Carolina Press, Chapel Hill, N.C., 1953.

McCloskey, Gordon: *Education and Public Understanding,* pp. 78–82, Harper & Row, Publishers, Incorporated, New York, 1959.

Mills, C. Wright: *The Power Elite,* Oxford University Press, Fair Lawn, N.J., 1956.

the role
of the
community
in education

3 Thousands of "complexes of human relationships clustered around the basic concerns of life" dot the land from coast to coast. Each has its pattern of life. Some are rural, some urban. Some are dynamic and aggressive; others are placid and retiring. Some have a liberal viewpoint; others are highly conservative. However, all have one thing in common—the recognition of the school as an essential community institution.

If the school is accepted as an integral part of the community, then its policies are of direct concern to the community. However, the policies of the school are not solely the concern of the community. In fact, the basic concept of the American educational system is that education is a function of the state. Furthermore, under the welfare clause of our Federal Constitution the national government has a stake in the educational process. National security, to no little extent, depends on effective and adequate education. However, many of the responsibilities and much of the authority of the state with respect to education has been delegated to the local community.

In delegating responsibility and authority to the local community, the state sets up certain minimum standards and often prescribes definite requirements with regard to subject matter, teacher certification, length of school term, and pupil attendance. On the other hand, a great deal is left to the community. The provision of physical facilities, the choice of curricula beyond state requirements, the selection of teachers, and a large part of the financing of education are responsibilities of the community. The administration of the school system is the task of a policy-making group of local citizens, usually referred to as the board of education, and a professional administrator who executes board policies.

Under this arrangement it is incumbent upon the local community to establish educational goals, to make plans for achieving these goals, and to develop educational policies consistent with the plans and goals.

What is the role of the community in establishing goals and developing plans and policies for their achievement? What is the proper relationship between the community and the school in this task? Where does the responsibility of the community begin? Where does it end? What is its proper sphere of influence in relation to long-range planning for educational progress?

determining the goals of the school

The determination of the goals of the school is the proper function of the people. The people of the state through their legislative body usually set up certain general goals for all schools on a statewide basis. However, much latitude is left to the local community since communities have varying educational needs. Taking the statewide goals as a start, the local community establishes additional goals in the light of its particular educational needs and interests.

In many communities these goals are never written and are seldom stated orally except as they may arise in unrelated contexts. Educational goals exist nevertheless, although they are unformulated, unwritten, and unrecognized. Every person expects something of the school system, but most people could state these expectations only in the most vague, general ways. There is no consensus. The teaching staff may work toward goals with which the majority of the people may not be in accord. People differ in their expectations of the school. When there are no stated goals, everyone is free to criticize the schools, using his own vague and unformulated expectations as criteria. Is it any wonder that conflict is characteristic of our educational scene?

Often, the professional staff of a school system adopts the philosophy of education which, in effect, sets forth the aims of the school. The people whom the school serves are seldom consulted, and they may not even be aware that such a statement of goals exists. If they did know, they might disagree seriously. The professionally established goals may, in some cases, be merely for the purpose of window dressing. The goals may be glibly accepted and then forgotten, each teacher substituting the personal goals to which he subscribes, vague, unformulated, and unsystematic though they may be. It is not difficult to understand why educational conflict arises under such conditions. There are no commonly accepted or openly stated purposes of the schools. Each individual is free to criticize the schools in the light of his personal frame of reference regarding the responsibility of the schools.

In the most desirable type of situation, which unfortunately is quite rare, representative lay citizens join with the educational staff in developing and setting forth a commonly accepted list of goals which are then formally adopted by the board of education.

An example of such a tentative list developed through cooperative effort of lay and professional citizens appears below:

GOALS FOR THE ELGIN, ILLINOIS, SCHOOL SYSTEM [1]

SELF-REALIZATION

The purpose of the school is:

To encourage and assist in the development of a desire for knowledge and self-improvement;

To develop appreciation and respect for thought and knowledge;

To inspire respect for intellectual freedom and creative thought;

To develop the basic skills of reading, writing, mathematics, and speech as aids to the acquiring of knowledge for the purpose of self-expression and communication;

To develop individual initiative, good study habits, the ability to think clearly and reason objectively; to recognize honest differences of opinion; and to develop a sense of judgment and confidence in one's own abilities;

To develop the basic elements of character, such as integrity, truthfulness, kindliness, courage, tolerance, and gratitude;

[1] The Citizens Survey Committee, *A Survey of the Elgin Public Schools,* 1956.

To teach students to recognize and appreciate the physical self, its requirements, its protection against disease and accident, its limitations, and its
constant dependence upon the good health of others; to recognize and
learn to live with one's own mental and physical limitations so that a failure
of effort will not result in mental or physical distress sufficient to harm or
retard good mental or physical well-being;

To help students to understand basic scientific facts concerning the nature
of the universe and of men, the methods of science, and the gathering
of scientific information; to recognize the importance of these facts and
their influence upon human progress; to develop an interest in the promotion of science for the betterment of all;

To encourage and aid the development of purely personal interests which
afford mental and physical satisfaction such as an appreciation of the
arts, the intelligent use of one's own leisure time, and the enjoyment of,
and participation in, sports and hobbies;

To teach a recognition of, and an ability to adapt to, ever-changing
economic, social, political, and scientific conditions and patterns.

ECONOMIC EVALUATION AND REALIZATION

The purpose of the school is:

To furnish guidance and information so as to assist individuals in the selection of a suitable and desirable occupation;

To develop natural aptitudes and abilities along particular lines of economic
endeavor;

To provide all educational prerequisites necessary for educational experience;

To furnish certain basic courses in trades and commercial subjects;

To help students learn basic economic theories and principles and to recognize the interrelation of all economic endeavor;

To help students appreciate the economic importance of, and recognize
the need for, conservation of our natural resources including wildlife;

To develop consideration of one's personal economic demands, requirements,
and limitations, the need for economic planning, and the acquisition of
good saving, buying, and spending habits.

POLITICAL INTEGRATION

The purpose of the school is:

To teach respect for the laws and a general knowledge of how they are
made and enforced;

To impart an understanding of the basic principles underlying the developments of the American system of government and the basic rights and
privileges guaranteed by our Constitution;

To impart a general knowledge of the Constitution of the United States,
the Constitution of the State of Illinois, the doctrine of separation of
powers, the Australian ballot system, and the important documents in
our history;

To develop a clear understanding of the history of the United States, the reasons for its growth, and its position in the community of the world;

To impart a knowledge of various types of government and an ability to compare and evaluate their principal characteristics;

To develop a loyalty to, and appreciation for, democratic ideals and a determination to protect them, preserve them, and assume personal responsibility for them.

SOCIAL ATTITUDES

The purpose of the school is:

To develop a thoughtful consideration for the welfare of all members of a society; to recognize the equality of all people, the equality of rights and duties of all members of the community, and the right to benefit commensurate with one's contribution, whether individual initiative, capital, skill, or labor;

To develop a charitable attitude and a sense of obligation to aid in the correction of social inequalities and relieve human misery and want;

To develop personality for a full social life, the friendship of others, and the ability to cooperate with others at work and at play;

To help students learn and respect the rules of social behavior and common courtesy;

To develop a recognition of the family as a vitally necessary social institution, and to prepare the student to be a contributor to its welfare and to accept its responsibilities.

The establishment of the goals of the school is the responsibility of all the people. The professional staff can and should give effective leadership in their development, and the board of education, as legal representatives of the people, should facilitate their implementation by formal adoption. However, the goals of education, if they are to be genuine, meaningful, and effective, must arise out of a consensus of the people and be recognized by the public.

making school plans and policies

School plans may be defined as systematic outlines of the steps to be taken in achieving the goals of the school. Such plans are a necessity in the case of the school administration which seriously accepts responsibility for education. Without well-conceived plans for the future, the development of education in a community is at best a hit-or-miss affair. Wise long-range planning is essential to economical use of school funds and effective development of the educational program.

The policies of the school may be defined as general basic principles of operation, the purpose of which is to facilitate the achievement of the goals of the school through a uniform, orderly, consistent, and equitable plan. Policies are equivalent to legislation. They differ from rules or procedures which are formulas established to carry out policies. Rules and procedures, except those adopted by boards of education to govern and systematize their own activities, are the proper concern of the professional people who execute policies.

The responsibility for school plans and policies, like that for school goals, rests with the entire citizenry. However, the actual adoption of long-range plans and the enactment of school policies is focused in representative citizens, elected or appointed, who are designated members of boards of education. Boards of education are required by law to refer many decisions on policy to the citizens at large. This is generally true of bond issues which obligate the constituents of the district for considerable sums of money for buildings and sites. All citizens, of course, have the right to protest policies and to petition for their revision. Ultimately, the people can remove from office their representatives who adopt policies contrary to the public will.

School board members are state officials who serve at the pleasure of the citizens they represent. Boards of education are comparable to the state legislatures and the Congress of the United States. Their principal function, similar to the functions of these other bodies, is that of policy enactment. Like legislators, school board members seek, formally or informally, the advice of constituents on policy issues. Often advice is given them voluntarily, and in some cases pressures are applied. It behooves the public school official, as well as his counterpart in the other legislative bodies, to remember that he represents all the people, not merely one segment of them.

Both individuals and organized groups can and do influence planning and policy making. Newspapers play an important role in policy making through their editorial pages and through their selection and treatment of school news. In some communities formal citizens advisory committees are set up for the specific purpose of developing long-range plans and advising boards of education on policy matters. Citizens participate, at the request of school officials, in surveys and studies of school programs. These projects ordinarily result in recommendations to boards in the form of plans which are usually basic to policy formation. Professional educators also influence policy making. Among them are the outside experts or specialists who may be consulted in the planning of buildings or in curriculum revision, as well as the local superintendents and their staffs of teachers and supervisors.

To summarize, the responsibility for school plans and policies is ultimately the responsibility of the entire citizenry. Duly selected and representative groups of citizens, usually called school boards, have the responsibility of adopting plans and enacting school policies. In the formulation of policy, board members need the assistance and advice of those for whom the policies are enacted. Assurance that proposed school policies are educationally sound may be obtained by consulting with professional educators before adopting them. Administrators, teachers, and other members of the professional staff should not be excluded from the initiation of school policies. They are citizens in their own right as well as educators.

The function of school plans

The most effective school system, like the most effective business enterprise, must plan for the future. Wise planning permits the orderly and consistent development of the educational enterprise. It tends to mitigate the problems which are bound to arise. The demands on education change both in nature and number with the changes in the society it serves. In order to meet these demands adequately and efficiently, careful planning must be done. When the community joins with the school in developing these plans, they are likely to be better conceived and more effective than if they are solely the product of one or the other.

Long-range plans are usually concerned with the reconstruction and expansion of the curriculum, the development of the physical plant to accommodate increased enrollments, and the financing of improved programs.

The function of school policies

In general, school policies have a threefold function to perform.

First, to translate the goals of education into operational principles.

Second, to make available the ways and means by which these educational goals may be achieved.

Third, to provide for continuous appraisal of the progress being made by the school in achieving these goals.

Good school policies have common characteristics which are identified with sound educational procedure. Some of the characteristics of a good system of policies are listed:

1. Policies are stated as general principles which have wide application over long periods of time.

2. Policies are stated in such a way as to be readily interpreted and easily applied.

3. Policies permit a maximum freedom of action to those who are to interpret them and execute them.
4. Policies are consistent one with the other.
5. Policies are stated in such a way as to be understandable to lay citizens as well as to professional educators.
6. Policies are subject to regular review and revision in the light of changing conditions.

determining the program of the school

The purposes of the school and the plans and policies for achieving them are given substance in the program of the school. The school's program in its broadest sense consists of all the experiences and services the school provides for the people of the community. The courses of study offered represent a major part of the program of the school. However, the program of the modern school also involves such things as student activities, counseling, and the maintenance of personnel records and health services. Many schools include transportation, hot lunches, and recreational programs among their services.

The planning, development, and execution of the school program is a professional function and should be the responsibility of professional people. This does not mean that help from lay people need not be secured by teachers and administrators. In fact, such help should be solicited, but the responsibility rests with those who are specifically trained for the job.

The goals and policies of the school will, of course, determine the nature of its program. For example, if one of the goals of the school is to prepare pupils for college, the general nature of at least a part of the program is determined. If a policy of offering the opportunity for every pupil to be served a hot lunch at noon is adopted, a plan for food services must be developed and administered. The planning of the courses of study and the administration of the program of college preparation is a professional responsibility. A hot lunch program should be planned and supervised by the professional staff. Rules governing the sequence in which college preparatory courses are to be taken and the timing of lunch periods are likewise professional responsibilities connected with the administration of the school program. They serve the purpose of guiding and systematizing the action necessary to carry out policy and should not be confused with policy itself.

Sometimes there is confusion among purpose, policy, and program.

It is not always easy to establish a line of cleavage. The analogy of the man visiting his doctor may be helpful. Let us say his purpose is to achieve and maintain good health and physical efficiency. He may have adopted a policy of taking annual physical examinations. His physician may well have advised this policy as an effective one for achieving the man's purpose. However, in any case the decision as to purpose and policy rightfully belongs to the layman. The doctor determines and administers the program of treatment which may be indicated since this is a professional matter. The layman relies upon the judgment of the doctor because of his specific knowledge of medicine. The layman will evaluate the program of treatment in terms of his purpose and policy. He may even change physicians if the program of treatment is not yielding satisfactory results. In the educative process, it is the professional educator who prescribes and administers the "treatment" in the form of the school's program.

When there is confusion with regard to this distinction, conflict is inevitable. When lay groups, including boards of education, attempt to prescribe courses of study, handle student discipline, and assume direction of student activities, they are venturing into areas of responsibility for which they are untrained, and unprepared. Board domination in such areas is wholly inconsistent with effective education.

However, to say that the responsibility for school programs should not be assumed by laymen does not imply that laymen should have no influence upon program development. Quite the contrary is true. As pointed out in preceding sections, it is the lay people who, by their establishment of the goals and policies of the schools, largely determine the nature of their programs. Their power and their influence upon the schools through the determination of purposes and policies, their provisions for continuous evaluation of these purposes and policies, and their financial support of school programs give ample responsibility to lay people. Indeed, these legitimate functions present a formidable challenge to all who subscribe to the cause of public education.

organizing for community participation

The direct participation of informal but organized lay groups in the determination of the purposes, plans, and policies of public education in the United States has been increasing rapidly in the last decade. This trend toward broader citizen participation in the educational process is of major significance for professional as well as lay people. But if education is to realize the notable values of this broader base of participation, ways and means must be provided whereby citizen groups may work most effectively and make maximum contributions to the schools.

Broad citizen participation presents both an opportunity and a challenge to the professional educator. A new and skillful type of leadership is called for if the professional administrator is to grasp the opportunity presented by lay people ready and willing to work for the improvement of education in their local communities.

If the educational leader of the community regards the citizen participation movement as a fad which will pass in a few years and as such should simply be tolerated, his school community is not likely to benefit greatly by lay participation. In fact, severe repercussions may occur as a result of such an attitude. An independently organized group of citizens with little access to the facts and operating without professional advice may understandably work at cross-purposes with the board of education and the professional educators.

It will be readily recognized by the more able educational leaders that regardless of the attitude of the school toward lay participation in school affairs, certain decisions about the school will be made by the people of the community. For example, the people will determine whether or not bonds will be issued to build a new school building. They will decide whether or not to levy additional taxes to improve and expand the school program.

Informal and often uninformed community pressures will force decisions about program, teaching methods, equipment, and even personnel upon the school. Pressure groups may exert strong influence on the nature and scope of the school program. Severe imbalances of the curriculum may result from such influences.

The question is not, therefore, "Shall the community participate?" but rather "How can community participation contribute most constructively?"

Constructive community participation can best be achieved through organized effort. A structure for participation which is mutually acceptable to school and community is essential to effective participation. Such a structure is a bridge over which school and community travel in the exchange of ideas, information, needs, and aspirations. It is a two-way bridge with traffic moving smoothly in both directions. The bridge should be open to all and encourage even the most eccentric traveler to cross over to the other side.

It is only by such an organized approach to school-community relations that a school may expect to achieve the larger benefits of active lay participation. Such a structure goes a long way to dissipate the undue influence which pressure groups may bring upon the school. If an established systematic procedure for participation is in operation, there is less likelihood of pressure groups and vested interests intervening in the program of the school.

additional reading

Grinnell, J. E., and Raymond Young: *The School and the Community,* The Ronald Press Company, New York, 1955.

Hamlin, Herbert M.: *Citizen Committees in the Public Schools,* pp. 2–47, Interstate Printers and Publishers, Inc., Danville, Ill., 1952.

Hamlin, Herbert M.: *The Public and Its Education,* pp. 9–25, 67–93, 203–235, Interstate Printers and Publishers, Inc., Danville, Ill., 1955.

Hand, Harold: *Principles of Public Secondary Education,* pp. 114–139, Harcourt, Brace & World, Inc., New York, 1958.

Melby, Ernest: *Administering Community Education,* pp. 205–219, 223–311, Prentice-Hall, Inc., Englewood Cliffs, N.J., 1955.

Stearns, Harry: *Community Relations and the Public Schools,* pp. 101–265, Prentice-Hall, Inc., Englewood Cliffs, N.J., 1955.

Sumption, Merle: *How to Conduct a Citizens School Survey,* Prentice-Hall, Inc., Englewood Cliffs, N.J., 1952.

how the
community
participates

The decade of the 1950s witnessed a phenomenal growth in lay citizen participation in educational planning and policy development. It is the same decade which produced probably the most widespread and severe criticism of public education that we have seen in the history of our public schools. A cause and effect relationship between the two seems a logical surmise. To a certain extent such a surmise is probably valid. However, it would be a serious error for the professional educator to assume that dissatisfaction is the only factor involved.

At least two other causal factors are present in the situation. First, the past decade, as the one before it, has seen the public schools given increasing responsibility as our pattern of living has become more and more complex. The universality of the use of the automobile has made driver training a common program in the public high schools of the country. A decade ago it was practically unknown in American secondary schools. New media of communication have presented new opportunities and new responsibilities. Changing economic patterns have challenged the school to adjust its program to meet changing needs.

Higher educational costs have inevitably followed expanded programs and most of the other steps taken by the school to meet the responsibilities thrust upon it. The hard economic law of supply and demand has raised the level of teacher salaries. Finally, the inflationary trends of recent years have drastically raised the price level in terms of dollars, and schools have felt the effects as much as other institutions.

Doubtless these factors have served to stimulate lay interest in educational planning and policy making even as they may be the source of some of the criticism.

Whatever the source of this expanding interest may be or however favorably or unfavorably professional educators may regard it, there is no doubt that it represents a most significant element in education today.

The participation of lay citizens of the community in school affairs is broad and varied. It takes place on both an individual and an organizational basis. It may be well-informed, uninformed, or misinformed participation. It is most often well-meaning but occasionally is inspired by selfish motives. The objectives of citizens in participating range from a sincere desire to improve education to a wish to "get" a superintendent or teacher who has in some way offended. Participation may involve direct contact with the school or it may be indirectly channeled through a student or school employee.

For purposes of discussion, citizen participation is divided into two categories, *formal* and *informal*. Under each category we have two subdivisions, organizational and individual. Such a classification is, of course, arbitrary but may serve to sharpen the general prospective of lay participation.

formal participation

Organizational

Formal participation is here defined as being that involvement which is provided by law, custom, or mutual agreement, and for which a format is provided. Probably the board of education is the most common vehicle for formal organized lay participation. The board is usually elected but in some instances is appointed. Thousands of local boards of education serve communities across the land, and most states also have lay boards of education to serve at the state level. The board of education is established by law and exercises powers delegated to it by the state legislature. It is designed to be representative of the community it serves. It has the legal responsibility to formulate and adopt plans for school development and the authority to enact policies designed to achieve those objectives and goals incorporated in the plans.

The Parent-Teachers Association is an example of nonlegal but nevertheless formalized participation. The organization operates not only at the local but also at the state and national levels. It has definite objectives and is organized to achieve them. It is recognized as a genuine asset in many schools and, in a few, benevolently tolerated.

School-sponsored citizens advisory committees, which may be temporary or continuous and which may be concerned with the total program or only a part of it, have no legal status but are organized by agreement and have established areas of action and channels of communication with the school. In most cases these committees or councils operate within a framework proposed by the school and agreed to by committee members.[1] This framework provides for study, deliberation, discussion, and finally, recommendation to the board. Such committees may or may not be affiliated with state or national citizens organizations.

Other formal organizations which are usually local but often involve many people include alumni associations, band-boosters clubs, and other school promotional groups of similar nature. They have specific objectives and, while loosely organized for the most part, do have a structure and procedures acceptable to the school and in some cases established by it. For example, a group of citizens may be invited by the school to promote a bond issue, given pertinent data, and assigned areas to canvass in support of the issue. Such a group is formal because it is established by mutual agreement and operates within a prescribed format.

Individual

Formal individual participation is most common in the form of the school vote. At the ballot box the individual expresses himself on issues formally presented to him. He may register his assent or dissent to a a proposal to increase the tax rate for educational purposes. He may express himself by his vote favorably or unfavorably toward a bond issue to build a new high school.

At budget hearings he is encouraged by law in many states to question

[1] For an example of such a framework developed by a board of education, see Appendix, page 223.

and comment on proposed financial allocations and expenditures. In the New England town meetings the school directors, commissioners, or trustees provide a medium for the local citizens to be heard.

Most boards of education provide any citizen who wishes it an opportunity to appear before the board and present his or her case. Such presentation may be in the nature of a complaint, a suggestion, or a request. Likewise, many superintendents maintain an "open-door policy" to allow citizens a direct contact with the administration.

informal participation

By far the greater amount of participation in school affairs is on an informal basis. This type of participation is by definition unstructured but, nevertheless, often quite effective in altering school plans and policies. It is sometimes frank and open and at other times cloaked in secrecy. Leadership of such participation is in some cases easily identified; in others, indistinguishable. In whatever form it may take, it should be a matter of direct concern to school officials and community leaders.

For purposes of discussion informal participation is divided into two categories, organizational and individual.

Organizational

The most common form of informal organizational participation is represented by the community group, often composed largely of parents, which is independently initiated to work for a change in the school's purposes, policies, program, or personnel. The group may call itself the "Sunshine Club" and work toward a more extensive program for handicapped children, or it may be the "Phonics Parents," seeking a change in the method employed by the school in the teaching of reading. Such groups usually are established as a result of dissatisfaction with some phase of the school program on the part of a number of people. If there is no way provided for an expression of this dissatisfaction or the way or ways provided are considered inadequate or ineffectual, the formation of such a group follows naturally. The fact that members often do not have a knowledge of the total school program does not deter them from pressing their case.

For the most part such organizations are essentially pressure groups. They are interested in the school even though their interests may be narrow and out of all proportion. The school administrator and the board of education may find themselves in the position of opposing the efforts of some of these groups even though they may sympathize with the organizational objectives. This is the case because often other parts of the school program have a prior call on the money and effort of the school officials. Informal groups seeking to dictate teaching methods are almost always sincere in their beliefs, but this does not make the task of the administrator any easier as he protects the right of the professional to determine his own methods (subject, of course, to appropriate evaluation of results).

The most undesirable of these groups is probably the kind which is organized to "get" the superintendent, the principal, or one or more teachers. In some cases the objective is openly stated and members solicited on this basis; in other cases the objective of dictating personnel practices is thinly veiled by designating the group the "School Improvement Association" or some similar title. Whether open or disguised, such groups are highly disruptive of school-community relations, to say nothing of their effect on the morale of school people.

Another kind of informal organization, the school caucus, concerns itself with the selection of candidates for the school board and the subsequent board election. It is a very informal group but one which may have a decided impact on the school system. Candidates for the board often appear before the caucus to state their positions on school policies and issues. The caucus may endorse a declared candidate or it may decide to select a candidate of its own and campaign for his election. In a number of communities the endorsement of the caucus is tantamount to election. Organized support of board candidates does not always take the form of a caucus but may be just as effective when extended by interested groups meeting in private homes. Informal coffee hours may be arranged by friends of candidates to promote their chances for election. Sometimes candidates are supported because of their personal qualifications and sometimes because they are known to favor or oppose certain school policies or practices.

The "family clan" is another powerful informal group which participates in school affairs in many ways. The family clan, consisting as it does of brothers, sisters-in-law, uncles, aunts, nephews, and nieces, is often quite large. In the older, rural communities it is often closely knit and quite powerful in community affairs. The clan usually convenes for Sunday dinner, and much of the day is spent in discussing local affairs as well as state and national politics. Attitudes toward the school and action proposals are often developed at these family gatherings. In some cases official family positions toward school consolidation or school bond issues are taken at the annual family reunion.

On the smallest scale the family clan consists of father, mother, sons, and daughters with occasionally a grandfather or grandmother who lives in the home. This group, by virtue of the fact that it is closely knit and has ample opportunity for face-to-face discussion about the schools, frequently forms strong opinions relative to school policies and practices. Especially is this true if one or more of the children are pupils. In such cases the family attitude is duly reflected by the children who are in school. The observations of the children often provide much of the basis for the family opinion. Family opinion makes itself felt in its support of candidates for board membership, in its influence on the participation of formal groups in school affairs, and at the polls when school tax referenda and bond issues are submitted to voters.

Individual

Many people participate informally in school affairs as individuals as well as members of organizations. Such participation often takes the form of praise or criticism of the local school. A basketball fan may criticize the school because it does not provide adequate seating for spectators at high school basketball games. Such criticism may lead to a new gymnasium. Others may criticize disciplinary practices for being either too rigid or too easy. Businessmen may complain that graduates of the local high school cannot spell or use good English or perform simple mathematical computations with accuracy. Such criticism is largely voiced in conversation with other citizens but not infrequently is expressed to board members and school officials.

On the other hand, individual citizens are quick to compliment the school on its success in athletics, drama productions, musical contests, and in producing national scholarship winners. Parents are complimented on the performance of their children in plays, concerts, spelling contests, school exhibits, and athletic contests. This in turn strengthens parents' faith in the school and leads to their more active participation.

Letters to the editor are a means of getting an individual's views about the school before the public. Most local newspapers are widely read in the community, and a letter from a reader receives considerable attention. The majority of papers publish unsigned letters as long as the writer is known to the editor. This permits people to give free rein to their opinions about the school without fear of retaliation against them or their children. On the other hand, signed letters often appear encouraging the support of school tax referenda or bond issues. In one community a series of such letters signed by community leaders appear in the two local papers during the month preceding every election in which more money is being sought for the schools.

The distribution of printed handbills usually opposing a tax referendum or bond issue is another way an individual sometimes expresses himself with regard to the school. In most cases such sheets are unsigned and contain statements of half-truths, accompanied by insinuations and innuendoes. Fortunately most people do not regard such publications as authoritative, but they do have an effect on the uninformed.

Informal individual criticism and praise both influence the nature of school policies and programs. Board members and school officials are usually quite sensitive to both praise and blame. It is not unusual for a few individuals to affect school policy significantly simply by noising their criticisms widely about the community.

types of organizations

Many kinds of organizations participate in the school program. They participate in various ways and in varying degrees. Some, which we shall refer to as school liaison groups, are school oriented and have been formed primarily for the achievement of educational objectives in the schools. They may or may not be school-sponsored groups. Their identifying characteristic is their primary and often sole concern with the school.

A second type of organization which commonly participates directly or indirectly in the school program is the general community organization which has only a secondary interest in the school. In many cases this secondary interest is a vital and aggressive one, but it is not the central purpose for which the group was organized or to which it directs its major attention. Such organizations, needless to say, are not school sponsored. Some are concerned with the school as an institution and some with the student as an individual.

Both types of groups from time to time exert strong influences on the school. The problem of the school is to capitalize on the interest and efforts of these groups and yet avoid exploitation. Demands upon the time and efforts of both teachers and pupils can become burdensome. Commercial materials, advertising, and propaganda may be cleverly injected into the school if caution is not exercised.

Unless the work of these groups is kept within its proper perspective, a highly unbalanced school program may be developed. The cooperation of such organizations can be valuable if kept in alignment with the overall program of the school. This is not always easy to do, but it is the task of leadership to see that it is done. Such leadership should be exerted by both school officials and organization officers.

The school liaison organizations

Most school liaison groups are school sponsored. They may and usually do have a specific concern or a special phase of the school program to which they direct their attention and efforts.

These organizations characteristically maintain continuing programs directed toward the improvement of the school and its program. Meetings usually are held in school buildings without cost to the organization. Clerical and duplicating service is often provided by the school. Teachers, administrators, and other school personnel take an active part in the work of the organization. The whole orientation of these groups is educational. While they are in some cases affiliates of national organizations, their principal efforts are directed toward the local school.

The services which they render include the advisement of school officials and school boards on school problems and policies, the transmission of information to and from the school, and the evaluation of community educational needs. Valuable contributions are made by such organizations in the development of the curriculum and the improvement of instruction. They help in the selection of equipment, the development of resource units of instruction, and the creation of community laboratory situations. In addition, they often donate teaching devices such as tape recorders and projectors as well as learning materials of various sorts, provide lunches for needy pupils, and contribute in the same ways in which general community organizations do.

The Parent-Teachers Association, the citizens school advisory council, the band parents club, and the vocational agriculture advisory committee are good examples of school liaison groups.

As with other organizations, there is the ever-present danger that they may become pressure groups. For example, the natural interest and enthusiasm of parents organized into a group to promote instrumental music in the school may, if not controlled, result in a distortion of the music program. Practice and preparation for musical events can consume an undue amount of the students' time and lead to their neglect of other areas of study. However, school sponsorship makes the problem of maintaining balance much easier, and able leadership can effectively utilize interest and enthusiasm without harm to the total program.

General community organizations

This category is by far the largest. Every community has a wide variety of civic organizations. Some are unique to the community while others have state, national, and even international affiliations. The term is used here to include cultural, economic, social, fraternal, patriotic, political, professional, religious, and governmental organizations. Although their primary concerns are in the fields of social welfare, economic well-being, health, recreation, safety, conservation, better government, law enforcement, and similar areas, most of them exhibit an interest in the school.

This interest is often closely associated with their primary concerns and may be directed toward individual students, a subject field, or the school program as a whole. For example, the Lions Club has long been interested in the child with defective sight and has provided thousands of needy pupils with glasses. The American Legion has actively promoted the study of American history and civics as well as encouraged emphasis on citizenship and patriotism in the school program. Organizations such as the American Association of University Women support the overall school program and are strong advocates of education in general.

The provision of glasses to needy students has furthered their education and thereby added to the effectiveness of the school. The school itself is not in a position to perform this type of service, yet it is a necessary concomitant of learning for some children. Thus, a community organization meets a real need which otherwise might not be met, and both the pupil as an individual and the school as an institution benefit.

Similarly, the school program can be strengthened by organizations which contribute learning materials, establish student loans and scholarships, furnish cultural opportunities in the form of musical, literary, or dramatic presentations, and provide community laboratory situations for learning.

Very effective support of tax referenda for increased financial support of the school can be provided by community organizations. Promotional efforts on the part of these organizations have made it possible for many school communities to have new buildings, better equipment, and well-paid instructional staffs. Those organizations which participate in the work of the school on a continuing basis are likely to give full and vigorous support to financing.

It should be emphasized that the cooperation and support of the type illustrated above must be on a basis determined by the school and must in no way impair its balance, objectivity, freedom, or independence.

Since this type of organization is not school sponsored, the matter of control is critical. While the potential for constructive participation is great, the danger of exploitation is always present. While the cooperation of all organizations on some level is desirable, the context in which they contribute should be established and maintained by the school. It is the responsibility of the school to conduct itself free from the influence of selfish interests. School officials must never sacrifice the integrity of the school as an objective, nonsectarian, truth-seeking institution for the support of any group. To do so would be to betray the trust of the people themselves.

The most common attempts at exploitation, either intentional or unintentional, involve the use of the time and efforts of pupils and teachers. Time and energy devoted to selling magazines, preparing food baskets for the indigent, making community chest appeals, aiding in membership drives and similar activities cannot be devoted to the work of the school. While such efforts may in themselves be quite worthwhile, they are not the responsibility of the school.

levels of participation

Lay citizens may be said to contribute to the work of the school on three levels. The first or primary level, the collection of information, is broadly based and may involve in varying degrees a major proportion of the citizens of a community. Especially is this true in the smaller community. Willingness and the ability to follow directions are all that is required at this level of participation. Participants serve somewhat like soldiers in an army. Each is aware that he is making a contribution to a common cause although he may not be privy to the grand strategy. If he does his assigned task well, he is assured that he contributes to the common good.

The second level of participation, which involves the analysis and interpretation of data, is usually characterized by a greater selectivity of personnel. In any given project, fewer people will ordinarily be required to analyze and interpret than to collect and assemble.

At the third level, judgments are made, conclusions are reached, and courses of action are recommended. In the case of the board of education this is the actual adoption of plans or the enactment of policy. Lay groups, such as citizens advisory committees and PTA groups without legal authority, offer a specific recommendation or series of recommendations for action. Selectivity of personnel is usually greatest at this level. In the case of a citizens advisory committee which is commissioned by the board to make recommendations, members are usually selected with great care to ensure that only the best-qualified people are represented on the committee.

The levels of lay participation may be likened to a pyramid. At the base we have the fact finding, the collection and assembly of data. A broad band represents the large number of people who can be involved at this level. The second level is considerably more narrow and involves fewer people. Here data are classified and interpreted. The third or peak level is the one at which judgments based on the data are made and recommendations developed. A relatively small and select representative group operates at this level.

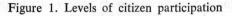

Figure 1. Levels of citizen participation

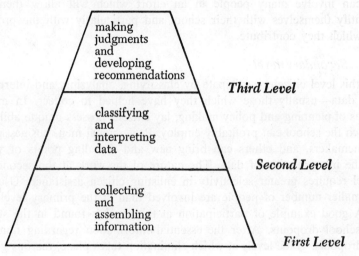

Primary level

The first level of participation is the collection of information or data necessary for planning or determining policy. A guide for the collection of pertinent data together with instructions is usually supplied by professional people. The lay citizen simply follows instructions and reports the information on forms provided. This procedure permits the assembly of large masses of data when participation is extensive. If instructions are clear and concise, the data collected are usually quite accurate. The assembled information is taken over by the professionals and forms the basis for planning and policy making.

A common example of citizen activity at this level is the taking of a child census. The geographic area to be covered is divided into sections, and a group of citizens is organized to cover each section. Each citizen reports to a sectional captain who is responsible for the child count in his section. The sectional captains, after assuring themselves that all children have been counted, turn in their reports to the person responsible for actually making enrollment projections.

Work on the primary level represents a genuine contribution. In the example given above, a group of citizens can secure an accurate child count which will prove invaluable not only for making enrollment projections but also for locating children who should be, but are not, enrolled in school. The job can be done quickly, accurately, adequately, and economically by lay citizens.

Primary-level participation is feasible in a wide variety of situations. It can involve many people in an effort which will allow them to identify themselves with their school and particularly with the project to which they contribute.

Secondary level

At this level citizens participate by classifying, analyzing, and interpreting data—usually those which they have helped to collect. In many areas of planning and policy making, lay citizens possess unique abilities which the school can profitably employ. Professional men, businessmen, homemakers, and others can bring new and revealing points of view to the interpretation of data. The nature of the work at the secondary level requires greater selectivity in enlisting citizen assistance. Usually a smaller number of people are involved than at the primary level.

A good example of participation at this level is found in the study of school dropouts. After the essential information regarding number of dropouts, grade levels at which elimination takes place, reasons given for leaving school, case histories, and similar data are assembled, the secondary-level task is to analyze and interpret the facts. What are the basic reasons for pupils leaving the local school before completion of their schooling? The answer requires careful study of the data and a look beneath the surface to discover the real reasons. The experience backgrounds of lawyers, doctors, social workers, business employers, and others provide helpful insights in this context. The net result of lay participation at this level is likely to be a clearer, more accurate perception of the broad base of causation than would otherwise be possible. The school can then seek out ways and means of combating pupil loss based on a broad knowledge of the cause or causes.

Tertiary level

The third and highest level of participation involves the making of specific recommendations on plans and policies. At this level the lay group, with the professional people acting as resource persons or advisers, propose courses of action for consideration by the board of education or other agency responsible for adopting plans or enacting policy. The recommendations of the lay people are based on the assembled data, analyzed and interpreted with the help of professional advisers. Usually the data have been collected by a larger group of lay citizens from whom a smaller group is selected to interpret the facts and figures and draw conclusions from them.

At this level lay citizens come face-to-face with the problems of planning and policy making. Although they have no legal responsibility, they do develop a genuine sense of responsibility for the welfare of the school. They fully realize that their recommendations bear considerable weight and strong likelihood of adoption. No responsible board would reject such recommendations without good and sufficient cause.

As is true at the secondary level, the varied experience and background of the lay group provide an unusually broad foundation upon which to make evaluations and form judgments. Add to this the intimate knowledge of the community which the group will ordinarily possess and the natural interest the members will have in how their children are educated and how their money is spent, and we have the essential ingredients for success. It is assumed, of course, that such judgments are made on the basis of accurate data and with the advice and counsel of professional people.

An example of third-level participation is the development of a broad, general plan for physical-plant expansion. Such a plan is usually developed after extensive study of community characteristics, economic developments, expected future enrollments, scope and nature of educational program, financial support, and existing physical plant. A study of this nature requires continuous consultation with appropriate professional educators and can be accomplished only with considerable time and effort. However, the unique abilities of lay citizens representing diverse occupations and professions make invaluable contributions to such a project. The banker, the building contractor, the engineer, the economist, the industrialist, the realtor, and many others bring a wealth of experience and usable skills and abilities to the project.

The plan for physical-plant development which results from a cooperative effort by lay citizens and professional educators is likely to be a better one than either could effect without the aid of the other. Furthermore, such a plan is far more likely to enlist the support of the community than is one which is developed by the professionals, all ready to be sold to the public.

ways of participating

There are many ways in which a community may participate in the school program. When the school is receptive to the involvement of local citizens, ways and means of effective participation are not difficult to find. The school has a responsibility to take the initiative and propose constructive methods and forms of citizen involvement in the educational process. The community has much of value to offer the school. It is incumbent on the school to assume a leadership role in tapping the wealth of human resources available in every community. The vast majority of the people of the community will welcome the opportunity to contribute time and energy to the school. However, they want to be assured that their efforts will be genuinely helpful. Few persons wish to spend time in fruitless discussion or passive listening to educational theory. Most are willing to listen and study if their work will help to improve education in the community. They recognize the necessity of acquiring information, of analytical discussion, and of intelligent evaluation. However, they want to be reasonably certain that their work will lead to action of one kind or another. Some of the major ways in which people can participate and produce wholesome effects on the school are discussed here.

In planning

The school, like any enterprise which hopes for success, must plan for the future. A school without a plan is like a ship without a charted course. Neither knows where it is going or even where it is trying to go.

For the modern school, long-range planning in the areas of curriculum, physical plant, and finances is vitally important. Too many examples of the effects of the failure to plan or inadequate planning are visible on the American educational scene to warrant the belaboring of this point. The question is, "How can school and community cooperate in planning?" The best plans will grow out of a joint effort to which each contributes according to its competences.

Probably the first step in planning is the determination of the goals or objectives toward which the school should be working. Certainly this determination is the proper function of the people. Some of the goals have already been established by society, by the nation or state, but many others are left to the community. With the advice and counsel of the professional educator, it is up to each community to establish these local goals in harmony with those of the larger community.

Once a list of goals is agreed upon, intelligent planning may begin. Since goals and objectives should be and are subject to change, planning to achieve these goals becomes a continuing process. The march of events will, from time to time, dictate changes in objectives and adjustment of plans. This is to be expected in a swiftly moving and complex society. However, change makes educational planning more imperative, not less so.

Legally there is considerable responsibility for planning vested in the state legislature. But such planning of a necessity must be broad and general. Major responsibility for specific planning has been delegated to the local district and the representative citizens who form the board of education, school commissioners, or trustees and have the power to enact local school policy.

Since board members typically serve without pay and devote only part of their time to school affairs, comprehensive long-range planning is a serious and sometimes neglected problem. Too many times it is left entirely to the professional educators. This is not fair to them. It places an undue burden on the administration. While the professional educator can and should exert leadership, he needs the help of his community in planning for the years ahead.

One very important and very valuable way in which citizens can participate is in the development of long-range plans for education in the community. How this can be done will be discussed in later chapters.

In policy making

It should be recognized that local school policy is being continuously developed in the community. Both individuals and organizations contribute to the development of school policy. When a mother complains to neighbors and friends that her child is being given too much homework, she is helping to shape policy. If enough parents join the protest, it will reach the ears of the teachers and principal either directly or indirectly or in both ways. The result may well be an informal change of policy. The principal may suggest to all teachers that less homework would be advisable under the circumstances. The teachers might decide for themselves that relations with parents would be more pleasant if less homework were assigned.

The suggestions, criticism, and complaints of citizens may also bring about formal changes of policy. Boards of education often revoke existing policies and enact new policies as a result of community pressures built up by individuals talking to their friends and in some cases voicing their criticism and suggestions directly to board members in board meetings.

Community organizations can be and often are influential in developing school policy. Clubs such as Rotary, Kiwanis, and Lions, by their interest and support, help shape policy with regard to the education of exceptional children. Local PTA groups influence policy in their association of parents and school people. In one instance a local taxpayers association proposed a more economical purchasing system for the school which was adopted by board action. Professional organizations of lawyers, doctors, teachers, and others influence educational policy at the national and state as well as the local level. Organizations such as the chamber of commerce, the retail merchants association, and labor unions influence policy in various ways.

Decisive influence is exerted by both individuals and organizations when school issues are presented at the polls. While voting is done by individuals, the endorsement or opposition of local organizations can be decisive. The plans, policies, and program of the school require financial support. Much of this support is contingent on the local community's approving tax referenda and school building bond issues. The best-laid plans of the school may be unrealized simply because the voters withhold financial support. Candidates for the board of education may be elected or defeated because they espouse or denounce certain school policies.

Policy making is a function of the people as a whole. That individuals and organizations influence school policy is a natural concomitant of our democratic system of education. At the state level representatives of the people, legislators, enact statewide school policy. At the community level representatives of the people, board members, school trustees, or commissioners, enact policy. In both cases the people they represent will ultimately determine school policy by the exercise of their influence at the polls and elsewhere.

While few will question the advantages of wide participation in our system of policy making, it is not without its dangers. In fact the dangers are inherent. They lie in three principal directions.

First, there is danger that policy development may be based on misinformation, inadequate information, or no information at all.

Second, there is danger that policies will be adopted on the basis of pressure rather than logical evidence, and as a result school policy may become inconsistent as well as unwise.

Third, danger lies in the fact that unrepresentative individuals and groups may by default assume the major role in policy development. As a result policies might be developed which would create an imbalance in the school program.

The dangers listed make it imperative that (1) the public be fully informed, (2) facts be basic to decisions, and (3) participation be broad and inclusive.

In communication

Adequate communication between school and community is basic to good relations. Adequate communication must be two-way in nature. It is not enough for the school to keep the community informed; it is equally important that the school be kept informed about the community. Educators have recognized for many years schools should change to meet changing conditions, but few have set up effective channels through which changing needs could be reported to the school.

While the school has a wide variety of media for communicating with the community it serves, available media cannot be truly effective unless the people participate. Even the traditional communication link between school and parent, the report card, requires the parent's signature. The teacher-parent conference establishes a closer tie and is in some schools replacing the report card. Home visits by teachers, open houses, graduation exercises, school newspapers, and bulletins to parents are all common methods of communication. School news columns in the local newspaper and radio and television presentations are gaining wider acceptance as media for disseminating information. All emphasize giving information about the school to the people, particularly the parents. Participation by the community is, of course, essential but is largely passive, consisting as it does of listening and watching.

Avenues of communication which emphasize giving information about the community to the school involve greater participation by lay citizens. Among the most common of these are community surveys of various types. They provide the school with information on educational needs, transportation facilities, financial resources, and community attitudes and opinions with regard to the school. Field trips during which not only pupils but teachers learn about government, business, and industry as well as the natural resources of the community are avenues of communication. Less common are extended field studies which involve several days or weeks of study of some aspect of the community.

Citizens councils and advisory committees are important instruments of communication. Through them the school may learn community attitudes, hopes, and aspirations. Studies undertaken by such groups can provide a wealth of valuable information about the number, characteristics, and educational needs of adults as well as children in the community. Councils composed of businessmen, labor union leaders, and professional men representative of the economic life of the community can provide information on current educational needs as well as some evaluation of the school program as reflected in the work of graduate employees.

Other valuable sources of information for the school include the city recreation department, the public park commission, the social welfare agencies, the juvenile courts, the various health services, and other civic agencies. It is important that clear channels for the exchange of information between these agencies and the school be established and maintained.

In problem solving

Every school, no matter how well administered, is constantly faced with problems. The fact that in too many cases problems are not recognized does not alter this condition. Problems are inherent in the social structure, and the school is an important institution in that structure. In the broadest sense the school was created to solve problems. Its purpose is to help solve the basic problems of providing food, shelter, government, communication, personal freedom, and protection against accident, disease, and other enemies.

The fact that the community is constantly changing means that educational needs are changing. Thus, the school which adequately meets the needs of today still has the problem of adjusting to the needs of tomorrow. The extreme mobility of our population imposes additional burdens and accompanying problems on the school. Modern technology opens new vistas not only of opportunities but also of problems. The traditional vocational program of the school is no longer suitable. The problem of retraining workers is a serious one for both school and industry. Social changes which affect individual and family life have their impact on the school.

Schools should face up to the fact that they have problems and will have problems in the future. There is no escape. The school can best serve its local community and the larger community by recognizing this fact and accepting it as a challenge which can and should be met. However, the school can not meet the challenge successfully alone. It must have the help of the community.

How can the local community help in problem solving? The principal way is by the formation of study groups which collect the pertinent data, analyze and interpret it, and make suggestions or recommendations designed to lead to the solution of the problem. Such groups may be made up entirely of lay citizens with professional people available for consultation and resource help; or they may be composed of both lay and professional people. In either case it is a cooperative endeavor in which the school usually takes the initiative but is strongly supported by lay citizens.

Typical problems which such groups undertake to study and propose solutions for include:

1. *The problem of school dropouts.* Why do students drop out? What becomes of them? What can be done to keep them in school?

2. *The problem of pupil transportation.* Who should be transported? How far should pupils be required to walk? By what means should pupils be transported?

3. *The problem of school housing.* Where should new schools be built? How large should they be? How should they be financed?

4. *The problem of after-school use of school facilities.* Who should be permitted to use school facilities? Under what conditions? For how long?

5. *The problem of cooperation with other social agencies in the community.* How can this best be accomplished? Under what conditions? By which officials?

These and many other problems yield to organized, cooperative effort of school and community.

More informal but more common are individual conferences between school officials and heads of various social agencies and civic organizations as well as business and professional leaders. Such conferences often lead to better understanding of the school's problems and valuable assistance in their solution. Few community leaders will decline an invitation to confer with the superintendent or principal about a school problem if invited to do so. The vast majority welcome the opportunity. Furthermore, their experience and training often give them some unique insights into situations which may be unfamiliar to the schoolman.

In developing the program

The people of the community can participate in program development in many significant ways. If the school is to be closely related to life, the community which it serves is its best laboratory. It is here that the pupil may study what Walter Lippmann, the distinguished news columnist, calls the "elementary experiences of humanity." It is here he can see at first hand the push and pull of our society and feel the pulse of the industrial complex which produces the material things of life. The fabric of community living reveals science at work, art created, languages spoken, and history made. It is here the enduring processes of human life are unfolded before the eyes of those who will observe.

However, if the community is to make its maximum contribution as a school laboratory, the people of the community must participate in the development and maintenance of the school program. This may be done in three major ways.

First, the community through its representatives can help in planning the school program so that community experiences may be most effectively incorporated in it. This in no way suggests that other than professional people be responsible for the curriculum. What it does say is that people of the community can help, particularly in relating the program to life processes.

Second, the community can provide wide opportunities for pupils to visit, observe, study, explore, discuss, and participate in the major economic and social processes of the community. With the cooperation of key people, factories, mines, ports, public utilities, refineries, television studios, publication houses, and banks become school laboratories. Welfare agencies, courts of law, museums, sanitation systems, hospitals, air-purification plants, conservation systems, and tax-collecting agencies become the "workbooks" which make the textbooks more meaningful. Even the problems of community living themselves are stimulants to learning.

The community can provide many students with work experience which contributes not only to their education but also to their subsistence. Many enterprises such as automobile service stations, department stores, supermarkets, and publishing houses are quite receptive to cooperative work experience programs. When supervised by the school, part-time work can be coordinated with the school program in such a way as to make learning richer and more meaningful.

Such a program can provide exploratory vocational experience and occupational orientation. Furthermore, it will stimulate a wholesome attitude toward work and its responsibilities. It also provides insights into the problems of employment, wages, fringe benefits, working conditions, employment grievances, and labor union and employee association membership.

In addition, the work experience program provides valuable contacts between school and community. Channels of communication are established which contribute to a clearer understanding of the role of the school in the community.

Third, appropriate persons can bring learning experiences from community life into the school. Many lawyers, doctors, merchants, labor union leaders, nurses, newspaper editors, and representatives of other professions and industries make excellent teachers for a class session or even a short course. They can serve as resource people in the study of economics, health, safety, civics, industrial arts, vocations, sociology, and many other fields of learning. Many who may be unable to contribute their time during the school day are quite willing to help in the evenings and on Saturdays. They can add much to special programs for the gifted as well as adult evening classes.

Guidance clinics featuring representatives of the various professions and industries can be very helpful in the high school program. Audiovisual materials from community industries and social agencies can contribute significantly to the elementary school program as well as to secondary school classes and seminars.

In some cases community sources have furnished the necessary objects for cultural and industrial exhibits which gave pupils firsthand knowledge of what they were studying in various types of study units. Occasionally appropriate persons from the community were present to explain in detail the nature and function of the objects on exhibit. In one instance a very interesting exhibit of papers and documents of a hundred years ago was provided by the local historical society.

In financing

Public schools like most public institutions are largely supported by taxes. Private schools depend for the most part on endowments, gifts, and tuition. In both cases the people in one way or another provide the money which enables the school to operate. Their participation in continued financing is essential if the school is to meet changing and expanding educational needs.

The participation of the citizens of a community in financing their schools is primary, formal, and direct. Their taxes at both the state and local level make the establishment and the operation of the school possible. Those school systems which seek to excel must look for the most part to the local community for the extra money required to forge ahead. To push beyond the minimum standards prescribed by the state and to expand the program to meet educational needs, community financial support is required.

In addition to supporting tax referenda and school bond issues by their votes, many citizens work hard to convince others of the need for a favorable vote on these issues. At times the school takes the initiative in organizing groups of citizens to promote school bond or tax issues. Such groups are invited to a meeting with school officials and given information on the financial needs and costs, the effect of the proposed levy on the individual tax bill, and similar information. Then the citizens are asked to relay this information to friends and neighbors and persuade them to vote favorably at the polls. They are also encouraged to appear before professional organizations, social clubs, and civic groups. In intensive campaigns they ring door bells and make telephone calls in behalf of the proposal. Such support when well organized and comprehensive can be quite effective. However, the facts presented must be convincing if people are to exert their strongest efforts.

There is also the danger that some citizens will resent being told by school officials what they should do and say. They prefer to examine the facts and act on their own judgment. Such a reaction can be avoided and the case for the proposal strengthened if a group of representative citizens are asked to study the situation for themselves. Since issues of this nature almost invariably involve the total school program at least indirectly, a survey type of procedure is indicated. The citizens school survey [2] has been employed successfully in many communities. It requires a considerable period of time and usually involves a comparatively large number of people. Although the citizens school survey represents a major effort and requires qualified professional consultants, its many benefits both direct and incidental make the project worthwhile. Especially is this true if school planning has not been emphasized or community financial support has been reluctant.

Several large school systems have named a budget advisory committee of businessmen who review the annual school budget before it is adopted. Suggestions made by the committee have proved valuable in planning the financial operation of the school.

Other school systems have sought and received the advice and assistance of local businessmen and accountants in establishing and revising their accounting policies and purchasing systems. Corporation executives can provide valuable advice relative to the feasibility of installing mechanical accounting systems and electronic computers for carrying on the financial transactions of the school system.

The school is usually one of the largest financial operations in the

---

[2] Merle R. Sumption, *How to Conduct a Citizens School Survey,* Prentice-Hall, Inc., Englewood Cliffs, N.J., 1952.

community, with a budget which exceeds that of any other public institution in the community. It would seem, therefore, the part of wisdom for the school to seek the advice and counsel of businessmen in conducting its financial affairs.

In evaluation

The school like every public institution is subject to evaluation by the public it serves. Formal evaluations by professional educators are provided for by state legislatures. This type of evaluation, usually conducted by the state department of education, is largely directed toward determining whether or not the school is meeting the minimum standards set up by the state. The criteria employed generally are objective in nature and have to do with the training of teachers, the provision of learning materials, and the adequacy and nature of space and equipment.

Important as these criteria are, the chief concern of the community is, "How good a job is the school doing?" While some citizens may be impressed with formal professional evaluations, many others do not even know of their existence. Among most citizens the only evaluation which exists is an informal one growing out of a combination of opinions, children's reports, newsworthy school incidents, and firsthand contacts with the teachers and pupils. Admittedly such evaluations are fragmentary, often distorted, and frequently based on very little information.

It is not uncommon to hear businessmen evaluate the school on the basis of the spelling or mathematical accuracy of a graduate employee. Too often the sports fan judges the school by its success in winning athletic scholarships. The parent with a mentally retarded or crippled child is prone to judge the school on the basis of its special education program. There are also those who measure the success of the school on how economically it is operated.

This informal type of evaluation, unfair as it often is, will doubtless continue in any community no matter what steps the school may take. However, if the school is willing to invite the community to assist it in evaluating the effectiveness of its program, the situation can be materially improved. A cooperative evaluation procedure not only will serve to guide school officials and teachers in revisions of the program, but will bind the school and community closer together in a common effort.

The lay citizens of the community in cooperation with the school can render valuable assistance in evaluating the school program. Some major ways by which this can be done are listed.

1. Follow-up studies of high school graduates to determine their opinions as to the strengths and weaknesses of the school program
2. Follow-up studies of high school graduates to determine their success in post-high school education
3. Surveys of local business and industry to determine the degree of success attained by products of the school
4. Studies of dropouts to ascertain in what respects the program failed to meet their needs
5. Surveys of unmet educational needs to determine to what extent the school program failed in meeting such needs
6. Comparative studies of other school systems of similar size and nature
7. Analyses and interpretations of evaluations made by state departmental and other accrediting agencies
8. Cost studies to determine trends in school costs in relation to offerings
9. Evaluation of the long-range plans of the school
10. Overall surveys in which representative lay citizens cooperate with professional educators in taking a close look at the school

The ten types of evaluation suggested all require considerable effort by both school and community, but their importance can hardly be overestimated. Since both school and community are changing, evaluation should be a progressive and continuous process. It should be an integral part of the school-community effort. In each case the goals must first be defined; then the evidence of achievement or lack of it must be collected, the degree of success or failure assessed, and, finally, inferences for future policy stated.

additional reading

Campbell, Roald F., and John A. Ramseyer: *The Dynamics of School-Community Relationships,* Allyn and Bacon, Inc., Boston, 1955.

Dreiman, David B.: *How to Get Better Schools,* pp. 89–247, Harper & Row, Publishers, Incorporated, New York, 1956.

Grinnell, J. E., and Raymond Young: *The School and the Community,* pp. 119–139, The Ronald Press Company, New York, 1955.

Hamlin, Herbert M.: *Citizens Committees in the Public Schools,* Interstate Printers and Publishers, Inc., Danville, Ill., 1952.

Hechinger, Fred: *An Adventure in Education,* The Macmillan Company, New York, 1956.

Kindred, Leslie: *School Public Relations,* pp. 148–242, Prentice-Hall, Inc., Englewood Cliffs, N.J., 1957.

McCloskey, Gordon: *Education and Public Understanding,* pp. 364–393, Harper & Row, Publishers, Incorporated, New York, 1959.

Sumption, Merle: *How to Conduct a Citizens School Survey,* Prentice-Hall, Inc., Englewood Cliffs, N.J., 1952.

Sumption, Merle, and Jack L. Landes: *Planning Functional School Buildings,* pp. 20–31, Harper & Row, Publishers, Incorporated, New York, 1957.

the citizens
advisory
committee

5 A citizens school advisory committee is usually made up of representative citizens who are willing to give time and thought to advising the local or state board of education and school officials with regard to the school. These committees have no legal authority and serve without compensation.

They are not always called committees but are referred to in some cases as councils or commissions. They are occasionally called study groups, consulting committees, or advisory councils. Regardless of the name, their essential functions are the same. Their primary purpose is to advise the board of education and school officials on policies and problems of the school. In so doing, they often develop and maintain communication between school and community and, in a sense, make evaluations of the school and its program.

A clear distinction should be made between the citizens advisory committee and promotional committees which school boards and school officials sometimes utilize in campaigns for new school buildings or increased educational taxes.

The promotional group is usually large, and its membership is non-selective. Often everyone is welcome to join. In a few instances it is limited to influential people invited to membership by the board of education. In either case the purpose is to convince the people of the community that they should support a school proposal or project. The procedure is to provide the group of citizens with facts, figures, and arguments; organize them for action; and persuade them to win community support for the project or proposal.

Citizens committees operate on the national level as well as on the state and local level. The National Citizens Commission for the Public Schools, the first such organization at the national level, was established in 1947. A number of states including Florida, New York, Delaware, Ohio, Arizona, and Illinois have advisory committees, councils, or commissions operating at the state level. In addition to advising on educational problems at the state level, most of these organizations encourage and sponsor local citizens advisory councils. One of the first such local organizations was known as the Public Education Association of New York City. It was organized in 1895 and has been in continuous operation since that date. A comparable group, the Chicago Citizens Committee, has been in existence since 1933 and is quite active at the present time. In rural areas agricultural education advisory councils have been in operation since 1911. Mitchell, South Dakota, has had a school advisory board composed of women since 1919.

In the United States today, thousands of citizens committees are in existence. Every state in the Union reports such committees in one form or another. They indicate in some measure the great interest and concern which people have in education. The most pressing problem in connection with citizens committees at present is how to provide them with experienced, competent professional advice so that they may make their maximum constructive contribution to the improvement of education.

types of citizens advisory committees

Advisory committees, whether on the local, state, or national level, can be classified as either (1) independent or (2) school sponsored. At the national and state level, while such organizations may have a variety of sponsoring agencies, they are ordinarily independent of local school sponsorship. At the local level the majority of citizens committees are school sponsored.

Citizens committees also divide themselves into (1) temporary or (2) continuing committees. The former are usually established for a special purpose, and when that purpose is achieved the committee is disbanded. The continuing committee, while its membership may change, has no terminal date. It serves in a more or less permanent capacity as an advisory group to the school or more specifically to the board of education.

A third classification divides committees into (1) "overall" committees or (2) "phase" committees. The overall committee is concerned with the total school system and its program. It is sometimes called a school-wide committee. The phase committee, as its name implies, devotes its attention and energy to one particular phase of the school system or program. It is sometimes referred to as a specialized committee.

The independent committee

The local independent citizens committee very frequently is a protest group. It is often established because local school officials or board members or both are out of touch with the community or turn deaf ears to criticism, complaints, or suggestions. When an administration becomes entrenched and, because of its connections with powerful segments of the community, tends to be complacent, independent citizens groups are sometimes organized to shake that complacency.

An example of this situation in a rural community may be cited here. The board of education consisting for the most part of older men whose children were in high school or college had been reelected year after year almost as a matter of course. When several young mothers pointed out to them that the forty-year-old elementary school building, which was of frame construction, not only was crowded and outmoded but also represented a distinct fire hazard, the board members showed little concern. One member suggested that women should attend to affairs of the home and not concern themselves with public matters. Another expressed himself to the effect that there was no fire hazard since fire drills were held semiannually. It was the general feeling of the board that any increase of the tax rate which a new elementary building would necessitate would be defeated by the voters anyway and therefore the board was not justified in doing anything. The superintendent, wishing to be agreeable in the eyes of his employers, supported this position.

It was at this point that the young mothers aided by their husbands formed an independent citizens committee with the avowed purpose of securing a new elementary school building. The committee numbered eighteen: six men and twelve women. A woman was chosen chairman. The first step was to send the chairman and two other members to seek professional advice as to how to proceed. They obtained such advice at a nearby university which provided educational extension services. Acting on the advice received, the committee began its work by taking an accurate preschool child census. Volunteer census takers working under the direction of the committee visited every home in the community school district. A careful compilation of the results indicated that enrollment in the elementary grades over the succeeding years would be greater than ever before.

Next the committee secured the services of a professional school-building specialist. He made a thorough appraisal of the wooden structure and furnished the committee with a detailed score sheet spotlighting the weaknesses and inadequacies of the building as a learning facility. His evaluation pointed out the danger of fire inherent in the school's old-fashioned basement furnace heating its wooden structure.

The committee gave the facts full publicity in the local newspaper as well as in a widely distributed mimeographed report to the people of the community. Next the committee circulated a petition requesting the board to call an election for the people to vote on a bond issue for a new elementary school. More than one-half the voters of the district signed, and when the petition was presented to the board it agreed to call an election. The issue carried by a substantial majority, and the old school building was replaced by a safe, adequate, and modern structure.

In this case an independent committee provided the initiative and leadership necessary to secure a much-needed improvement in the school system. Fortunately most school communities are not as devoid of responsible school leadership, but in cases such as the one cited the independent committee serves a valuable purpose. It can lead to improved school community relations over the long term.

On the other hand an independent citizens committee may be another name for a pressure group. Some groups recognizing the prestige which may be associated with citizens committees often adopt the name. Also a well-intentioned committee may, without proper guidance in the form of professional advice, become a pressure group. In either case, the committee usually does not conduct an impartial, objective study of the issue or issues in question, but rather proceeds on the basis of an established point of view.

An example of such a committee in a Midwestern community of twenty-five thousand is cited. The issue was the location of a proposed new high school. The board of education had employed a professional survey team to study the problem, and the professionals had recommended a site on the western edge of the city where adequate acreage was available. When the report was released, a number of east-side residents formed a citizens committee with the avowed purpose of getting the high school located on the east side of the city. The site which they proposed contained only 15 acres and was adjacent to a shoe factory. When the board asked the voters to approve a bond issue for a new west-side high school, the committee waged a successful fight to defeat the issue.

In order to win the support of the independent committee, the board of education committed itself to the small east-side site and called a second election. Again the issue was defeated since many voters felt that the board, in endorsing the small site, had yielded to pressure instead of standing on the merits of its original plan. Some citizens raised the question, "Why get professional advice if it is to be disregarded?"

In this case the independent committee almost certainly rendered a disservice not only to the board but to the school community. The situation might have been different had the school maintained communication channels which operated in both directions.

As can be seen from these examples, independent committees can be constructive or destructive. The constructive committee will usually be one or more of the following:

> Representative of the people of the community rather than a segment of the population
>
> Willing to study a problem or issue rather than take a position in advance
>
> Receptive to professional counsel and advice
>
> Organized in such a way as to involve many people of varied opinions yet maintain a relatively small executive or action group

The destructive committee usually has opposite characteristics. It is frequently unrepresentative, unwilling to study, without professional counsel, and willing to take into its ranks only those who are in full accord with its avowed aims.

The school-sponsored committee

School-sponsored advisory committees are usually school initiated and have rules for operation which have been proposed by the school and adopted with or without revisions by the committee. Thus a mutual understanding is established before the committee starts to work. The possibility of friction between board and committee is considerably minimized by this procedure.

These committees may be temporary or continuous; they may be overall or phase committees. Their principal function, typically, is to study problem issues between school and community.

Their membership is usually selected by the board of education or a selection committee named by it. The number of members varies from seven to twenty-five. Sometimes large groups called together to promote a bond issue or tax referendum are called citizens advisory committees, but this is a misnomer. They are in reality promotional groups such as are described earlier in this chapter even though they may assimilate a certain amount of information in the course of their work. They are typically captive groups of the board. The true advisory committee membership must be kept relatively small to allow face-to-face deliberations.

Membership in continuing committees is usually rotating so that in the course of years a comparatively large number of people may be involved. The school-sponsored committee ordinarily holds most of its meetings in the school after school hours. Materials, books, and duplicating and secretarial service are sometimes provided by the school. Administrators and board members offer their services as resource people. In some situations the board employs a professional consultant from a nearby college or university to work with the committee.

The problems for study and recommendations are sometimes presented to the advisory committee by the board with some indication as to their relative importance and urgency. Some boards stipulate that only the problems presented are to be studied. Others are nondirective and give the committee a free hand to choose its own area of study. Probably a combination of these two approaches is best; that is, to present the committee with a list of topics with some indication of priorities, while at the same time making it known that the committee is free to choose any topic it deems fit whether on the list or not. In the case of a phase or special committee the choice is limited by the nature of the committee. In the case of temporary committees time may be a limiting factor. However, most temporary committees are chosen for a particular task and confine their inquiry to the matter at hand. Nevertheless, this may lead to many ramifications since the school system is so closely interrelated. Almost every phase has implications which reach throughout the school system.

The organization of the school-sponsored committee is usually left to the committee after it has convened and its members have become acquainted. Sometimes the sponsoring board provides for officers in its rules for committee operation, but seldom does it assume the prerogative of naming those officers. Provisions are often made for reports to the board, joint meetings with the board, and orientation sessions with selected teachers and members of the administrative and supervisory staff. Sometimes visitations to the various schools of the system are arranged for committee members as an orientation measure.

the case for the citizens advisory committee

Advisory committees of lay citizens in their various forms have demonstrated their worth in many school communities over the United States. There have also been some cases in which the citizens advisory committee has not proved helpful. In fact, some school administrators have had very unpleasant experiences with such committees.

What is the place of the advisory committee in school-community relations? Is it to be encouraged, tolerated, or opposed? Let us look at the facts.

Today's schools face a multitude of problems as a result of rapidly increasing enrollments and greatly expanded programs. Enrollments are growing not only because the population is increasing but also because a greater proportion of that population is in school. Programs must expand to meet the needs of an expanding economy spurred by technological advances. Furthermore, the increase in the number and complexity of social problems places responsibilities on our educational system which were not dreamed of several decades ago.

These facts suggest that the school needs and should actively seek the best advice it can get. From its own community the school can secure, free of charge, sound advice on many of the major problems it faces. A wealth of resource people is available in every community. It awaits only the farsighted school administrator and his board who are willing to tap it.

Also, if the school is to meet expanded needs and solve attendant problems, it must have the understanding of the community. The achievement of such an understanding is not easy with hundreds of agencies and institutions, both public and private, competing for public attention. A direct, continuing, organized contact with *all* the community is essential. The citizens advisory committee offers such a contact.

The development and maintenance of a program geared to changing needs requires frequent critical evaluation. Once again, one logical source for help in such an evaluation is the community the school serves. However, if the appraisal which the community makes of its schools is to be valid, it must be based on facts and study. Under such circumstances community judgments can effectively supplement the judgment of professional people in the appraisal of the program of the school.

Finally, the basic concept on which our public school system is based, namely, that the schools belong to the people, dictates the involvement of lay people to the full extent that they can constructively contribute.

In view of these facts, citizen participation in the school program on a sound, organized basis can and should be the keystone principle of school-community relations. Once this principle is accepted we must move quickly to the problem of implementation. To accept the principle without providing constructive means for its implementation can bring disaster. An analysis of the cases of reported failure of citizen participation reveals almost universal inadequacy at this point. It is the responsibility of the school to provide the ways, the means, the procedures, the organization, and the tools with which the lay citizen can work. He has proved again and again his interest, his competency, and his willingness to help. He should be provided with the framework in which he can operate effectively and constructively. If the school fails to so provide, then citizen participation itself is not on trial. If failure results, it is the failure of the school.

An example of failure to provide for implementation of citizen participation in a small Midwestern community is cited. In this case the school superintendent convinced his board of education of the values to be accrued from broad lay participation. As a result a call was issued throughout the school community inviting all and sundry who wished to participate in improving the school to attend a meeting at the high school. Approximately 150 people or almost 10 percent of the population of the community attended. The first hour of the meeting was taken up by the superintendent and the board president portraying the values of citizen participation and indicating some of the problems which the school faced. Then the meeting was thrown open to the audience for suggestions. Some off-the-cuff suggestions were made, and a number of complaints followed. Before the meeting concluded, some criticism of the board and professional administration was voiced. The meeting adjourned sine die without any plans or program. Some board members, nettled by the criticism, were quick to blame the superintendent. This made him reluctant to propose further citizen participation, and thus a well-intentioned effort died at birth. A comparatively large number of people offered their services to the school only to find that the school was not prepared to utilize them.

The example cited illustrates the necessity of an intelligent, knowledgeable approach to citizen participation. Without a sound approach, both community and school reactions are likely to be unfavorable. Certainly a group of 150 people is too large to draw up a mutually acceptable program of cooperation with school officials. The open invitation to a mass meeting encouraged the attendance of those who had complaints against the school and, by virtue of the size of the group, precluded any thoughtful discussion.

The approach to citizen participation recommended here is by way of the school-sponsored, continuing, overall, advisory committee. If lay participation is to reach maximum effectiveness, such a committee must be established and must function as a basic instrument of school policy. It must be accepted by the board, the administration, the teaching staff, and other school personnel as an advisory group which has as vital an interest in the success of the school as they have. Properly selected, organized, and assigned responsibilities, the citizens advisory committee usurps no one's authority but rather strengthens the hands of all who work for the school.

It is in no sense a superboard. It can and often does act as a bulwark for the board which acts on its recommendations. It provides a valuable link between school and community. It does not duplicate the functions of the board but advises how to perform those functions most satisfactorily. The committee serves as the focal point of community contact with the school.

The overall committee is the focal advisory group in a properly organized participatory system. The work of temporary and specialized committees should be coordinated by the overall committee. Their work should be in close cooperation to ensure best results. In no sense does the overall committee limit community participation, but, on the contrary, it serves to encourage wider and more effective efforts by all those in the community who desire to contribute to the improvement of their school system.

In summary, the case for the citizens advisory committee rests upon:

First, the need of the school for advice on policies, plans, and problems from the community it serves.

Second, the necessity of direct, clear, and accurate communication between school and community.

Third, the advisability of supplementing the professional appraisal of the school program with community judgments.

Fourth, the basic concept that the public schools belong to the people.

the functions of the advisory committee

If the school-sponsored advisory committee is to make the contribution of which it is capable, its functions must be not only legitimate but clearly defined and agreed upon by school and committee. Regardless of its type, the advisory committee has one or more of the major functions discussed below. The overall committee when it is of the continuous type should at some time or other in the course of years perform all these functions.

To aid in developing educational policy. It is the legal responsibility of the board of education to enact school policies. However, anyone and everyone is free to propose policies. In fact, one of the principal duties of the professional school administrator is to propose policies to his board. An advisory committee is in the most advantageous position to propose policy. It is in touch with the wishes, desires, and opinions of the people of the community. The nature of its function requires that it be a study committee. Probably no other group is in a better position to propose policies to the board of education. Whether it is a matter of adopting new policies, revising existing policies, or discarding outworn ones, an advisory committee can give sound advice to the board. In many cases the advisory committee has time to give policy matters much more careful study and analysis than does the board itself.

One advisory committee, for example, gave three months' study to public use of school facilities after school hours. A complete list was made to show the organizations which used school facilities, the amount of time they were used, the nature of the meetings, types of facilities used, cost to the school, and remuneration received. After careful analysis of the data, the committee proposed a policy for public use of school facilities which was adopted by the board and which has been in effect over ten years to the general satisfaction of all concerned.

Prior to the advisory committee's study, complaints regarding the manner in which the board handled requests for use of school facilities had been commonplace for years, yet the board had continued to decide on each request with only a vague, unwritten understanding of its policy. As the board changed in membership, so did its understanding of policy. One organization which was refused use of facilities could cite similar requests which two or three years before had been granted. Before the advent of the advisory committee there was no task force willing and able to conduct a study. Certainly the members of the board did not feel that they had the time to do so. However, once the study was made, the board was happy to adopt a policy based on the facts of the case and the judgment of representative citizens of the community.

To aid in developing long-range plans. Every school system, like every business, must plan ahead if it is to meet the compelling needs of future years. In our rapidly changing society the developments in science, economics, art, and politics are often upon us before we realize it. The school has an obligation to anticipate these changes and develop long-range plans to accommodate them. The advisory committee, if properly chosen, can be invaluable in such planning. The insights and experience which businessmen, industrialists, lawyers, bankers, and other laymen of the community possess can be effectively utilized in planning. The wealth of resources for educational planning which every sizable community possesses constitutes a veritable "gold mine" for school officials who are not content to operate on a day-to-day basis.

To help in solving school-community problems. Every school has such problems. They are inherent in a situation which requires close cooperation with divergent groups. Most communities have widely different types of people making widely different claims on the school. Some claims may be legitimate; others may not be. In either case problems may and do develop. The advisory committee is in a strategic position to deal with such problems and recommend solutions to the school. The intimate knowledge of the community possessed by committee members gives them a distinct advantage in dealing with problems of school-community relationships. They have the ear of both the lay people of the community and school officials. They can listen to both sides of any controversy and go far to resolve differences.

To assist in evaluating the work of the school. Some educators are dubious of the ability of any lay group to evaluate educational proficiency. However, we must never lose sight of the fact that the school turns out a product, the graduate, and society at large places a valuation on the education he received. His success or failure in vocational, social, and civic life is in part a measure of the success or failure of the school. In the case of the student who drops out, where does the failure lie? Is it the student who fails, or is it the school? Among the multiple factors causing an individual student to leave school, which were the more influential, those originating in the school or those originating elsewhere?

Is the school adequately meeting the educational needs of the community? If not, what significant needs are unmet? Are segments of the school program outmoded by changes in our economic or social structure?

These are some of the questions which the lay people of a community can help answer. Frank and perceptive answers are essential to any valid appraisal of the school program. And an objective evaluation of the existing program is the first step in improving it. It seems quite clear that intelligent lay participation in the evaluative process will contribute significantly to both the objectivity and the perceptiveness of any appraisal.

A number of schools have profited by follow-up studies of graduates and dropouts conducted by lay citizens in cooperation with the school. Surveys of educational needs of communities, areas, and even regions can be readily conducted by organized lay groups.

To aid in maintaining two-way communication between community and school. Many of the misunderstandings between school and community are caused by a breakdown of communication. In many cases the community doesn't understand what the school is trying to do or the school doesn't understand what the community expects it to do or both. Furthermore, there are frequently differences in opinion on how things should be done. The advisory committee can perform a very valuable service in facilitating the exchange of accurate and timely information between school and community. Its position as a school liaison group which has access to the ears of both school officials and community leaders is strategic.

An overall, or system-wide, committee, for example, will in the course of time become familiar with a large part of the school program, and, as a result of its studies, it may become intimately acquainted with the various problems which a school faces. It is usually aware of the financial picture the school presents. In brief, it is a group of citizens with no official connection with the school but a vital interest in it. Information coming from such a group either by word of mouth or in written form is usually accepted at face value by the man in the street. It is not discounted or discredited as school propaganda. It often reaches an audience which is not reached directly by the school.

The advisory committee also serves to stimulate the flow of information to the school. Many people who will not approach a school official or appear before a board of education will express themselves freely on school matters to an advisory committee or a member of it. Opinions from the community may be sought by the committee, analyzed, interpreted, and reported to the school. This may be done informally, or it may be done by opinion polls in which members of the advisory committee serve as interviewers. In larger communities the advisory committee enlists the aid of civic organizations and school liaison groups to furnish interviewers to contact people of the community. An example of an instrument developed by an advisory committee and used to secure community opinion of the school appears in the Appendix, page 231.

While sometimes referred to as an incidental function of a school advisory committee, the facilitation of two-way communication between school and community is an important service which the committee can render—and render perhaps more effectively than any other group.

the professional consultant

The importance of a competent professional consultant to an advisory committee of lay citizens can hardly be overestimated. All types of citizens advisory committees need consultant service, but the continuing committee probably has the greatest need. This is true because of the variety of problems which faces such a committee as well as its need for developing processes and procedures on a long-term basis.

The sources of professional consultants are of two kinds. First there is the local school professional staff which may provide teachers, supervisors, principals, and superintendents as well as specialists in areas such as remedial reading, special education, and business management. Then there is the nonlocal school educator who may come from a college or university, the state department of education, or the staff of another school system. While local school consultants have the advantage of a familiarity with the school and community, they suffer a distinct disadvantage because of the vested interest which they have in the school system. No matter what degree of objectivity they may achieve for themselves, they are still open to criticism because of their connection with the school. On the other hand the outside consultant is in a position where objectivity and impartiality can be expected. Such a position is ordinarily of greater importance in working with lay advisory committees than is familiarity with the school since a reasonable working knowledge of the local educational situation may be rather easily obtained by the consultant. Often a combination of local and outside consultants is the best solution to the problem of consultant service.

Consultants to citizens advisory committees are of two types. They are (1) the general consultant who provides guidance and counsel to the committee in methods and procedures, and (2) the special consultant, sometimes referred to as a resource person, who provides information in the area in which he is specialized. For example, the general consultant will advise the lay committee on the correct organization for attacking a problem, appropriate methods to use, suitable techniques of study, and proper forms of reporting. In short, he acts as an operational guide. The special consultant, on the other hand, is responsible for supplying information on his field, interpreting it in relation to the local situation, and aiding the committee in drawing conclusions.

The general consultant is usually associated with the advisory committee over a long period of time, while the special consultant limits his efforts to helping the committee while it is concerned with his area of specialization. The former is doubtless the more important to the success of a committee, but adequate and qualified special consultants or resource people are quite valuable to a committee. The well-qualified and experienced general consultant is a rare figure on the educational scene. He will be found in most cases in the extension or field services departments of universities or occasionally in state departments of education. Once in a while, a superintendent of schools who has had experience working with citizens committees in his own school will be available to serve as a general consultant, but this is comparatively rare.

On the other hand, special consultants are readily available from the sources mentioned and from the local teaching or supervisory staff. Of course, some are much more adept than others in speaking the layman's language and bridging the gap between the lay and professional worlds.

Utilization of consultants

The qualified consultant is essential to the success of a citizens advisory committee. The need for the general consultant precedes even the selection of a committee. In fact, the general consultant should be called upon when the school board and administration are considering the establishment of an advisory committee. He can inform them, first of all, of the nature, procedures, and mode of operation of, and values to be expected from, such a committee. He can advise them of which problems are appropriate to refer to a citizens committee and which are not. He can counsel them on selecting the committee and on developing tentative ground rules for the operation of the group. He can make sure that there is a clear understanding of the relationship of the committee to the board, the administration, and the teaching staff.

Once the committee is selected, the general consultant becomes a liaison agent between the committee and the school. He keeps in close touch with both and is constantly anticipating possible misunderstandings and in general smoothing the path to a close and mutually satisfactory relationship between school and committee. While the typical citizens advisory committee will possess much talent and ability, it will find the general consultant invaluable in helping its members to utilize their abilities effectively in attacking educational problems. His educational background combined with a knowledge of processes makes him the ideal person to guide committee members in channeling their efforts along educational lines. It is also the general consultant who will suggest the use of special consultants at appropriate times. He may even help secure such consultants from the local school system as well as from nearby institutions of higher education.

The general consultant, to be most effective, must secure and maintain the confidence of not only the advisory committee but also the board of education, the administrative staff, and the teachers and other resource people with whom he works. In order to do this, he must be intellectually honest at all times and willing to admit it when he does not know an answer. He should recognize his role as that of a facilitating agent, never a lecturer or a manager. The general consultant will guide the committee in its search for data. He will help its members decide what data are necessary and pertinent. It is his responsibility to aid them in securing, classifying, analyzing, and interpreting those data.

He represents the profession of education and provides the measuring stick of educational validity to the ideas, conclusions, and recommendations of the committee. However, he should also stimulate thinking and encourage expressions of opinions on the part of the committee members. He should always recognize that recommendations for the solution of problems and development of plans are the prerogatives of the committee, not the consultant. He is not to provide the answers but rather to give all possible aid to the committee so that it may arrive at logical decisions based on facts and possessing educational validity.

During the first year of a committee's existence it is generally wise to have a consultant at every meeting of the group. Subcommittee meetings do not ordinarily require the presence of a consultant since the results of their studies are reported to the full committee for action. Often a subcommittee may need help from the consultant in the form of materials or suggestions on procedures, but these may be supplied by correspondence.

The role of the special consultant or resource person, while not as vital as that of the general consultant, is strategically important. The committee should as far as possible utilize the services of local teachers, supervisors, and administrators in informing itself of the educational considerations involved in the particular problem being studied or the plan being developed. For example, in a study of school dropouts probably the most valuable insights into the problem may be secured from a session with the school guidance director and some of the counselors. An evaluation of the physical facilities of a school might well involve both teachers and custodians as resource people. Occasionally the need for a resource person from the state department of education or a nearby college faculty will be indicated by the size or complexity of the problem. Many of the local problems studied will have state or even national implications, and in such cases a special consultant with a broad background of experience can serve the committee best.

It should always be recognized that the consultant, whether general or special, is a facilitator. His purpose is to aid and advise the committee to the end that its efforts will be effective and its recommendations educationally sound and constructive.

selecting and organizing the committee

Both the selection and organization of citizens committees are important factors in determining their success. Improperly selected committees often are so handicapped that they fail to do any constructive work. In fact, some selection procedures prejudice the people of the community against a committee before it even begins its work. Poorly organized committees suffer significant disadvantages in carrying out their functions.

Selecting the committee

The independent citizens committee is usually a self-selected group. That is to say that those who have a strong interest in the formation of such a committee assume membership in it. After it is organized, new members are usually invited to join as a result of committee action. Often this selection procedure leads to a committee which is not truly representative of the community and may even cause the committee to take on the character of a pressure group.

The school-initiated committees lend themselves to better selection procedures. Two selection plans have evolved as the most satisfactory. The first is direct selection by the board of education with a planned effort to secure a thoroughly representative group. The second is the use of a selection committee composed of three to five substantial citizens chosen by the board of education with the same objective. This latter procedure is particularly recommended when a continuing committee is being chosen. A once popular practice of asking each organized group in the community to name a member has proven unsatisfactory. First of all it cannot be truly representative, and in the second place people so named often tend to think of the interests of the organizations they represent rather than of the whole community.

The selection process in the case of the school-sponsored committee should be initiated only after the board of education, with the aid of the superintendent and a consultant, has developed a set of ground rules for the operation of the committee. An example of such an operational code appears on page 223 in the Appendix. In cases where a selection committee is employed, its members should be supplied with copies of the code for use in their task. The selection committee should be charged with the responsibility of nominating a representative group of citizens who are interested in education and are willing to devote a portion of their free time to the improvement of the local schools. It should be emphasized that committee members should be chosen on the basis of their ability to contribute to the making of plans and the solution of school problems. "Rubber stamp" committees composed of "yes" people are to be avoided at all costs.

In selecting a list of people as nominees, it is usually wise to provide a companion list of alternates. In cases where a refusal to serve is encountered, an alternate can then be invited. The invitation to serve on the citizens advisory committee should be extended by the board of education and accompanied by a clear statement of the duties and responsibilities of the proposed committee as well as the relationship of the committee to the board of education. This information is sometimes incorporated in a code of operation or a set of ground rules referred to earlier. In any case it is the responsibility of the board of education to provide this type of information to those whom it invites. A clear understanding between board and advisory committee is basic to the success of the committee.

The size of the advisory committee varies with the type of committee and its function. The typical committee has about fifteen to eighteen members. The number should not exceed twenty-five in any case, since larger numbers preclude the face-to-face discussion which is such an important part of committee deliberations. The committee can effectively augment its working force by enlisting the aid of many other citizens through temporary subcommittees reporting to the parent committee.

Organizing the committee

Usually at the first meeting of a citizens committee the superintendent, the president of the board of education, or the consultant acts as a presiding officer. Sometimes the nonmember serves as chairman pro tempore for several meetings so that the members of the committee may become reasonably well acquainted with each other. However, when the group is ready to organize itself, it should be given full rein to organize as the members see fit. Ordinarily the permanent officers are a chairman, vice-chairman, and recorder or secretary. It is customary to elect these officers by secret ballot. In no case should anyone outside the committee seek to influence the choices of the group. If the committee leadership choices are poor, it will have only itself to blame and can replace its leaders at the first opportunity. Officers of continuing committees usually are limited to one-year terms.

As has been indicated earlier in this section, the working force of the committee may be expanded almost without limit by the formation of subcommittees for special tasks. For example, a subcommittee of businessmen may be selected to serve under the chairmanship of a committee member in making an inventory of job opportunities in the local area. Once the project is complete the subcommittee makes its report to the advisory committee and disbands, its function performed.

Another way of expanding the working force of a committee is the utilization of other groups or organizations as affiliated committees. For example, an advisory committee might enlist the local Parent-Teachers Association as an affiliate to take a child census. In such a case the PTA might accept the responsibility of furnishing personnel for the door-to-door contacts necessary, while the advisory committee would design the project, furnish census cards, maps, and other materials, and compile the results.

operation of the committee

The operation of an advisory committee, if it is to be most effective, should be governed by a set of guidelines. The ground rules described in the preceding section form the base upon which the committee operates. The ground rules in effect are commitment by the board of education to the principle that public education belongs to the people and their advice and aid are needed. Furthermore, the ground rules clarify the relationship of the committee to the board of education and school personnel and define its responsibilities.

Once the ground rules are adopted by the committee, it launches out on its mission. A typical first step is one of orientation to the school system which is to be served. Usually the superintendent and his staff appear before the committee to supply information about the many facets of the school system and its program. Such appearances give the committee members a chance to get acquainted with school personnel as well as to ask questions about the school. School personnel in turn get acquainted with the lay citizens and learn of their interests and concerns.

Areas of study

One of the first questions raised by committee members concerns the area of study to be undertaken. "What are the proper and legitimate areas of study for the committee, and who should make the selection?" The help of a qualified consultant is extremely valuable at this point. He will point out to the committee the five major areas of study and recommendation: (1) development of policy, (2) development of long-range plans, (3) school-community problems, (4) evaluation, and (5) school-community communication. Within these major areas are a large number of specific topics which can be explored profitably by the committee.

Many kinds of educational policies involve the community in a very direct way. These and others which indirectly affect the community offer opportunities for committee study and recommendation. A few illustrations are listed.

Policy governing after-school use of school buildings by community groups

Policy governing transportation of pupils

Policy governing public performances of athletic teams, bands, orchestras, and drama students

Policy with regard to reporting to parents

Suitable topics of study in the area of long-range planning include:

The development of a long-range plan for financing the schools

The development of a long-range plan for acquiring school sites

The development of a long-range plan for school plant development

The development of a school-community plan for recruitment of
superior teachers

In the area of problem solving, an advisory committee can usually
be most helpful by analyzing the problem and then suggesting a solution,
which often takes the form of a recommendation to revise an existing
policy or enact a new one.

Typical problems which citizens committees have studied and for
which they have proposed solutions include:

The high school dropout problem

The problem of juvenile delinquency among pupils

Problems of faculty housing

Problems of school district reorganization and consolidation

Problems of financing additions to the school program or plant

While the academic evaluation of the school program is the job of
the professional educator, it can only be properly evaluated in relation
to educational needs of pupils. It is in this area that the citizens committee can probably render its most valuable service. Another aspect
of evaluation which such committees can explore with profit is the
product of the school, the graduate. His success or failure in some
measure is a reflection of the adequacy and quality of the school program. His reactions to a questionnaire on his local school experiences
often shed valuable light on the strengths, weaknesses, adequacies, and
inadequacies of the school program.

Evaluation studies which advisory committees are qualified to make
include:

Appraisal of the goals of the school in relation to community
educational needs

Survey of unmet educational needs in the community

Analysis of the use of community resources by the school

Study of the holding power of the school with particular reference
to curriculum revision

Follow-up study of high school graduates

Study of the coordination of the school program with those of
other community educational agencies

In very few communities is communication with the school entirely
satisfactory. Failure to establish and maintain clear and effective channels

of communication between school and community is probably the cause of more misunderstanding and criticism than any other single inadequacy. Study and recommendations in this area by citizens committees alone would amply justify an advisory committee in many school communities. Typical activities of committees in this area include:

Study of community opinion and attitude toward the schools

Appraisal of the use of available communication media by the school

Study of system of reporting to parents on pupil progress

Development of a comprehensive plan for communication between school and community

The list of studies in the five major areas of committee work is by no means exhaustive. Many other aspects of the school community are legitimate topics for study and recommendation by a citizens committee. Although the committee usually assumes responsibility for studies, it seeks and receives help from teachers, administrators, and board members as well as organizations and individuals of the community. Some aspects of the school community lend themselves best to joint efforts in which responsibility is shared. For example, any study of teacher recruitment policies might well be a joint effort of the lay committee and a representative committee of the teaching staff.

What areas, on the other hand, are not suitable for committee study? Briefly, lay citizens should leave to qualified professional people the planning of courses, the choosing of textbooks, the methods of instruction, the employment of teachers, teacher promotion and transfer, and the selection and use of instructional materials. As an advisory group, the committee should not recommend or endorse candidates for the board of education.

The results of committee studies together with recommendations should be reported to the board of education, which in turn releases them to the public in the same way other reports are made.

Who determines what aspects of the school community should be studied, and how are priorities established? In general the committee should have the freedom of choice. The best practice is probably for the board of education to present its suggestions to the committee and leave the choice to the group. Usually if the board explains the need for study and recommendations on one or more aspects of the school program, the committee will give these topics high priority. Most committees are guided by the board in their choices.

Guidelines for operation

A list of guidelines based on the experience of school administrators, board members, educational consultants, and citizens committee members is presented below. Although not purporting to be exhaustive, the list, if observed, will do much to keep the committee operating effectively.

1. A regular schedule of meetings should be established as early as possible. Interim meetings may be held if the work requires them. No less than one meeting should be held each month of the school year.

2. The board should provide a regular meeting place for the committee, preferably at a centrally located school.

3. If possible some secretarial, clerical, and duplicating service should be provided for the committee.

4. A citizens committee should be primarily a study group making recommendations and only secondarily a promotional group.

5. A good way to orient the citizens committee with the program of the school system is to start with a tour of the schools.

6. While a citizens committee should not be limited as to the scope of problems it may study, it should undertake only one or two problems at any one time.

7. A citizens committee should, when possible, select for its first problem for study one which it is possible to solve in a relatively short time.

8. A citizens committee, when it is starting, should avoid issues which are likely to split the community and should attack this type of problem only after it has become well established.

9. A consultant should assume the responsibility for seeing that the advisory committee maintains its proper relationship to the school board, the school staff, and the people of the community.

10. Resource persons, those who have a special competence in one or more areas, should be called on for help as needed. The superintendent of schools is one of the most valuable resource persons available to the committee.

11. The citizens committee should fully utilize the services of the teaching staff as resource persons.

12. There should be close communication between the citizens committee and the board of education at all times. A member

of the board of education should often be invited to sit with the committee as a resource person, and one annual joint meeting between the board of education and the citizens committee should be held.

13. While working cooperatively with the board of education, the citizens committee should arrive at its own decision and never be a rubber stamp for the board.

14. The committee should enlist the aid of citizens of the community by establishing temporary subcommittees as needed to work on specific phases of a problem.

15. All meetings of the citizens committee should be open to the public.

16. The committee should report its recommendations and suggestions to the board, never to the public directly.

17. When the board appoints a citizens committee, it assumes an obligation to consider the opinions of the committee carefully, and while the board is not obligated to act favorably on all committee recommendations, it should be prepared to state specific reasons when it does not act favorably.

Dangers to be avoided

The properly selected, suitably organized, and adequately guided committee can serve as a unifying agent for the school community. It can be expected to make the school more sensitive to the needs of the community and the community aware of the plans and program of the school. However, it would be unrealistic to assume that there are no dangers or pitfalls in an advisory committee program. In any activity involving people's working together, there is always danger of misunderstanding, personality conflicts, friction, and frustration.

A common practice which is unwise and sometimes dangerous is the selection of unrepresentative committees. A committee may be unrepresentative in that it was chosen to reflect the thinking of the board or to assure that a majority of the committee came from the professional or business groups. Or it could be unrepresentative because some substantial segments of the population were bypassed or certain large geographic areas were unrepresented. Selecting a committee by asking organizations to each name a committee member usually produces an unrepresentative group. All these and any other selection process which may result in an unrepresentative committee should be avoided.

The reaction of a community to such a committee is often quite critical. Unrepresented elements of the community seldom have confidence in a group which is skewed in favor of a particular cultural level or has an occupational or economic bias of any kind. Furthermore, such a committee is not likely to provide the school with an accurate reflection of community attitudes and opinions.

A second common danger involved in utilizing citizens committees is the possibility of their assuming the prerogatives of the board of education and in effect becoming a superboard. Many school board members are dubious with regard to citizens committees for this reason. Some school superintendents advise their boards against citizens committees because of this danger. Nor is this fear wholly without grounds. In some cases energetic, zealous committees have invaded the field of administration and figuratively stepped on the toes of board members. However, such a situation is, in most cases, the fault of the school administration which failed to establish the ground rules by which the committee was to operate. Without such guidance, enthusiastic citizens may well encroach on established authority. With the rules of the game made known to them at the time of their invitations to become members, they accept with a full knowledge of their responsibilities and the limitations of their authority. It is of utmost importance that a good relationship be established and maintained between committee and board. The ground rules are the best assurance that such a relationship gets a good start and continues for the life of the committee.

Another danger to the effective operation of a committee is a tendency on the part of some committee members at times to want to express opinions and make pronouncements without adequate information. The consultant will help avoid this danger by pointing out from time to time the necessity of getting the facts before giving opinions or making recommendations. He will also remind the group that it is a study committee and so should never resort to off-the-cuff pronouncements. Study is especially important to a group of lay citizens who are working in the field of education. Their own experiences in school hardly qualify them to deal with educational planning, policies, problems, and evaluation without some careful information collecting and thoughtful analysis.

Still another danger is that the committee will stray from its proper fields of study. Some committees contain members who would like to dabble in personnel matters. Occasionally a committee wants to have a voice in the transfer or promotion of teachers. Pupil discipline is another area that a few committee members would like to invade.

Once in a while a committee assumes the role of a complaint bureau and encourages people to bring their complaints about the school to the committee. A committee operating in this role usually disintegrates rather rapidly.

Not infrequently, a committee will want to assume a role in choosing textbooks and in planning courses of instruction. Usually this desire is motivated by some incident in which a parent criticizes the nature of some school experience or the contents of a textbook.

The above activities are all professional responsibilities, and the only concern the citizens committee need have is that they are discharged effectively by competent professionals.

Still another common error is for the committee to act without adequate professional assistance. While a good consultant costs money, it is money well spent. Committees attempting to operate without competent professional assistance can easily become lost or, worse yet, stray into paths which lead to conflict and frustration. It is usually advisable for a committee to have a consultant in attendance at every meeting during the first year. It is false economy on the part of the board of education to limit the consultant's aid until after the committee has had a chance to become oriented to its work.

Finally, an ever-present danger is that of the committee's voicing recommendations and making formal or informal reports directly to the community. This practice places the board at a distinct disadvantage. It often leads the committee into errors which could have easily been avoided by channeling reports through the superintendent of schools and the board. Even independent committees will find it advantageous to report first to the school administration, as in this way errors will be quickly pointed out, and the committee may be saved considerable embarrassment.

Independent reports by committees can cause confusion in the public mind and often lead to duplication of effort and in some cases apparent contradictions. Most boards and superintendents resent reports by groups which have no official responsibility in connection with the schools.

Difficulties of this nature can be avoided by establishing a rule that all committee publicity be released through the school administration and all reports and recommendations be made originally to the board of education. In the case of school-sponsored committees, this represents a logical procedure since the committee is set up to advise the school. In the rare cases where boards attempt to squelch a committee recommendation or report, a judicious appeal to public opinion will usually force the board to release the information. Seldom is such action necessary when a board and committee have established the proper relationship.

additional reading

American Association of School Administrators: *Lay Advisory Committees,* National Education Association, Washington, D.C., 1951.

Campbell, Roald F., and John A. Ramseyer: *The Dynamics of School-Community Relationships,* pp. 107–186, Allyn and Bacon, Inc., Boston, 1955.

Davies, Daniel R., and Kenneth Heller: *Citizen Committees,* Arthur C. Craft Publications, New London, Conn., 1954.

Dreiman, David B.: *How to Get Better Schools,* pp. 6–59, Harper & Row, Publishers, Incorporated, New York, 1956.

Hamlin, Herbert M.: *Citizen Committees in the Public Schools,* Interstate Printers and Publishers, Inc., Danville, Ill., 1952.

Jones, James J., and Irving W. Stout: *School Public Relations,* pp. 165–178, G. P. Putnam's Sons, New York, 1960.

Stearns, Harry: *Community Relations and the Public Schools,* pp. 293–310, Prentice-Hall, Inc., Englewood Cliffs, N.J., 1955.

Sumption, Merle: *How to Conduct a Citizens School Survey,* Prentice-Hall, Inc., Englewood Cliffs, N.J., 1952.

communication between school and community

6 It is clear that if a school system is to serve the community with maximum effectiveness, there must be continuous communication between school and community. Furthermore, this communication must be of a two-way nature. It is just as important that the school hear from the community as it is that the community receive the message of the school. Too many schools have been satisfied with one-way communication—getting the program of the school before the people. Little attempt has been made in such schools to look at the other side of the communication coin. Thus even information which might be very helpful in facilitating the process of presenting the school program to the people is not secured.

The importance of effective communication in the context of the school community can hardly be overestimated. Communication is the nervous system of the school community. Through this system impulses are received, messages sent out, and reactions stimulated. If the network of communication nerves breaks down in any area of the school-community body, the whole complex suffers.

The American tradition of education, the statutes of the several states, and the very mores of our society proclaim the fact that the public schools belong to the people. Their interest, concerns, and criticisms are strong indicators of this close relationship. In most communities the people naturally assume a conscious responsibility for providing adequate and suitable education. It would be difficult to conceive of a societal relationship which depends more on effective communication for its success.

The competition for public attention and interest is intense. People are exposed to many, many messages every day. Advertising on television, radio, billboards, and neon signs and in magazines, newspapers, and letters conveys messages designed to create good will, an appetite for some product, or an urge to buy, or in some way to influence people. Organizations of various kinds seek to communicate in order to secure support or new members. Institutions other than schools through broad communication networks seek a sympathetic public ear.

If the school is to compete successfully with the many and varied interests seeking a hearing, it must develop and maintain an effective system of communication. The nature, objectives, principles, structure, processes, and media of such a system are discussed in this chapter.

the nature and objectives of communication

Characteristics

As indicated earlier, the communication system of a school community is quite similar to the nervous system of the human body. The school represents the head or brain which sends out and receives messages. The limbs and various organs of the body represent the various elements of the community in such an analogy. The coordination of efforts is a function of communication. The most important feature of the analogy is probably the impulse-response relationship. In the highly complex network of nerves in the human body each action brings a reaction. Each message brings a reply. The hand touches and reports on the nature of the object touched—whether it is rough or smooth, round or square, hot or cold. The nerves of the stomach protest overindulgence in food or drink. The neglected tooth reports the pain of a cavity. While the brain directs to a large extent the actions of the body just as the school to a lesser extent determines the course of community action, it is quite sensitive to the responses of the body. It is in much the same way that the school, if it is to be truly effective, must respond to the community. It should be recognized, of course, that the response may not and should not always be an accession to the wishes or demands of the community, but these wishes or demands should be known and given consideration.

Another important parallel to be drawn is the inclusiveness of the nervous system. It reaches every part of the body. It carries messages to and from the remotest parts. So also should the school-community communication system. If it fails to reach every segment of the community, it is incomplete in structure and function. Such failure can have serious implications for the school which needs the support and understanding of those it serves. Not a few communities have suffered defeats of proposed bond issues and tax levies, which were badly needed and fully justified, simply because a segment of the community was not reached by the communication structure.

One superintendent stated the case for comprehensive overall communication when he said, "Every person in our school district is part of our school system." If this concept of the school is accepted, then it follows logically that the communication system should strive to reach everyone in the community. Hit-or-miss communication has no place in the modern school community. The achievement of an effective communication system requires careful planning based on a thorough knowledge of the social structure of the community. It is never established overnight. It often requires several years to develop a reasonably comprehensive communication system. It is not a one-man job, but rather a task requiring the cooperative efforts of many persons.

A third characteristic of the desirable communication system is flexibility. Present-day populations are characterized by a degree of mobility undreamed of twenty years ago. In some communities the population turnover runs as high as 15 or 20 percent annually. Over a period of five years, this results in almost an entirely new population. Natural population growth is another factor which must be taken into account because growth represents change. Economic and social and political changes also affect the nature of the community. In brief, as has been said earlier, the modern community is changing, and the modern communication structure must be flexible enough to accommodate these changes.

A fourth requirement of good communication is accuracy. The communication system which does not provide a reasonably accurate transmission of information can be embarrassing and in some cases disastrous. Accuracy is not easy to achieve since people are inclined to place their own interpretation on news and this sometimes leads to considerable ambiguity and actual variance from the truth.

The most effective communication system is usually carefully structured. A structure is an established framework of communication channels which is designed to promote the efficient flow of information. Structure in a communication system helps to achieve accuracy, increases speed, and tends to eliminate duplication and conflict. The community is structured, and it logically follows that the most effective communication with it will be structured also. A full discussion of the structure of communication appears in a subsequent section.

Closely allied to structure is the organization which directs and controls the flow of information through the communication structure. Sometimes this is referred to as the administration of communication. Regardless of the term used, the concept is one of ensuring that information is properly forwarded, through the proper channels, to the proper persons at the proper times. Organization provides communicants with a precise knowledge of their responsibilities and the authority to discharge those responsibilities. The organization naturally must have at its head a person who assumes overall responsibility. In the case of the large school system this person may have the title of director of public relations. In the smaller school system he may be the superintendent of schools, an assistant superintendent, or a teacher of journalism or English.

Last, but not least, the most effective communication will be that which is developed and operated on a long-range basis. Communication is a long-range process and requires long-range planning. Today's program is not for today only. It provides the foundation on which tomorrow's program is built. A desirable image of the school is the result of years of communication consistently directed toward desired goals. Short-term gains in public relations, if not consistent with long-range goals, may eventually prove disadvantageous to the school system. The public school is a very long-term institution, and its communication system should be geared to long-range plans.

In summary, the characteristics of effective communication between school and community include a two-way nature, comprehensiveness, flexibility, accuracy, structure, organization, and long-range planning.

Objectives

What is the objective of school-community communication? The answer in simplest form is to make education as effective as possible. Or in other words, to achieve the best possible education for the community. This is, of course, a very broad and inclusive objective. Upon analysis we can subdivide this major objective into a number of component parts. Such a subdivision will serve to aid the reader in seeing the communication picture in more detail.

1. *The first objective is to provide the people with information about their schools.* This information comes in a multitude of forms and from many sources within and without the school. If may be in the form of news, or it may be an interpretation of the program of the school or an analysis of its activities. In any event the objective is to get the information to the people of the community at such times, in such form, and in such a way that it is accepted and assimilated.

2. The second objective is a corollary of the first. *It is to provide the school with information about the community.* This takes even more effort than does the first. Perhaps this is true because we have too little experience in this aspect of communication.

3. Another objective and one which is closely tied to the first two on the list and goes far in helping to achieve the others which follow is *to establish and maintain public confidence in the schools.* Of course, communication alone is not likely to accomplish this unless the work of the school merits confidence. In advertising, a strong promotional campaign may temporarily increase sales, but if the product is poor, sales are not likely to continue to be good. So it is in communication. The school must merit confidence if this important objective of communication is to be achieved. It should be recognized, however, that the failure to communicate with the public even by an excellent school system can breed suspicion and mistrust under some circumstances.

4. *A fourth objective is to secure community support for the school and its program.* Intelligent support comes only with an understanding of the school and its needs.

5. *An important objective of communication is to develop a commonality of purpose, effort, and achievement.* Good communication can develop a feeling of sharing by the community in the program of the school. Such a feeling serves to identify the community with the school, to give it a sense of participating in the accomplishments of the school, and to establish a feeling of responsibility for the success of school projects.

6. *A sixth objective is to develop in the community a recognition of the vital importance of education in our social and economic life.* This is a broad objective but one which, if achieved, will be reflected in the local attitude toward the school and its program. The evidence is readily available but it is seldom presented to the people in clear, concise, and meaningful terms. This objective is prominent in the long-range approach to communication. It is a strong segment of the foundation on which such an approach can be built.

7. *A corollary objective is one of keeping the people informed of new developments and trends in education.* Educational research and experimentation are searching for and formulating new and, hopefully, better methods of teaching and learning. The school may and should from time to time adopt new ideas which promise educational improvement. If the community is aware in a general way of new educational developments, it is more likely to accept new methods in the classroom. The radical change in the method of teaching mathematics introduced only a few years ago is a case in point. The school system which has a long-range communication program which includes keeping the people informed of educational developments will certainly encounter less opposition and criticism if and when the new concept of mathematics instruction is adopted.

8. *Another objective is to develop, through a continuous exchange of information, an atmosphere of cooperation between the school and the other social institutions of the community.* Close cooperation of this nature promises considerable advantages both to the school and to such agencies as the library, the public health service, the recreation system, the museum, and many others. It is not unusual in the American school community for one institution to be almost unaware of what another is doing. This often leads to useless duplication of effort and sometimes to open conflict. Effective communication can go a long way to avoid this situation. It can also lead to some very productive programs in which the school joins hands with another public institution to the benefit of all concerned.

9. *A ninth objective is to secure an unofficial but frank evaluation of the program of the school in terms of educational needs as the community sees them.* This is in part a function of the

return flow of information. Value judgments often are included in the flow of information from community to school, but specific evaluations may be obtained by questionnaires and interviews. Such inquiries often produce results which surprise school officials. Few schools will fail to profit by this type of specialized communication.

10. A tenth and final objective is in many respects and to a considerable degree an outcome of the successful achievement of the preceding objectives. *It is to develop public good will toward the school.* Private institutions and business enterprises spend millions of dollars each year to secure public good will. It has proven to be good business for them, and it is even more important for the public school which depends on the public for financial support. Although its monetary value is impossible to measure, it is a decisive influence in public education as well as in business and industry.

the structure of communication

As has been indicated earlier, the advantages of a structured communication system over an unstructured one are difficult to overestimate. Some might well contend that unless communication is structured, it should not be referred to as a system.

The elements of communication briefly are (1) a source from which information emanates, (2) a message to be transmitted, (3) a medium of transmission, (4) a receiver that picks up the message, and (5) a reactor that accepts or rejects the message. This is one-way communication. If we reverse the process and the reactor becomes the source of a message which was stimulated by the original message received, we have two-way communication. The feedback takes the same route but flows in the opposite direction.

Now if the school had but one family, or one group, or one institution with which it needed to communicate, the establishment of a single two-way communication system would be all that was necessary. However, such is not the case. Every school community includes many families, groups, and institutions. The school must strive to communicate with all. Different messages in different forms at different times must be sent to different people. Likewise, dissimilar reactions to these messages will and should be elicited from the community, and original messages inspired. Thus it is easily seen that comprehensive communication is a very complicated and complex task.

The necessity of a formal structure for communication is quite evident when one examines the facts presented above. The next question then is how to establish such a structure. The first step is a study of the community to learn as much about its structure as possible. The effective communication structure is the one which best fits the community in which it operates. There are, of course, structural elements which will be found common to all communities. On the other hand, there will be distinctive elements as we move from one community to another. This is true not only because of the variation of the components of communities but also because of the differences in the percentages of the population at the various interest levels.

In every community there exists what may arbitrarily be designated as three major interest levels with regard to the school: They are as follows:

Level One. At the top level are those who are very interested in the school. Their interest is consistent and continuous. The motivation for this interest may be children in school, taxes, a recognition of the importance of education, personal participation in the educational process as a worker or supplier, a critical attitude toward modern education, or any number of reasons. These people belong to parent-teacher groups, attend school affairs, appear at school board meetings, and discuss the school program with their neighbors.

Level Two. People at this level show interest in the school only on occasion. Their interest at best is characteristically subordinate to other interests and varies greatly in degree from time to time. They become active in school affairs only when some widely publicized issue is being argued or decided. Their attention to education is intermittent, and their interest for the most part superficial. They seldom join school liaison groups, and when they do, attend meetings irregularly. Both parents and nonparents are included in this grouping.

Level Three. The lowest level of interest includes those who seldom, if ever, exhibit concern about educational matters. For the most part the school is for them an unknown factor in community life. Many are uneducated and occupy underprivileged social positions in the community. They are typically from the lower economic levels. Many of them would be considered culturally deprived. Those on this level are not reached by the channels of communication and media of the typical school community.

They seldom vote on school issues and when they do they typically cast a negative vote. Response is almost nonexistent at this level.

These levels of interest include both individuals and groups. There are, of course, individuals on one level of interest who belong to organizations which occupy another level of interest. However, there is a tendency for those at one level of interest to align themselves with

Figure 2. A communication structure design

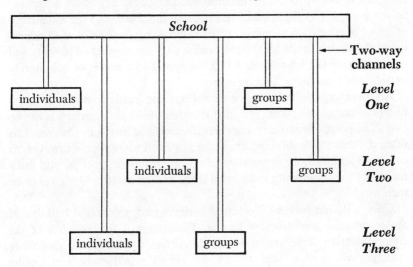

groups or organizations which represent a comparable level of interest as related to education. Interest levels are, of course, not static, and there is some movement between levels. In fact, one of the objectives of a communication system is to encourage upward movement from the lower interest levels.

In order to reach all levels, a communication structure must be developed which provides information channels to and from all levels and finds media which will carry messages through these channels to and from all three levels. Figure 2 illustrates the type of design involved. Once the design for the communication structure is set up, the problem becomes one of selecting and using the appropriate media to get the best results.

In the majority of communities, the largest proportion of the population will occupy the middle interest level. Only in some suburban high-income population centers and a few communities with a traditional educational orientation will a large proportion of the people be found at the top interest level. In the typical heavily industrial community with large areas of cultural deprivement, the number of people at the lowest interest level may exceed the number at the upper levels.

A careful analysis of a community will make possible a fairly accurate assessment of the percentage of people at each interest level. Some of the more important indicators include (1) the number of voters at school elections as compared to the number of voters on other issues and to the total of eligible voters, (2) the number of people belonging to school liaison groups, (3) the attendance at school functions, (4) the attendance at board of education meetings, (5) the frequency and amount of educational discussion in the local news media, (6) the number of parents and others visiting the schools, and (7) the type and amount of community participation in the school program.

An inventory of the formal organizations and institutions of a community presents no difficulty. The identification of informal groups is not so easy. The power structure, which was discussed at length in Chapter 2, is often difficult to identify and even more difficult to analyze. However, as complete an inventory as possible of all organizations, groups, and institutions of the community is essential if the communication design is to be inclusive.

Once a design such as illustrated is developed, the actual building of the communication structure begins. The design is the skeleton of the communication structure and will determine the size and shape the structure will assume. The media which are discussed in the next section provide the flesh and blood of the communication structure. The design of the structure is largely determined by the number and the media by the nature of the occupants of the various interest levels.

the processes of communication

The processes of communication may be divided into two broad classifications: person-to-person and mass communication. Most communication is probably of the person-to-person type, but the advent of radio and television has greatly increased the volume of mass communication. Each classification has its characteristic media. Face-to-face dialogues, telephone conversations, letters, speeches, sales talks, and personal acts influence millions of people every day in a very powerful way. Likewise, newspapers, magazines, advertising materials, radio, television, and the other mass media exert a profound effect upon community life.

In developing a school-community communication structure, a thorough knowledge of both types of communication is essential. Each has an important role to play. Each has advantages and disadvantages in relation to the varied situations which are confronted in developing and maintaining an effective communication structure.

Before discussing the media of each of these classifications, it might be well to point out that under each classification there are four major means of communication: the spoken word, the written word, the picture, and the physical act. Technically speaking, some authorities may question the physical act as a means of communication although few will question the communicative effect of a nod, a shrug of the shoulders, a wry facial expression, or a clapping of the hands. Advertising has used the physical act extensively to deliver the sales message. Examples are the sense of deep satisfaction conveyed to the audience by the lighting of a cigarette or the pouring of a bottle of foaming beer into a glass.

The spoken word is the common means of communication over the backyard fence, at the Rotary Club meeting, in the teacher-pupil conference, and over the telephone. The spoken word has in recent years become a major means of mass communication also, by virtue of radio and television.

The written word is still the principal means of mass communication despite the inroads of radio and television verbal presentations. Millions of pages of printed material are read every day in books, newspapers, and magazines. Although largely a means of mass communication, the written word is also used to convey thoughts between persons through the media of letters, notes, and telegrams.

Pictures are powerful means of communication. The old proverb, "One picture is worth a thousand words," is quite true in many situations. Movies and television pictures convey messages of one kind or another to millions every day. The artist seeks to convey an impression, a mood, or an emotion in his work. Maps are one of the most common and valuable picture media. Schools have made effective use of pictures in the form of exhibits, posters, and pupil sketches and paintings. Newspaper cartoons are picture presentations of the moods, attitudes, emotions, and opinions of the times as well as caricatures of prominent public figures. Occasionally, pictures are used in person-to-person communication where the spoken or written word is inadequate. Who has not found himself in the position on some occasions of wishing he could draw a picture or diagram to explain a situation? It is often easier to draw a map than to give verbal directions on how to reach a certain place. Correspondents exchange pictures of themselves to convey their likenesses to each other—a task for which words are not fully adequate.

Physical acts deliver messages in many ways both in person-to-person situations and via mass media. The dramatic arts rely heavily on physical actions to convey the most subtle meanings. Expressions on people's faces often speak louder than words. A wink or a smile conveys a message or an attitude which it might take many words to express. Charitable contributions, gifts to employees, provision of parks and recreational facilities for public use are all types of institutional acts which communicate good will. The school in making its plant facilities available for various legitimate community activities is communicating its feeling of public responsibility and cooperation. In fact, the total school program, aside from formal public relations efforts, can be effective in delivering a message of faith in and good will toward the community. A good school program is the foundation on which effective communication is built. In turn, effective communication of the two-way variety is helpful in building a good school program.

Those responsible for communication between school and community should be fully cognizant of the processes and means of communication as well as the media. The school is in an enviable position to take advantage of both person-to-person and mass communication. Probably no institution has more and better opportunities for person-to-person communication with the people it serves. Few institutions have the number of mass media available to them, and none can secure their use at a lower cost. Many school systems, however, not only have failed to utilize these media, but have not even recognized them.

The spoken and written word, the picture or illustration, and the physical act can and should all find a useful place in the comprehensive communication structure of the school community. Each has its peculiar and, in some cases, unique functions in conveying ideas, attitudes, opinions, and facts. To neglect any one means is to fail to seize the opportunity to reach someone, at some place, sometime.

the media of communication

Media are here defined as the transmission agents which can be utilized to convey messages. For example, the telephone is a common medium through which the spoken word expresses the thoughts of one person to another. The telegram serves in a like way for transmission of the written word.

Mass media such as the newspaper, radio, and television transmit identical messages to large numbers of people. With the advent of large television networks, it is estimated that as many as eighty million people have received the same message at the same time. The number of books and magazines and the amount of other printed materials have increased enormously in the last decade. These mass media in many instances are profusely illustrated, making use of pictures, sketches, and drawings to supplement the written word in striving for more effective communication.

It is the purpose of this section to discuss the principal media in relation to their use in school-community communication.

Person-to-person communication media

The media in this classification have one important advantage in all situations over mass media. They provide an opportunity for, and encouragement of, immediate response. Person-to-person communication is inherently a two-way process almost without exception. The media of conversation, for example, is by definition a two-way process. For this reason, if for no other, this type of communication is of great importance for school-community use.

In person-to-person situations the message sender can appraise the reactions of his listener. He has some basis for deciding whether his message is received with pleasure, anger, or indifference. He gets what is sometimes called "feedback." It may be in the form of nodded approval, expressions of interest, questions, or even argument. Sometimes his message may be misunderstood or his motives questioned. In the person-to-person situation there is immediate opportunity to remedy the situation. Clues are also often provided regarding possibilities for increasing the effectiveness of the message. The more feedback the school gets from its messages to the community, the greater is the opportunity to reach a common understanding.

Direct contact with individuals encourages them to identify themselves more closely with the school. They have an opportunity to contribute their ideas, their desires, and their aspirations for the development of the school program. This tends to create an attitude of sharing, of cooperation between the individual and the school.

Let us now turn our attention to the direct personal contact media which are available to the school in communicating with the people it serves. They are both numerous and varied. One of the most common is the telephone which is the medium parents most often use to reach the superintendent, the principal, and, less frequently, the school board members. To some administrators this type of call is unwelcome, to put it mildly. Too often it is associated in their minds with a complaint, a criticism, or even a denunciation of some teacher or other school employee. On the other hand, in many schools calls by school officials to parents are usually made as a result of the truancy or misbehavior of pupils. The direct contact by telephone can be used to communicate an attitude of good will and concern on the part of the school not only for its pupils but for parents. School officials can call parents to offer congratulations on some achievement of their children, to extend an invitation to some school affair, or simply to give some bit of information about the school. Frequently a call to a school patron or taxpayer will not only secure information or advice, but will create a feeling of sharing in a common endeavor.

Reporting to parents on the scholastic progress of pupils is a custom as old as the public schools themselves. Yet only a comparative few have seen and utilized the great potential for communication which is inherent in it. Reporting systems vary, but probably the most common is the report card which is usually issued at the end of the month or six-week period. It typically contains the bare facts of scholastic achievement with an indication of satisfaction or dissatisfaction with the deportment or conduct of the pupil. Some reports enlarge the area reported on to include sociological and psychological aspects of the pupil's development. In a few schools the progress report is descriptive in form, giving the parent more detailed information and often suggesting measures that the home may take to benefit the pupil's achievement. In still fewer schools individual conferences with parents are used to report pupil achievement. Combinations of these methods are not uncommon.

In any school-community system of communication the pupil progress report merits special consideration. It is a ready-made channel of communication with those who are or should be most vitally concerned with the school. It provides an opportunity to reach the parent in an area which readily commands his interest. No topic is of greater concern to the typical parent than his child's welfare. With this interest as a base, the progress report can be utilized in a number of ways to bring the parent into closer contact with the school. It can be expanded to carry relevant information to the home and provide a feedback to the school. It should be an integral part of the communication system.

Direct contacts by school personnel with individuals and organizations can be valuable in conveying information about the school, interpreting the school program, clearing up misunderstandings, and evaluating the effects of the use of other media. Firsthand reactions which are frank and objective may be secured in this fashion. Every member of the school staff can participate to a greater or lesser degree. The school should make a conscious effort to make its staff aware of the importance of face-to-face contacts in relating the school to the community. If each teacher, each administrator, and each member of the custodial staff were to take it upon himself to bring an item of information about the school to one person each day, the volume of information would be tremendous. This presupposes, of course, that these people have a working knowledge of the school program and the goals toward which it is directed. It is a responsibility of the person who administers public relations to see that the staff is aware of the opportunities in this area and is prepared to take advantage of them. Opportunities occur in face-to-face conversations in stores, laboratories, offices, homes, theaters, and in family gatherings and club meetings, at service organization luncheons, chambers of commerce, and labor union meetings. Most of these opportunities will occur in informal conversations, but not infrequently school personnel are asked to speak on school-community matters or appear on panels or participate in formal question-and-answer periods. The school itself may provide such opportunities by inviting individuals to visit the school and by having visitation days for parents and other people of the community. Open house at a new school building, high school graduation exercises, honors day programs for recognition of outstanding students, dramatic and musical productions, and athletic contests all provide opportunities for direct contacts which can, if school people are prepared and alerted, result in very effective two-way communication.

Personal letters, informal notes, and even telegrams are useful media for person-to-person contacts between school and community. Personal letters from the superintendent of schools or the director of public relations to organizational officers and business and industrial leaders are quite effective. On the occasion of the introduction of a program of adult education, letters from the superintendent of schools to community leaders are very well received. Personal letters to business and professional men asking for suggestions on how to present the need for school tax increases usually produce both information and good will. A request for permission to have a science class visit a chemical plant or oil refinery can convey a lot about the school science program as a justification for such a request. An informal note of thanks for an individual's support of a bond issue may well include a brief summary on how the money will be spent and the benefits which are expected to accrue.

One superintendent wired the editor of the local newspaper from Atlantic City, New Jersey, that the building plans for the new high school had been awarded first prize in an architectural exhibit. Almost immediately the whole community was informed. A day or so later the same news appeared in the metropolitan papers of the state. In this case the telegram proved a useful medium not only to get the news back home but to build good will with a strategic person in the school-community communication system.

Formal person-to-person contacts include systematic interviews, house-to-house canvasses for information, opinion surveys, and child census taking. Such contacts should be planned carefully and the purposes fully explained to the community. Advance notices in local newspapers help to expedite the work of the canvassers and census takers. Adequate training of those workers is essential if complete and reliable data are to be secured.

Valuable information can be secured by such organized contacts with cross sections or random samplings of the community. In some cases, such as the child census, every home is contacted. Harold Hand in his book *What People Think about Their Schools* [1] suggests a number of areas for inquiry. Among them are school discipline, adequacy of offerings, financial demands, homework, lunch arrangements, teacher attitudes, guidance, and extracurricular activities. Information about community satisfaction or dissatisfaction in regard to these and many other facets of the school program is invaluable to the school.

While the principal objective of such inventories and opinion polls is to discover what people think about their schools, an incidental benefit accrues as most people, if properly interviewed, will experience a feeling of helping and sharing in the work of the school. The public relations effect is usually quite good.

Mass media

The number and diversity of the mass media available to the school is almost overwhelming. In most communities the problem is one of selecting the proper media rather than of securing them. Effective use of mass media depends largely upon an understanding of their nature, their potential, their limitations, and the ways in which they function. Certain messages, at certain times, to certain people will perhaps find one medium which is most appropriate, while the same message at another

[1] Harold Hand, *What People Think about Their Schools,* pp. 33–47, Harcourt, Brace & World, Inc., New York, 1948.

time, or directed to another element of the population, will be better transmitted by another medium. Much is yet to be learned about how people react to different media, what the impact of secondary or incidental transmission is on persons who receive mass media messages, and how messages can be most effectively encoded for each medium.

The most common mass media available to the school may be divided into two classes; namely, those sponsored by the school and those of nonschool sponsorship. In the first class are school newspapers, school exhibits, tape recorders, and projectors; posters, pamphlets, and brochures issued by the school; class yearbooks, annual reports, and similar publications. At the university level some institutions have their own radio and television broadcasting stations which are noncommercial These stations, while largely used for instructional purposes, also present a great deal of information about the college or university of which they are a part.

The greater volume of school-community communication carried by mass media travels through channels which the school does not own or control. The principal ones are newspapers, magazines, television, radio, and community publications of various types. Since media of this class are beyond the control of the school, it is necessary for the school to establish a mutually satisfactory working relationship with those who do control these media. This is one of the tasks of developing and maintaining a comprehensive communication system.

Mass media as a whole have the distinct advantage of making it possible to reach a large number of people in a relatively short time. A report of a change in the school curriculum or method of teaching science appearing in the local newspaper may be read by 60 percent of the people in the community in one day. To reach the same number of people by person-to-person contacts might take months.

Furthermore, mass media messages usually can be delivered in the exact form in which they are encoded. This is manifestly impossible in person-to-person situations. Finally, mass media provide the most economical means of conveying messages to large numbers of people.

On the other hand, mass media have certain limitations which affect their use in the school-community communication system. First among these limitations is the one-way nature of mass communication. The receiver cannot talk back to or question the television or radio set, the local newspaper, or school publication. It is true he may call the broadcasting station by telephone or write a letter to the editors, but these at best are delayed reactions of relatively low frequency. The urge to respond to a mass-media message even when invited to do so is usually short-lived unless the receiver has some compelling motivation. The situation may be improved to some extent by inviting response and providing return communication channels for reactions. This usually involves another medium except in the case of letters to the editor in response to news or editorial comments.

In the second place, since mass media by definition carry identical messages, it is impossible to adapt news material to the various types of readers. This lack of flexibility is a serious disadvantage in a school community with a diverse social and economic structure.

Furthermore, mass media are subject to reinterpretations which are often inaccurate. Mr. Jones, for example, may read in the local newspaper an article about the promotion policies of the school. He then, in conversation with his fellow workers, tells them about the article. His interpretation may be colored by his own background and prejudices to the extent that the content of the news item is radically misinterpreted. As a result of the distortion, a dozen people may assume an antagonistic attitude toward the school because "they promote kids whether they know anything or not." A more sophisticated reader might accurately interpret the policies to mean that some children whose social and physical maturation was considerably ahead of their scholastic attainment were allowed to proceed to the next grade with their age groups.

Finally, any evaluation of the results of the use of mass media by the school is difficult if not impossible. This is, of course, a characteristic of one-way communication. On a national scale radio and television rating systems provide fairly reliable estimates of the number of listeners or viewers, and newspapers and magazines have accurate counts of their circulation. However, it is the number of viewers, listeners, and readers, not the nature of the response, which is involved. Advertising results in mass media can be fairly well evaluated in terms of product sales. But this evaluation procedure is applicable to the school-community communication problem in only a very limited way.

This brief discussion of the advantages and limitations of mass media points up the fact that to be most effective for school-community use as well as any other, a message must be properly and carefully encoded, presented through the most suitable medium, and provided with response channels which may well involve person-to-person communication. Mass media are of great value, but their greatest value can be achieved only after careful study of their characteristics and the nature and structure of the population to be reached.

Of the school-sponsored media the school newspaper is probably the most common. While its circulation outside the school is largely limited to parents, it is read by almost all students who, in turn, relate its contents to parents and friends. Although the paper is primarily designed to give students journalistic experience, it does provide an avenue of contact with the home and should be utilized to provide readers with information about the school, along with the personal items which characterize this type of publication.

School exhibits, when well done, give the community an idea of the nature and quality of work done by the school. Exhibits featuring the graphic arts, metalwork, machine-tool products, and scientific phenomena are appreciated by school patrons. Dramatic presentations, musical productions, and athletic contests convey vivid impressions of the atmosphere and achievements of the school. Posters which are usually made by art classes advertise some feature of the school or announce a school production or in some instances illustrate an issue, such as overcrowded classrooms or the need for more financial support.

Tape recorders and projectors have only recently achieved common usage. They can be valuable in presenting the work of the school to community groups. Tape recordings of class proceedings, student discussions, faculty meetings, and similar events hold the interest of PTA members and other school liaison groups. Even greater possibilities are inherent in projectors. Series of slides may be developed which depict class procedures, scientific experiments, laboratory exercises, school equipment, plant facilities, and building conditions. Sound film projections of teaching and learning situations, graduation ceremonies, student council meetings, guidance procedures, and many other activities make very effective presentations.

The annual school report, which is required in many states, is a typically neglected medium for communication with the public. A few school systems have recognized the potential in the annual report and produced handsomely illustrated and carefully composed editions of the usually staid report. The school should take a leaf from the book of the publicly held business corporation which typically puts out a colorful, well-illustrated, easily read annual report to its shareholders. The shareholder of the public schools merits similar treatment.

A special type of school medium which is usually employed only on occasion is known as promotional material. It consists of leaflets, pamphlets, brochures, and other kinds of printed material which are designed to influence people to take a desired action. For the most part, promotional materials are used by the school to help secure the passage of a bond issue, a tax increase, or a school-district reorganization or consolidation proposal. Such publications vary from informative presentations to "hard sell" messages which prophesy educational disaster if the issue they are promoting is rejected by the voters. While the former type is ordinarily in the public interest, the latter is not. The people should be fully informed, but to predict dire things for the future is not in the public interest unless the facts are incontrovertible. If there is an effective school-community system of communication, the facts will already be known and only a brief synopsis of the background of the issue and a timely reminder of the time and place of the election will be necessary.

The community newspaper stands at the head of the list of non-school-sponsored media. It is usually powerful in developing public opinion. Fortunately, the typical community newspaper is pro education. The newspaper characteristically recognizes its responsibility to the community and particularly public institutions of the community. The editor, in the majority of cases, is more than willing to extend full cooperation to the school. Most community newspapers, furthermore, are aware of the close relationship of the local educational program to the state and national scene.

With such a background, the local newspaper is an essential medium in the school-community communication system. A close-working relationship should be established with the editor by the head of the school system. The editor should be one of the best-informed persons on educational matters in the community. It is the job of the school to see that he is. The editor should be fully aware of the goals of the school and if possible be convinced that these goals are legitimate and desirable. If there is a disagreement in this area, the editor may be invited to discuss any differences with the policy-developing and policy-making bodies of the school. Any disagreement is likely to be in the interpretation of goals and purposes or in their implementation rather than over the goals themselves. Often an editorial point of view changes when all the facts are known. Letters of appreciation for school news coverage help to build good will with the local paper. Some papers prefer that advance copies of school news items be prepared by school officials and sent to the paper. Others prefer to do their own news reports. The school should take its cue from the newspaper and give full cooperation in either case.

Most local newspapers provide space for readers to express their views on public issues. These "Letters from the People" columns can be utilized in a very effective way to secure community opinion. Challenging articles on the various aspects of the school program and on school policies may be written with the express purpose of stimulating discussion in the letter column. In fact basic issues can be raised in such a way as to motivate replies. An article on an educational issue may conclude with the question, "What do you think?"

Finally, it should be recognized by school people that ordinary events are not news. A story of long and faithful service is not as newsworthy as one on the embezzlement of funds by the school board treasurer. The rehiring of the superintendent of schools will not receive the headlines accorded to his dismissal. These are the facts of newspaper life. However, there are many things going on in the school which are new if the school is keeping abreast of the times. A new course, a new appointment, a new honor won by a student or teacher, new equipment, and new ideas can be the basis of newsworthy articles.

In the relationship of school to newspaper each has definite responsibilities and obligations. The school should at all times remember that it is a public institution and make its operation an open book. Only minor exceptions with regard to certain phases of personnel and finances are permissible. The school should make all other information freely available. Information should be reported accurately and fully since incomplete disclosures breed suspicion. Half-truths and evasions reflect on the integrity of the school and on the profession itself. It is the responsibility of the school to see that no favoritism is shown among newspapers or between the newspaper and other news media. This is not always easy with differing datelines and deadlines, but among reasonable people a set of policies can be developed which will be reasonably acceptable to all.

The responsibility of the press is well stated by Louis B. Seltzer of *The Cleveland Press,* who says,

> The newspaper, if it is to discharge its duty to the schools, must serve them by being their civic "report card." The paper has an obligation to give the public a periodic accounting of what schools are costing and just what this money is buying in these important intangibles: the development of skills, talents and character of the community's young people. It has a duty to report accurately, objectively and dramatically on classroom work and other activities within the school in order that the public, responsible for the support and control of its education, can wisely appraise the school's purposes, accomplishments, and needs. Only a thoroughly informed public can determine accurately whether the schools are strong or weak and just what should be done about it.

Radio and television are fast gaining ground as media of school-community communication. Most population centers of 35,000 or more have local radio stations which are to a greater or lesser degree available to school systems within their coverage area. The key people in the typical local radio station organization are the program director and the news editor. Their cooperation is essential to the effective use of radio. It is important that they become well versed in the program of the school. Messages for radio broadcasting must first of all be brief, for time is money in the radio world. Second, they must be carefully and simply stated, preferably in the present tense to indicate ongoing action.

Half-time breaks in the broadcasting of high school football and basketball games provide an excellent opportunity for informing the public about other aspects of the school program. Most stations have a neighborhood news program which will include school news items. Some school systems have cooperative arrangements with their local stations which include students' announcing and reporting school events. This arrangement provides laboratory experience for students interested in the radio field as well as a news outlet.

Tapes of school events of the day may be produced for evening broadcasts. Radio dates the news much more closely than newspapers. Yesterday's events are ordinarily of no interest to the radio program director.

Television is a much more difficult medium. Most stations have network commitments which take up a large proportion of the available time. Television is also a difficult medium in the sense that presentations involve both the spoken word and the picture or image. Many people are self-conscious before the camera. Notes and outlines are seldom permissible. Time allotments are quite rigid. Nevertheless television can be a very effective medium of school-community communication under favorable conditions. The school should take the initiative in creating such conditions. Executives of the television station should be kept fully informed of the program of the school on a continuing basis, not just when time is wanted for promoting school bond issues and tax increases. National educational events and such occasions as American Education Week offer opportunities for local school-sponsored programs. Stations usually provide a half-hour or an hour per week for public information programs. The school should be prepared to capitalize on this opportunity. Both teachers and students, with careful preparation, can present classroom demonstrations, panel discussions, demonstrations of guidance and counseling techniques, musicales, and dramatic sketches. Exhibits of student work in the various forms of art can be presented effectively through the medium of television. Some of the larger cities have stations that provide instructional programs for both youngsters and adults. In such cases, the opportunity to communicate more than just the instructional courses should be utilized, thus making educational television all that the name implies.

The responsibility of the school to the radio and television media is much the same as that owed to the newspaper. Continuous contact with station officials must be maintained. These media should be represented at school press conferences. Full, accurate, truthful, timely, up-to-the-minute, interesting, and carefully prepared information is essential. Station officials should be provided with regular news releases even though they cannot be expected to use all of them or even a substantial number of them. They should be kept continuously informed so they can intelligently select those items they do use. Brevity, simplicity, and clarity are of major importance since time is valuable and seldom is there a repeat performance for those who do not get the message the first time.

These media have a responsibility to the school. Unlike the press, these media do not have a lengthy tradition of carrying educational news. Their time is in a real sense their money, and there are no educational "commercials" to provide financial compensation. However, as public media, most stations recognize an obligation to the public and provide some time for noncommercial broadcasting. A fair proportion of this time should be allocated to the school system. Remote-control broadcasting, while expensive, is justified on special educational occasions. These media have a particular obligation to cover those school events which are most effectively reported by them. The press can only describe the newly organized orchestra or band; radio can transmit the music; but television can bring to its viewing audience both the sound and the picture of the musical performance.

Finally, those who control these media should offer the help of their technical staffs to school people in the preparation, organization, and presentation of education programs. This will not only benefit the school; it will help to create good will among future community leaders.

Magazines, particularly those of national circulation, provide only very rare opportunities for a local school to break into print. Occasionally a school with some unique feature is the subject of a national magazine article. How some common educational problem was solved in your community is good magazine material. Outstanding performances by students as individuals or groups sometimes receive attention from magazines. Professional magazines for teachers, administrators, and other personnel frequently carry articles about local school systems. They afford an opportunity for local school people to achieve some recognition for their school and also provide good copy for the local newspaper. Such publicity enhances the image of the school in the community.

Almost every community has a variety of publications which have wide circulation in the local area. Included among these are neighborhood weeklies, church bulletins, shopping guides, organization publications, newsletters, guides to community activities, foreign language papers, corporation magazines, and house organs of various kinds. Many small towns have a weekly newspaper which gladly accepts school news. Often a column is turned over to the school for a weekly account of school events and other items of educational interest.

Church bulletin editors will usually accept brief news releases about schools, which are of interest to the parishioners. Stories of cooperative efforts among schools and churches are particularly welcome. Joint programs aimed at combating delinquency make excellent items for church bulletins.

Shopping guides are read largely by women, and thus offer a direct contact with a segment of the population which characteristically is concerned with children and youth. These publications are unusually receptive to articles about children and their education.

Most clubs, civic organizations, and associations have a printed or mimeographed medium of communication with members. Such publications usually are glad to get school news, announcements of educational events, and school calendars of events. Guest editorials by the superintendent of schools, the guidance director, or the supervisor of special education are usually welcomed. Organizations like the Rotary, Kiwanis, and Lions Clubs which have a special interest in a particular phase of education appreciate articles featuring their joint efforts with the school.

The newsletter is a medium which both public and private agencies use to keep their clientele informed of what is going on in their respective agencies. Banks make use of the newsletter to advise patrons of developments in the money markets. Investment brokers offer a similar service to their accounts. Some libraries use the newsletter to keep patrons informed of new books available and improved services offered. These newsletters are often distributed at the place of origin but occasionally are mailed. Their editors are usually quite receptive to brief school items, especially announcements.

Some communities publish guides to entertainment, professional services, public institutions, recreational facilities, and other community resources. While the school system is usually mentioned in terms of numbers of pupils or size of buildings, there is no reason to limit the reference to these items. The program of the school should be of greater interest to the reader.

Foreign-language newspapers offer an opportunity to reach some people who are comparatively isolated from the school by language barriers. Providing school news in the language of the readers of these papers, along with announcements of evening and adult classes, is a real service to foreign-born residents as well as a unique communication contact.

Many of the larger corporations publish a magazine for employees and stockholders. These magazines are for the most part well illustrated, colorful, and interesting, especially to employees and stockholders to whom they are primarily directed. However, they often appear in dentists' and doctors' waiting rooms and sometimes in public libraries. In cases where the company has a plant or an office in the local community, school people will find the editors of these magazines willing to consider well-written articles for publication. Business corporations are taking increasing interest in education and are providing substantial support to education at the collegiate level. This interest can be extended to the lower educational levels if school officials make a concentrated effort along these lines. The corporation magazine provides a good opportunity to present the case for the elementary and secondary school.

The circulation of the house organ is usually limited to the employees of a particular business enterprise. Companies with a small number of employees usually resort to mimeograph or ditto. Larger enterprises use the most modern photographic processes of printing to produce their publications. A well-defined group can be reached through the house organ. However, some of these publications have a policy of carrying only their own materials. In such a case, the editor may be persuaded to put out a special edition during American Education Week or just prior to an education-industry program. Another approach is through the employees. Employees who are members of school boards, PTAs, or citizens school advisory committees can become subjects of feature articles at the suggestion of the school superintendent or public relations director. The publicity given the schools will be incidental but nevertheless will add to the sum total of school-community communication.

additional reading

American Association of School Administrators: "Educational Administration in a Changing Community," pp. 158–174, in *Thirty-seventh Year-book,* National Education Association, Washington, D.C., 1959.

Bryson, Lyman (ed.): *The Communication of Ideas,* Harper & Row, Publishers, Incorporated, New York, 1948.

Dapper, Gloria: *Public Relations for Educators,* pp. 32–104, The Macmillan Company, New York, 1964.

Hand, Harold: *What People Think about Their Schools,* Harcourt, Brace & World, Inc., New York, 1948.

Kindred, Leslie: *School Public Relations,* pp. 269–418, Prentice-Hall, Inc., Englewood Cliffs, N.J., 1957.

Lynd, Robert: *Knowledge for What?* pp. 193–197, Princeton University Press, Princeton, N.J., 1939.

Schramm, Wilbur (ed.): *The Process and Effects of Mass Communication,* University of Illinois Press, Urbana, Ill., 1955.

the development
and maintenance
of communication

7 Communication is the basis of all learning. It is the process through which knowledge is acquired and disseminated. It is at the heart of the educative process. We learn from books, from pictures, from teachers, and from fellow students. We learn from the spoken and the written word, from the likeness on the page or on the screen, and from the acts of ourselves and others. The educative process is simply planned, controlled, and directed communication. Messages stimulate other messages so that a chain reaction is carried on. The teacher stimulates discussion among her students. Effective messages should be encoded in a form which is least susceptible to misinterpretation by the receivers. Every teacher has the problem of presenting material in such a way that her pupils will understand. Appropriate media for the various kinds of messages must be carefully selected. The

good teacher not only lectures; she uses audio-visual materials; she assigns reading; and she plans field trips. The effectiveness of communication should be evaluated. The teacher does this by oral and written examination.

Thus we see that developing and maintaining a communication system involving both school and community is merely a matter of extending horizons. The professional educator is eminently fitted for the task. He needs only to recognize and accept the wider and greater responsibility of dealing with the total community. He will find this rewarding as well as challenging, for there is much to be learned from the community which is in close contact with the school.

Effective communication between school and community can be developed and maintained only through conscious, planned effort. It must be designed to serve a particular school community, not just any community. The agents of communication, which include both school personnel and the people of the community, should in a lesser or greater degree participate in the communication process. Their responsibilities and relationships should be set forth in a clear and understandable fashion. Their efforts should be organized for greatest effectiveness. Available media should be mobilized for the task. A structure of communication must be developed which will help to ensure comprehensive, accurate, flexible, long-range, two-way communication. Finally, there should be provision for periodic evaluation of the communication system in order to spot weaknesses and develop overall efficiency. It is the purpose of this chapter to discuss how this may be done.

the agents of communication

For our purposes the agents of communication may be defined as those who send and receive messages. Therefore, the agents of school-community communication include all of those who convey and those who receive information in this context. The board of education, the superintendent, his administrative staff, the teachers, the maintenance workers, and the pupils are all agents of communication who convey impressions and information about the school to others. The agents of communication in the community may for convenience be divided into two classes: individuals and groups. The latter classification includes formal organizations, institutions, and informal groups.

The casual observer will usually overlook teachers, custodians, and pupils as communication agents. He regards the board of education, the administrative staff, and the director of public relations, if there is such a person, as the school's agents of communication. Often they are the only members of the school staff involved in a formal way. However, every member of the school system to a greater or lesser degree contributes to the image which the school conveys to the community. By far the majority of the school's contacts with the community are made by teachers and pupils. Their very number ensures this. Few teachers and fewer pupils regard themselves as communication agents. Most are never charged with any formal responsibility along these lines. And yet their contacts with parents, civic organizations, business and professional people of the community, and others make them informal agents. Their words and actions create impressions and attitudes regarding the school among people of the community. A child who loves to go to school, admires his teachers, and brings home reports of events at school is an effective agent of communication. So is the teacher who enjoys her work, likes her students, and radiates enthusiasm for the school program. The custodian who keeps the school plant well heated and ventilated, spotlessly clean, and free of hazards contributes to a favorable image of the school even if he never says a word about his job. His actions speak for him.

On the other hand, a dissatisfied, complaining teacher, a discouraged, resentful pupil, or a careless, untidy custodian can convey a very unfavorable or negative impression of the school to the community. Unfortunately, there are instances in which this type of impression is justified. However, one of the functions of communication is to make such conditions known so that they may be remedied. The better the communications, the sooner conditions are known and can be improved.

The community agents outside the school may include all local persons both as individuals and as members of groups. The distinction is made in this context because of the difference in the manner in which individuals and groups or organizations originate, encode, and react to messages. Organizations often assume positions on issues, make pronouncements, and convey impressions from which some of their members strongly dissent. Occasionally a minority with a leader will break away from an established organization and form a new one. Some groups have considerable prestige which adds weight to their positions on issues. An informal group, such as a community power structure, sometimes wields power greatly disproportionate to its numbers.

The family with children in school, for example, is a close-knit group which usually forms a common opinion of the school from children's reports, teacher contacts, and discussions around the table at dinner. Its response to the school is ordinarily uniform. On the other hand, a childless couple, a widow, or a bachelor are more likely to act as individuals in the communication process except when they are participating as a member of an organization or informal group.

Because of the fact that people form organizations and other types of groups to achieve goals which are difficult or impossible to achieve individually and because these groups operate in a different fashion and pose different communication problems, it is imperative in developing a communication system that these groups should be recognized as separate and distinct from the individuals who compose them.

analyzing the school community

The nature and program of the school are or should be well known to those responsible for developing and maintaining the communication system. The nature and composition of the community which the school serves is ordinarily considerably less well known. Effective communication requires that the community as well as the school be familiar to those who develop a system of communication.

In most instances a study of the community is indicated. There are a variety of ways to secure the necessary information about a community. The formal sociological survey may be useful in some cases. In others, an informal analysis carried on by knowledgeable people is a better procedure. The objective of these and other types of studies is to secure an accurate picture of the nature and structure of the community.

The study should seek to answer such questions as follow:

> What is the educational level of the people in the community?
>
> What proportion of the population is at each school-interest level?
>
> What organizations are interested in education, and how large is their membership?
>
> How well developed is the power structure?
>
> What school liaison groups exist, and how effective are they?
>
> What media of communication does the school community possess?
>
> How effective are these media?
>
> Which are available to the school, and which might be made available?

The answer to these questions will provide a foundation of information upon which the communication structure can be built.

The responsibility for getting the desired information rests with the school, usually through the superintendent or, in the larger school systems, an assistant superintendent or a director of public relations. However, it is obvious that no one individual can effectively make such a study. It is essential that a number of people participate if the study is to be reasonably accurate and comprehensive.

A formal sociological study by an outside agency is usually of extended duration and expensive. Few school systems have the funds or the inclination to sponsor such a study.

The informal compilation of data by local people is usually better, quicker, and less expensive. There is also the advantage of familiarity with the community which local people have and the outside agency ordinarily does not have.

The local citizens school advisory committee discussed in earlier chapters is an ideal agency to conduct such a study. A joint effort with a carefully selected group of teachers analyzing the school communication picture can prove quite effective, not only in getting the data but also in familiarizing each group with the other's area of study. A joint project has the advantage of providing the opportunity for a coordinated report dealing with both school and community. Students in high school journalism and sociology classes may profitably participate in such a study.

If no citizens advisory committee is in existence, such a study presents a favorable occasion to establish one on either a temporary or a continuing basis. The latter is preferable, since it makes organized and knowledgeable citizen aid available in developing the communication system and carrying out the long-range communication program.

Regardless of the method used to collect the information, it should be organized and presented in a written report. This report on the school community will include:

1. A brief history of the community
2. A brief history of the educational system
3. A description of the material and human resources of the community
4. An analysis of the nature of the population
   a. Numbers in various age groups
   b. Educational status
   c. Occupational status
   d. Social structure
5. A description of the agencies and the institutional life of the community

6. Identification and analysis of organizations and groups
7. An analysis of the communication media
8. A description of the school program
9. An analysis of the economic structure
10. An analysis of community attitudes, opinions, and morale

This report serves as a foundation upon which to develop the communication system. It should be consulted from time to time and revised as events may dictate. It will serve as a guide to those working in the communication field, both inside and outside the school system.

organization and administration

A good communication system does not operate without organization and administration. There must be a clear allocation of responsibility and authority. Good organization reduces the amount of duplication and conflict. It outlines the various roles individuals are to play in contributing to the total enterprise.

The leadership role falls naturally on the school since it is or should be an institution of leadership responsibilities. Furthermore, it is in an excellent position to organize and develop the communication system. However, the community beyond the school has definite responsibilities in the undertaking. In fact, essential features of a good system require active community participation.

In school communities which have pupil enrollments in excess of 5,000, a director of public relations is usually justified and logically assumes the leadership role in the organization. In the smaller system this role often is assumed by the superintendent. In some cases he delegates this responsibility to an assistant superintendent, a business manager, or a teacher. Whoever it may be, he should assume responsibility and have the necessary cooperation to successfully establish and administer the system. It should be recognized, of course, that his job is only one facet of a total operation, and he, therefore, works within a larger administrative structure.

Figure 3 illustrates a suggested basic pattern of organization for the school-community communication system. As indicated, final authority and responsibility rest with the board of education, which is the policy-making body. The enactment of a board policy establishing a formal communication system is a prerequisite. The organization and administration of the system is delegated to the superintendent, who may assume the responsibility himself or delegate it to another employee of the board. Assuming he does so delegate, the director of public relations, if there is such, is the logical person to be assigned the responsibility of coordinating the communication system. He may then

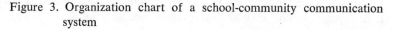

Figure 3. Organization chart of a school-community communication system

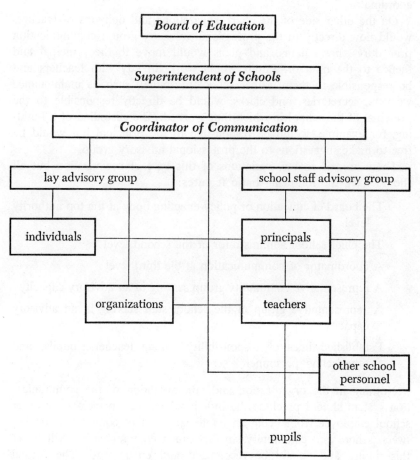

select a cabinet or planning committee, a representative group carefully chosen from both the community and the school. The function of such a group is to counsel, advise, and plan with the coordinator. As the name indicates it is advisory in character and does not have administrative powers. Its role, however, is quite important since the coordinator must rely on it to recommend policy and appraise results. Individuals and organizations of the community communicate directly with both the lay advisory group and the coordinator, depending on the nature of the communication. A suggestion for the improvement of the system by an individual of the community would be channeled to the advisory group; a newspaper editor seeking information would deal directly with the coordinator.

On the other side of the chart, suggestions and opinions of teachers would flow directly to the professional advisory group; communication procedures, news items, and plans would move to the principal and thence to the director. Pupils would work directly with teachers and be responsible to them. Other school personnel, such as maintenance workers, secretaries, and clerks, would be directly responsible to the principal of the school in which they worked. The custodian of a building, for example, would be responsible to the principal but would be free to make suggestions to the professional advisory group.

There are, of course, variations of this type of organization but all should have the following basic features:

> The board of education or policy-enacting body at the top authority level
>
> The chief school administrator at the second level
>
> A coordinator of communication at the third level
>
> A representative community group serving in an advisory capacity
>
> A representative group of the school staff serving in an advisory capacity
>
> Established lines of responsibility among teachers, pupils, and other school personnel

Nothing in the organization and administration of the communication system should preclude the individual teacher, principal, or other school employee from being an unofficial agent of communication between school and community. In fact much communication will be of this nature and should be recognized and encouraged. The formal structure suggested is designed to coordinate these efforts, supply accurate information for dissemination, and enlarge the areas of communication. Officially it defines responsibilities, provides internal communication channels, helps develop new and better procedures, provides a center for all formal news releases, and directs efforts in accordance with a planned design.

responsibilities of communication agents

Both school personnel and the people of the community have unique responsibilities in a successful communication system. In some cases these responsibilities are fairly well defined, in others they are not. All have the responsibility of striving for truth, accuracy, and fairness in all communication. All school personnel have the responsibility indicated by the motto, "If satisfied tell others; if not, tell us." This means that those who work in the school have an obligation to tell others about a system in which they are proud to work. If they are unhappy with conditions, their first responsibility is to tell the proper administrative officer and suggest changes.

While the members of the board of education are, with few exceptions, lay people, they are treated in this context with school personnel because of their key role in the school system. In connection with the communication system the major responsibility of the board is to enact a written policy which recognizes the vital importance of school-community communication and provides for securing and maintaining it. Once this is done, the board should delegate to the chief administrative officer and his staff the task of implementing that policy. Such funds as are necessary for implementation should be allocated by the board. Another responsibility of board members is to be available as individuals to serve as speakers, panel members, and discussion leaders on such topics as school goals and policies. The board also has the obligation to conduct its meetings in such fashion as to inspire and merit full public confidence. Complaints and criticisms of pupil discipline and similar areas of the school program should be referred to the proper school official. Finally, it is the responsibility of the board from time to time to have the communication system evaluated and revisions made where indicated.

The superintendent has the original responsibility of acquainting the board with the essential nature of school-community communication, pointing out its value to the community as well as to the school. His is the responsibility of developing the plans for implementing the communication policy established by the board. He is responsible for seeing that an effective organization is set up and personnel are designated to assume the various roles required. He will also make himself available to translate the program of the school to the people and will invite their reactions. He will aid and advise those school personnel working in the communication system. It is his duty to submit data necessary for evaluating the system to the board of education and, finally, to check continuously on the organization to see that it is working properly.

The work of the coordinator of communication is usually done by the coordinator of school-community relations, or the public relations director, or the director of community relations, whichever he may be called. As has been pointed out earlier, communication is the foundation and a substantial part of the superstructure of good school-community relations. Therefore, the coordination assignment is not something extra, but rather a basic part of the job. No new position is created unless the school system has been without an organized school-community relations program.

As the name indicates, the coordinator is the key figure in the organization. All formal news releases or announcements clear through his office. He meets with both advisory groups, separately and jointly as the situation dictates. He, with the advice of these groups, will make decisions with regard to utilization of media, encoding of messages, timing of news releases, and procedural matters. He will be the principal contact for individuals and organizations of the community. He is responsible for the development of community contacts which will ensure that the system reaches all the community. The report of the school-community study will be his guidebook. In short, he is the administrator of the communication system. It is for him to weld personnel, materials, and ideas into an effective unit for the achievement of the desired goals. He also must set up procedures to evaluate progress and point to needed revisions.

The school principal is the leader in his school. He, with his staff, develops communication to and from his school within the procedural framework established. He keeps in contact with the staff advisory committee, channeling suggestions and recommendations to it. His lines of responsibility go directly to the coordinator. He reports and interprets the attitudes and opinions of his school neighborhood. He tells the story of his school to the community. He aids his teachers in performing their communication duties. He evaluates the communication system in terms of his own school and reports to the coordinator.

The teacher is indirectly in contact with the home through her pupils. Much that goes into the image of the school is a direct reflection of the teacher and her activities. By virtue of numbers alone, teachers rate a very important place in the communication system. The teacher cooperates with the principal in the development of communication in the school where she teaches. She accepts assignments to explain the purposes and program of her school in general and her teaching field or grade in particular. She appraises the attitudes, opinions, and ambitions of the patrons of the school as she observes them and as they are reflected in her pupils. She has a further obligation to acquire a general knowledge of the school system, so as to be able to represent it adequately in individual conversation and before groups. And finally, she has the responsibility of doing the very best job of teaching possible, which, after all, may be her most important contribution to the image of the school.

The pupil is a close contact with the community five days per week. He is a valuable communication agent because he moves regularly between home and school. His reports of school activities and classroom procedures are influential in the formation of parent opinion. He is in effect an "inside" agent for the school in the family circle. Pupil appearances in public as performers in plays, musical presentations, and athletic contests reflect in a large measure the influence of the school. A well-acted play or a fine musical performance brings a favorable reaction toward the school as well as the performers. A high type of sportsmanship exhibited by high school athletes cannot help but reflect favorably on the school they represent. Each student should be made fully aware of his role as a communication agent with the community and encouraged to conduct himself so as to bring credit to the school. In his case actions will invariably speak louder than words.

Other personnel consist, for the most part, of maintenance workers, secretaries, business managers, and other noninstructional personnel. All should acquire a general knowledge of the operation of the school and the nature of its program. Such information is not only necessary from the standpoint of communicating with the public, but is also helpful in the effective performance of regular duties. Noninstructional personnel usually have contacts with certain segments of the population which instructional personnel do not have. These contacts can be utilized to secure information on the opinions, attitudes, and desires of a portion of the population which might otherwise not be directly reached. It is the responsibility of noninstructional personnel, as part of the school system, to supply information and report newsworthy items to the proper person in the communication organization. In most cases this would be the school principal; in a few cases, such as the business manager of the school system or a supervisor of buildings and grounds for the whole school system, the report should be made directly to the coordinator of communication.

A few school personnel in this category are involved in work which, while not instructional, is closely associated with instruction. Reference is made to such people as assistant superintendents in charge of instruction, curriculum supervisors or consultants, directors of special education, and similar school personnel. In addition to the responsibilities suggested for teachers and noninstructional personnel, these people have the obligation to interpret their specialties to the public. A director of special education, for example, has at his command a wealth of information about exceptional children and how they learn, which is of genuine interest to the public. There is still another responsibility which this type of personnel is peculiarly qualified to perform, and that is taking charge of communication activities that require a broad knowledge of the school system as well as specialized ability. For example, a director of adult education might be assigned the task of exploring the educational needs of the adult population of the community. The director of special education might be given the job of finding out how the people of the community regard the special education program and what the attitude of parents who have children in the program is toward it.

The communication agents of the community have been arbitrarily divided into two classes: individuals and groups. The primary obligation of individuals is to obtain a basic knowledge of the local school system and program in particular, and of the total educational picture in general. Education is of such vital importance to both community and national welfare that no citizen has the right to be ignorant of its purposes, policies, and program. It is true that some by virtue of parenthood will be more concerned than others who may have only grandchildren or possibly no relatives at all attending school. Still every person in the community has vital interests in the school whether or not he recognizes them. First of all, the public school is one of the most important institutions in the community, and the quality and adequacy of its program is reflected in the community. It has been said that a community can be no better than its school system. In its vital leadership role the school can go a long way toward determining the quality of living in the community.

In the second place, whether or not he likes it, every citizen is a taxpayer. In some form or other he makes a financial contribution to the public school. He pays an income, property, sales, excise, nuisance, or luxury tax. He cannot escape paying taxes, and if he accumulates sufficient wealth, his heirs will be paying inheritance taxes on his money after he is dead. As a financial contributor every citizen has a stake in the school and owes it to himself to know how his tax dollar is spent and what it buys.

As a citizen of the United States, the local community member should be deeply concerned with education in general as well as with the local schools. Education is essential to the economic, social, and political welfare of our country as well as for its defense. State and Federal government are and will be making greater and greater efforts to educate our people for the challenges of a technological revolution in a rapidly changing social order. Every citizen has a vital interest in education as a potent force in national and international life. No person who holds citizenship in the country can in good faith dis-associate himself from education in the community or in the nation.

A primary responsibility of citizens is to help define the goals and purposes of the school in the community. This requires direct contact with the school if it is to be done effectively. As pointed out in Chapter 3, this responsibility can be discharged best through organized participation. Assistance in developing plans and policies is a further responsibility which was likewise discussed earlier.

The lay citizen is also responsible for providing the school with information about the educational needs of the community. This is not an easy task unless a communication structure has been established. Nevertheless, it must be done if the school is to be sensitive to, and adequately meet, the needs of the community.

Another responsibility is that of cooperating in the program of the school. This may involve answering questionnaires, serving on advisory committees, or providing laboratory situations in the community for classes in economics, government, and other fields. In a few cases it may mean serving as guidance counselors to high school students who are deciding on a career. These and similar activities provide direct communication with the school and are extremely valuable in building an integrated school community.

Organizations and informal groups have a unique role to play in the school-community communication system. In addition to the responsibilities which individual members should assume, the organized group in its meetings can provide a platform for discussion of education both on the local and on the national level. For example, a civic club may invite a school official to explain an educational trend or present an educational problem, and follow the presentation by a full discussion. Thus ideas are presented, clarified, explored; suggestions are made; and, in some cases, solutions are offered.

Organizations themselves have communication structures which can be utilized to disseminate educational information. To a reasonable degree, it is the responsibility of non-school-sponsored groups as well as school liaison groups to make these channels available to the school.

If properly selected, much of the information provided by such organizations will be of interest and value to the majority of their members, if they are civic-minded people.

Endorsements of school projects by community organizations can be very helpful. A public endorsement of a proposed tax increase to expand the school program is a form of communication within the community and one which is of great value to the school. A bond issue to enlarge the physical plant is an opportunity for community organizations to express themselves. Regardless of whether they favor or oppose such an issue, school liaison groups and civic organizations have a responsibility to communicate their attitudes to the people.

Organizations such as school advisory committees, of course, have specific responsibilities assigned to them. They include formulating goals, developing plans and policies for consideration of the board, working on school-community problems, aiding in maintaining communication, and assisting in evaluation of the school program. All these require direct communication with the school. They also involve communication with the people of the community. Thus, such groups act as valuable two-way communication agents and, therefore, should be a part of every school-community communication system.

what the community should know about education

As has been indicated earlier, people of any given community need to know not only about their schools but also about education generally. Now, as perhaps never before, education has assumed a dominant place in our national life. Its significance in all phases of the economic, social, and political scene is more clearly recognized now than ever before. President Lyndon B. Johnson in talking of his quest for the Great Society said, "Poverty has many roots, but the tap root is ignorance." The essential nature of education for our national welfare, even for our survival as a free country, is indisputable.. It follows, therefore, that people need to know about education as a vital force in national as well as community life.

It is the responsibility of the school to assume leadership in disseminating information about education in general as well as education in the community it serves. What types of general educational information should the local school disseminate? Certainly we cannot expect to inform the lay person about the technical aspects of education, nor is there any value to be achieved in so doing. Education is a profession, and its procedures, techniques, and methods are not essential to the layman's understanding of education as a vital force in national or even community life. What he does need to know is what education does and how it affects the basic areas of human life.

A few examples will serve to indicate the nature and content of general educational information which the school should provide its community.

1. *The essential nature of education in the preservation and progress of a democracy.* In a democracy people have a freedom of choice, but that freedom can be preserved only if people make enough right choices. Ignorance is a handicap in making right choices of governmental officials and on public issues. Democracy depends to a great extent on the common man, and his educational level is a crucial factor in his ability to make wise choices.

2. *The relationship between education and freedom.* The Bible states, "Ye shall know the truth and the truth shall make you free." That statement is as true today as it was two thousand years ago. It is the ignorant masses who live beneath the heel of the oppressor. In no country in the world is freedom so cherished and so enjoyed as in our own. It is hardly a coincidence that although our country has only about 6 percent of the world's population, it includes more than half of the high school graduates in the world.

3. *The concept of equal educational opportunity for all.* This is an ideal which is fundamental to the democratic way of life. It is not easy to achieve, yet it is important that people be reminded of it and the necessity of constantly striving for it. As educational demands grow and educational tax rates rise, it is essential that the school keep the ideal of equal educational opportunity before the people at all times.

4. *The social and economic values of education.* The social and economic values of education are, of course, immense. Educational expenditures are in a real sense an investment. In the technological age in which we live education is an investment we must make to ensure reasonable productivity and a minimum of unemployment. Adlai E. Stevenson, onetime United States Ambassador to the United Nations, said,

From the start of the Republic we in America have recognized that our strength as a nation, our wealth, our welfare, yes, our love of country all depend on what happens in our schools. Now in the middle of the twentieth century, in an increasingly crowded and complex world, we understand more urgently than ever how necessary it is to give our children the education they need to play an effective role in modern life.[1]

5. *The concept of individual needs.* It is important that people understand the significance of individual differences and consequent individual educational needs. The school must make clear that the diversity of human abilities and interests requires a broad curriculum. The parents of a student bound for college must be made to realize that his neighbor's son who will not go beyond high school needs and deserves a different type of education.

6. *The trend in education.* If the eductional process is to keep pace with changing times and conditions, it must innovate. Some innovations are not welcomed by the community largely because of lack of information. It is the duty of the school to keep the community informed of educational trends and to explain why they developed and how they affect learning and teaching.

There are, of course, other examples, but these will suffice to present a picture of the type of general educational information which should reach the community. Information about the local school system which should be disseminated is nearly all-inclusive. With the exception of certain personnel and acquisition problems, the public is entitled to know all about the school all of the time, and it is the job of the administration to see that as far as possible such is the case.

A few examples of interesting and essential information about the local school which should flow through the communication system to the people of the community follow:

1. The nature and scope of the school program
2. The measurement of pupil progress
3. Promotion policies and the reasoning behind them
4. The policy of the school with regard to homework and the reason for it
5. The importance of well-trained teachers in the school and the cost of getting them
6. The nature of the guidance and counseling program

[1] *NEA Journal,* vol. 45, p. 411, October, 1956.

7. The nature and policies with regard to extracurricular activities
8. Pupil transportation
9. The school's methods of obtaining its money and its use of the funds it receives
10. Honors and recognition received by the school and its teachers and pupils

what the school should know about the community

The importance of the two-way nature of communication has been pointed out. The question then arises as to what type of information should flow from the community to the school. Some of the information which the school needs is found in the sociological survey described in a preceding section of this chapter. This is basic information, and once obtained should be kept up-to-date by way of a carefully designed communication system.

In addition to the basic information provided by such a study, there are certain types of information which should flow from community to school on a more or less continuous basis. Examples of these types of information are listed.

1. What the emerging educational needs of the community are
2. What the attitudinal climate of the community with regard to its school is
3. What opinions of the people are on local educational issues
4. What the opinions of the people are on major educational issues of the state and nation
5. What the people of the community think about the teaching staff with regard to its
   a. instructional ability
   b. fairness to pupils
   c. discipline
   d. participation in the life of the community
6. What the people of the community think about the administration of the school with regard to its
   a. administrative ability
   b. fairness to employees
   c. vision and foresight
   d. participation in the life of the community

7. What the people of the community think about the board of
   education with regard to its
   a. effectiveness in policy making
   b. judgment in school matters
   c. vision and imagination
   d. faithfulness in attending meetings and devoting time to the
      job
8. What parents think about pupils'
   a. work load
   b. homework
   c. lunch arrangements
   d. transportation
   e. progress
9. What the people of the community think about the school plant
   and equipment, its maintenance and use
10. How the people of the community regard the use of school
    funds as they are expended for administration, instruction, and
    physical plant
11. What features of the school are most popular with people of
    the community, and why
12. What features of the school are most unpopular, and why
13. What opportunities are available in the community for profit-
    able field trips by pupils to see manufacturing processes,
    industrial developments, governmental processes, and similar
    activities
14. What opportunities are available for the school to utilize the
    community as a learning laboratory in projects of considerable
    length and depth
15. What opportunities are available for cooperation with commu-
    nity organizations and institutions such as health service,
    organizations, libraries, and museums

utilization of available media

The effectiveness of the school-community communication system will
depend in some measure on the availability of media and the nature of
their use. No single medium is best in all cases or at all times. When
special segments of the population are to be reached special media may
be required. Some messages are much more effective in one medium
than in another. Seldom will a single medium do the whole job. A con-

stellation of media, each medium supplementing the others, usually is required to achieve comprehensive coverage.

The primary responsibility for selecting the media of communication falls upon the person we have designated coordinator of communication. In the larger systems, he is the person in charge of school-community relations, while in smaller systems he is the superintendent of schools or one of his assistants. He will do well to seek and heed the advice of both the staff and the lay advisory group, particularly the latter. No one person can be expected to have all the knowledge necessary to select and utilize proper media all the time. He must rely on others, and it is best to have the others consciously organized for the purpose. The organization suggested earlier in the chapter provides the coordinator with a rich source of counsel and advice.

The general principles which should govern the selection and use of communication media in the school community are listed here.

1. Identify and catalog all available media.

2. Develop long-range plans for the utilization of the most promising media.

3. Choose the medium or media best adapted to the time, the message, and the coverage desired.

4. As far as possible, develop a balanced usage of available media.

5. Establish and maintain a fair and equitable policy for news releases through the various media available.

6. If possible, make use of all available media over a period of time.

7. Utilize media in such a way as to involve a maximum number of people in the transmission of messages as long as it does not detract from the effectiveness of the message.

8. Other factors being equal, select the media which require the least time and effort to encode the message since facility of preparation is important.

9. Encode the message to suit the medium to be used in order to achieve maximum effectiveness.

10. Maintain a close professional relationship with those in charge of community-based media, and respect requirements as to form, space, accuracy, and deadlines.

11. Accord public recognition to media and individuals who have made special contributions or rendered outstanding service to school-community communication.

12. Conduct periodic evaluations of the adequacy, appropriateness, and effectiveness of the media used.

additional reading

American Association of School Administrators: *Public Relations for America's Schools,* pp. 275–305, National Education Association, Washington, D.C., 1950.

Fine, Benjamin: *Educational Publicity,* rev. ed., pp. 145–244, Harper & Row, Publishers, Incorporated, New York, 1951.

Griffiths, Daniel E., David Clark, D. Richard Wynn, and Laurence Iannaccone: *Organizing Schools for Effective Education,* pp. 189–210, Interstate Printers and Publishers, Inc., Danville, Ill., 1962.

Grinnell, J. E., and Raymond Young: *The School and the Community,* pp. 195–421, The Ronald Press Company, New York, 1955.

Olsen, Edward G.: *School and Community,* pp. 73–288, Prentice-Hall, Inc., Englewood Cliffs, N.J., 1945.

Stearns, Harry: *Community Relations and the Public Schools,* pp. 41–207, Prentice-Hall, Inc., Englewood Cliffs, N.J., 1955.

principles of operation

8 The broad concept of a changing school in a changing community is not new or essentially different. This situation has been recognized by perceptive and imaginative school people for some time. However, its implications for school-community relations have received only the most meager attention. And the possibilities for educational development and improvement through a school-community relations program have received even less attention. The typical school-community relations approach has been predicated on the necessity of bringing the community along with predetermined school plans and programs. The approach has been one of "selling" rather than "buying," of telling rather than asking. If the opportunities of a changing school in a changing community are to be realized, the approach to school-community relations must be consistent with basic principles which will serve to implement the concept in the most effective manner.

The approach to school-community relations which is suggested in preceding chapters is based upon four essential principles. Each of these major principles has a number of subordinate and related principles which serve as operational guides to effective school-community relations. Preceding chapters have attempted to translate a concept of the school community into an operational structure designed to make possible the achievement of a high degree of cooperation between school and community for their mutual benefit. However, no structure, no matter how carefully developed, will in itself assure good school-community relations. Granted that such a structure will usually predispose and invariably precede an effective school-community relations program, we still must recognize, understand, and observe certain operational principles which grow out of the concept upon which the structure is based.

It is the purpose of this chapter to examine the four major principles on which the suggested approach to school-community relations is based and establish the subordinate and related principles which are so necessary to effective operation. In so doing, some attention will be given to the social and psychological dynamics which are inherent in each of the four major principles proposed.

the public school as a public enterprise

The first major principle may be stated as follows: *The public school is a public enterprise.* At first glance this may be accepted as a truism which requires no further examination. However, such is not the case. The implications are broad and vital, yet seldom explored.

The public school belongs to the public—to all the people. It is their instrument for the achievement of essential social goals. It occupies a unique and commanding position in the community. It is an institution with a mission—a mission of transcendent importance to all the people. It is challenged by the very course of events in a rapidly changing world.

The significance of public ownership has to a considerable degree been overlooked by many educators and most lay people. Ownership implies responsibilities, and the effective discharge of responsibilities requires knowledge and effort. Translated, this means communication and participation. Both of these will be discussed later in the chapter.

The public school, as has been indicated earlier, is quite comparable to a corporation which is owned by the public. The people are shareholders in their public schools. They will reap the benefits, along with the people of the state and nation, of a good school system. They, along with the people of the state and nation, will suffer from a poor one. It is in their own self-interest to accept the serious responsibility of a shareholder in a vital community institution. What this implies is spelled out elsewhere in this volume.

The public school is an instrument to serve all the people, not just those who fit a prescribed set of characteristics. This obligation is inherent in the concept of public education. Yet it is not accepted in its broadest sense by many laymen and even some educators. Public education is not a privilege for the few; it is the right of all who live in this democracy of ours. Democratic government in a large measure will stand or fall on the effectiveness and universality of its educational program. Public education for all is a public necessity.

In the last analysis the public school can only be truly public when both the educator and the layman recognize the challenge, the opportunity, the responsibility, and the vital necessity of universal public education.

Let us turn for a moment to the final words of the statement that the public school is a public enterprise. The word enterprise itself connotes initiative, imagination, boldness, faith, courage, and planning. Is the typical school system an enterprise? Is it characterized by boldness, imagination, courage, initiative, and well-laid plans? Or does it plod unimaginatively and timidly in the ruts of tradition down yesterday's well-trodden paths? Does it respond to the challenges of changing patterns of life, or is it content to pass on the traditions of the society which it serves?

It might be said with considerable justification that a business venture is more like an enterprise than is the typical school system. In fact the name business enterprise is frequently applied to a commercial venture. A group of men may form a corporation to launch a business enterprise designed to return a profit. They invest their money, their time, and their efforts in the project. They lay plans, assume responsibilities, perform duties, and evaluate their efforts—all to help ensure the success of the venture. That success which they seek will depend to a large extent on how well they have gauged the need for their product or service, how well they have analyzed the market, how boldly and imaginatively they have operated, how effectively they have communicated with the market, and finally how good their products or services are.

The school system which regards itself as an enterprise will function in much the same way. Substitute the people of the community for the shareholders and the school for the business enterprise, and you have a close parallel.

Finally, the social dynamics of our times demand that the public school be, in the true sense, a public enterprise. The economic importance of education can hardly be overestimated. With rapidly developing technology creating both new jobs and new unemployment, maximum production demands new skills, more specialized training, and universal education. Public education is challenged to meet the demands of a technological revolution. It will require boldness, imagination, and courage as well as enlarged facilities and increased finances. The problem is both local and national. Each community has an obligation to the nation as well as to itself. If this country is to achieve and maintain a working force which can keep abreast of technological change, the public schools must do a more effective job of educating than ever before. But if the challenge is greater, so are the rewards. The possibilities for further raising the standard of living in our country and abroad stagger the imagination. And furthermore, as the school meets the challenge, it contributes to technological progress by educating those who will be responsible for future progress. The public school at all levels plays a vital role in preparing both youth and adults for effective life and at the same time contributes incalculably to economic progress.

Operational principles

In school-community relations the basic principle that the public school is a public enterprise generates a number of subordinate or related principles which should serve to guide the development and maintenance of sound, effective, school-community relations. A number of these principles are listed here.

1. *The public schools belong to all the people.* This means that no one group, class, or individual should by virtue of position or influence dominate the school. Each and every person has the right to be heard. Each person is a shareowner in the public school. Each one has invested some of his tax money in education. Each one has a stake in the public school.

2. *The public schools should serve all the people.* This principle is usually accepted at the verbal level but often resisted on the practical level. Programs in vocational education and special education are often denied to those who need them simply because they are "too expensive." Little recognition is given to the fact that the students in the academic program who have no physical or mental defects are receiving the type of education most suitable for them at the expense of others. To serve all,

the school must adapt its program to the individual differences of its students.

3. *The purpose of the public school is a public purpose which should serve individual aims to the extent they coincide with the public purpose.* It is clear that the school cannot and should not meet the demands of every group and every individual. It is in the best interests of the public for the school to attempt to develop the constructive abilities of its students to their highest potential. In fact one of the major purposes of the public school in America is just that. But the line must be drawn at the point where the program fails to meet the public interest.

4. *The resources of the community, both human and material, should be utilized by the school.* Every modern community has a wealth of resources which the school should utilize fully. Human resources in the form of interested citizens who can contribute as speakers, advisers, counselors, information suppliers, and leaders can greatly enrich and broaden the school program. School liaison groups, citizens advisory committees, and civic organizations have much to contribute.

The material resources of communities vary greatly, but all can provide laboratory experiences for the school, and many can provide the locale for interesting and informative field trips. The media of communication which the community can supply are usually much more effective than those of the school.

5. *The school should cooperate impartially with the other institutions of the community.* The many institutions of a community often include private and parochial schools. Cooperation with such schools as well as other types of institutions such as hospitals, recreation agencies, welfare homes, and libraries is consistent with achieving the best possible educational program for the students of the public schools.

Cooperation between public and parochial schools is discussed at length in a later chapter. Cooperation with all types of social agencies should be based on a mutual understanding of goals, policies, and programs. The school can assume leadership in forming a council of community social agencies if none exists, and if one has been organized, the school should have effective representation on it. The council should develop coordinated long-range plans for securing financial support for all agencies and present a united front in seeking funds. This will tend to eliminate unwholesome competition for money and provide a schedule of priorities for the component agencies. Social agencies can contribute much to the program of the school, and the school can, in turn, provide them with personnel and training resources which are invaluable.

the principle of intellectual freedom

The second major principle is that the public school in America has the essential function of seeking truth in an atmosphere of intellectual freedom. It starts with no predetermined point of view. It fosters freedom of thought and discussion. It is independent and must remain so if it is to serve the highest ideal of democracy—free men in a free society.

Any attempt by any individual or group or organization or even any class of society to restrict or deny freedom of inquiry to the school is a threat to our democratic way of life. Intellectual freedom is essential to a free society. The first act of a dictator is to seize the educational system and subordinate it to his doctrine. Through the educational system he can shape the minds of men. They become subjugated when they lose the right of free inquiry.

The school from the kindergarten to the graduate college has the magnificent goal of helping to achieve and maintain a free society of free people. To do this, the right of unlimited inquiry is essential. The school should foster the spirit of intellectual freedom, the right to doubt, and the privilege of utilizing all available resources in the search for truth.

The forces of inertia, the resistance to change, the power of vested interests all are on occasion roadblocks in the paths of academic freedom, but they must never be allowed to form an insurmountable barrier. The public school is the one instrument of democracy that has the potential power to clear the roadway and maintain a continuous, persistent quest for truth. The atmosphere of intellectual freedom must be created and maintained at all educational levels.

At the elementary level free inquiry by pupils in the world of science will permit them to establish for themselves certain basic scientific truths. These principles can then be translated into guides in everyday living as well as made to form a foundation for further scientific study. In fact, one of the most productive ways of teaching science is known as the inquiry training method in which pupils are given the opportunity and training to learn by asking questions.

In the secondary school the exercise of intellectual freedom often involves controversial social issues. The obligation of the school is clear. It must ensure the acquisition by the student of all the relevant information available on the issue and allow him to determine his position for himself. The constant criterion to be applied in the exploration and analyses of the data is the simple but vital one which the school must uphold, namely, "Is it true?"

The quest for truth to which the right of free inquiry is essential is a complex and hazardous undertaking. However, neither its complexity nor its dangers relieve the school of its unique institutional responsibility for nurturing intellectual freedom. Rather it presents a challenge to education as a bulwark against any force or forces which seek to control and direct the minds of men. In no other institution, public or private, is there greater opportunity or greater responsibility for maintaining and expanding the freedom of thought and inquiry that alone can ensure a free society.

This concept of the role of the school should be shared by school and community alike. If accepted by one and not the other, conflict is certain to arise. The alignment of the school with private interests, the banning of books, the censorship of school texts are symptoms of such a conflict. It is essential for good school-community relations that this unique role of the school be continuously emphasized not merely as a local responsibility but as a national obligation—even a global one if we are to accept leadership in the free world.

Unfortunately, there are citizens of some communities who regard the school as solely a community institution which may be bent to the popular will. They fail to recognize that the community is only a part of an indivisible nation and has obligations which, while local in their performance, are national in significance. Perhaps much of the blame for this attitude may be attributed to the failure of the school to make clear its responsibilities in this area.

The Constitution of the United States leaves education to the states in an attempt to ensure that no Federal power should exploit the schools. The states have uniformly guarded the public schools against the encroachment of private interests which might seek to use them for selfish purposes.

The courts of the land have zealously maintained the separation of religion from education. The duty of the school in this context is clear. It must, at all costs, maintain and exercise the independence which allows it to perform its unique function in our democracy.

Operational principles

The achievement of a common understanding and acceptance of the unique institutional role of the school in the search for truth and its resultant obligation to maintain intellectual freedom is not easy. It requires continuous effort on the part of the school. Some operational principles which may serve as a guide in this important area of school-community relations are listed.

1. *The public school has obligations which reach far beyond the boundaries of the community.* The community must recognize the larger role of the school in fulfilling its historic obligation as a democratic institution. It must not allow local prejudice or bias to restrict or circumscribe the intellectual freedom essential to the discharge of this wider responsibility.

2. *The public school must maintain its independence in order to be effective in its search for truth.* Domination by any individual, organization, group, or social class would render the school impotent as an agency of free inquiry. To be effective as an instrument of freeaom, the public school must itself be free. Only when it is free is it possible for its students to exercise the freedom to learn.

3. *The use of reason based on intelligent and free inquiry is the best way to solve the problems of society.* The acceptance of this principle by the school community allows the school to function as it should. If reason is so recognized, the school can proceed with its major task of developing the intellectual potentialities of the student so that he may participate effectively in the solution of problems. This precludes the possibility of imposing any theory or point of view on him. It also decreases the likelihood of the community's attempting to impose a doctrine or point of view on the school. Ready-made solutions proposed by groups or organizations are subject to examination and intellectual inquiry, not accepted blindly.

4. *The community interest in the broadest sense is the interest of democracy itself.* It is easy to become provincial in our thinking, and in so doing we often disassociate the interests of community from those of the larger society in which we live. Therefore, the school should point out the indissoluble bonds which tie together the thousands of communities in our broad land. No community is a law unto itself. Each and every community in our democracy will find itself bound more closely to the others as they face ever-growing and ever more complex common problems. The school is an institution committed to the basic concerns of our democ-

racy. As such it has no alternative but to seek for truth in the maze of issues which confront a free people.

5. *The school has an obligation to aid in improving the quality of life of the community.* Values and ideals which have stood the test of truth and time possess enduring worth for all men. They serve to improve the quality of life when applied to communities as well as to nations. The school as a free institution teaches the individual and the community it serves to seek out these values and ideals, to test them in the light of modern culture, and (if they pass the test of truth today) to live by them. This is more than passing on the essentials of the culture; it is critically examining the values of the past, selecting and using those which will improve the quality of life today, and then moving forward in the pursuit of new truth which may be added to the accumulated store by which men may be taught to live. By doing all this, the school can contribute significantly to the quality of community life.

6. *The people of the community have the right to originate educational ideas, express judgments, and criticize the schools.* The community, like the school, has the right to exercise free inquiry, to search for truth in education, and to criticize what it regards as deserving criticism. The school should foster the spirit of inquiry in the community as well as in the schoolroom. It can profit by the new ideas, thoughtful judgments, and constructive criticism of the people it serves.

However, if these ideas are to be useful, the judgments valid, and the criticism helpful, the people must have the facts about the school and its program. It is the responsibility of the school to provide accurate, honest, and full information for the community.

the need for participation of the people

James Conant succinctly stated the third major principle, "The community and the school are inseparable." Only by the closest cooperation can the full values of education be realized in the school community. Such cooperation can be achieved through intelligent participation by the school in community life and by the people of the community in the planning, policy making, problem solving, and evaluation of the school. By the very nature of its function the school is a major participant in the life of the community. School attendance is almost universal in the youth age group, and is being extended upward to include adult programs in many communities. While, admittedly, participation by the school in community life could in many communities be expanded and improved, it is immeasurably greater than the participation of the community in the educational process. This situation is due at least in part to the failure of the school to enlist the community in the total process of education. In too many communities the people are onlookers and bystanders rather than active partners and shareholders in the school. Often the board of education is the sole organized contact between the school and the community it serves. This is the minimum required by the law.

The problems which society faces today are of such magnitude and complexity that every effort must be made toward their solution if man is to survive and realize his potential. The eminent historian, Arnold Toynbee, described our age as a "time of troubles." Our problems are planetary; their solutions involve complexities without precedent in human affairs. If, as H. G. Wells stated, human history is a race between education and catastrophe, we cannot move too fast to strengthen our educational system. The public school is but one of a number of educational agencies, but it is the most important one and offers the greatest opportunity for effectively meeting the challenge of the times.

However, if the public school is to meet the educational needs of the individual and at the same time fulfill its destiny as a great societal agency, it must have a degree of cooperation never before achieved.

The case for public participation in education has never been stronger than it is today. The task of education is more vast, more complex, and more difficult than ever before. Its challenges have never been of greater magnitude or importance. The issues have never been more crucial, the outcomes never more vital to our country and to the world. Under these conditions the school must enlist the help of all those who have the ability to contribute to its program.

These will include, of course, the scholars not only in the field of education but in the arts and sciences. Education can learn much from the economist, the political scientist, the sociologist, the psychologist, and many others. They have much to contribute in the improvement of the general educative process. Supplementing these sources, education must have the aid of the local community if the specifics of the educative process are to receive equal attention. The public school in the local community, if it is to maintain a close contact with the realities of the life situation, must maintain a close contact with the community it serves. Here the specifics of educational need and program resources are found. It is here that the school must look for immediate, perceptive, self-interested, and vitally concerned participation. Scholars may come and go, but the people of the community are with the school always.

However, if community participation in the educational process is to be of maximum effectiveness, the school must establish a format for such participation. Random, intermittent, unorganized, unguided, and selfish participation will certainly not produce maximum benefits, and in many cases will harm the school program and reduce the effectiveness of the school as a social agency with influence far beyond the confines of the local community. The necessity for leadership in establishing a design or format for participation is clear. Such patterns do not evolve by themselves. They must be thought out, worked out, and tried out. The school must assume this responsibility for its own good and for the welfare of the community. Suggested formats and procedural patterns appear in earlier chapters. They can be adapted to fit the community. Regardless, however, of what adaptations are made, there are certain operational principles which can serve as guides for active community participation. A number of these principles are listed here.

Operational principles

1. *The cooperative efforts of professional and lay people are necessary to make the school what it ought to be.* This principle is demonstrable and should be fully recognized by the people of the school community. No school can operate with maximum effectiveness without the cooperation of the people it serves.

2. *What the school is to do and be must be decided by the citizens.* In our country education is in the hands of the people. They must decide directly, or indirectly, what kind of an institution the school will be. Societal and national goals will be determined by the people of the nation; state educational goals, by the citizens of the state; and community goals, by the people of the community.

   The proper role of the professional educator in this context is to be an adviser, a resource person, a specialist, and a guide. The scope and character of the school will and should be, in the final analysis, decided by the citizens.

3. *The actual operation of the school is the responsibility of the professional schoolworkers.* While it is the responsibility of the citizens to determine what the school shall be, it is the responsibility of the professionals to operate the school in such a fashion as to ensure that it will be what the citizens have

determined it should be. The citizens establish the goals of education; the professionals direct the forces of education toward the achievement of these goals. The citizens determine the "what" of education; the professionals, the "how."

4. *Public participation in education is essential at all levels.* Education is a national, a state, and a local concern. Important decisions in education are made at all levels, and the decisions at each level affect education at all levels. The benefits of citizen participation should accrue to all levels. The White House Conferences of the 1950s provide an example of effective citizen participation at the national level. A national board of education has been suggested as a means of bringing lay citizens more fully into the national educational scene. On the state level almost all states have state boards of education composed of lay people. State citizens study and advisory committees have been quite effective in dealing with educational problems. A number of states, including Connecticut, Massachusetts, and Michigan, have made remarkable educational advances as a result of wide citizen participation at the state level. Participation at the local community level, district-wide, in each school building and even in each schoolroom, yields many benefits.

5. *Lay participation requires professional guidance and counsel for maximum effectiveness.* The lay citizen has much to contribute but needs assistance from the professional educator. Such assistance may well be in the form of a carefully developed design for participation, an orientation program, a format for interaction between lay citizens and school personnel, an organizational pattern for work, resource people and material, counsel in analyzing and interpreting data, evaluation procedures, and an effective system of translating the results of citizens' efforts into educational practice. Such assistance must be initiated by the professional educator; his is the responsibility of leadership.

It is true lay people in many instances can and do make contributions without professional assistance. Interest, enthusiasm, concern, and dedication even without guidance may achieve some gains. On the other hand, if misdirected, they can bring irreparable harm to a school system. Cooperation between lay and professional people is essential if the full fruits of participation are to be realized.

6. *The legally constituted body for enacting school policy is the school board.* Citizens and school people have a duty to help develop policies for education in the community. They should help in developing long-range plans for education in the community. They can give valuable help in the solution of school-community problems. They can make significant contributions in evaluation of education both in the local community and beyond it.

However, the enactment of educational policy is the responsibility of the legally constituted board of education just as the enactment of municipal policies is the obligation of duly selected representatives of the people. The adoption of school plans and solutions to problems is a function of the board of education. The responsibility for evaluation of the school program also rests with the board even though it usually designates others to perform this task.

It is important to good school-community relations that the school board be recognized as having comprehensive and final authority, subject to the limitations imposed by the state. All other citizens serve as advisers, counselors, guides, resource people, and executors. School boards almost without exception are composed of lay citizens, so that in effect the decisions made are those of lay people.

7. *Participation should be geared to the total school community.* Efforts of lay people as well as professional people should be directed toward the total school community rather than any segment of it. Although participants are representative of various elements of the school community, they should represent the total community in their efforts to improve the school. A selfish attempt to advance the interests of one segment of the population at the expense of another defeats the very purpose of participation. Policies should be developed, plans formulated, problems attacked, and evaluations made in the light of total school community needs.

8. *Participation should be based on careful study.* The problems of education are complex and difficult. They are many-faceted and have implications which extend far beyond the boundaries of the community. If they are to be dealt with effectively, exhaustive study, thoughtful discussion, and mature judgment will be required. Lay citizens and professional educators often push for action based on a hunch or at best incomplete knowledge

of the relevant facts. Time must be taken to define the problem or issue, analyze its implications, collect and examine the available evidence, interpret it, and consider alternative solutions or courses of action before arriving at a solution or proposing a recommended course of action.

9. *Participation should be organized.* The most effective participation requires an organizational pattern designed to ensure an orderly approach to participation. The coordination of the efforts of many individuals and groups is essential to successful participation. A pattern for participation helps ensure study and analysis of problems and issues as opposed to impulsive action based on misinformation or no information at all. A representative citizens committee may serve as a screening agency to ensure that recommendations to the board of education are the result of careful study and thoughtful discussion rather than hasty action or selfish actions.

10. *Participation should be comprehensive.* All people in the community should be given the *opportunity* to participate. All will not participate, of course, but the opportunity should be provided. At present probably the largest percentage of participation occurs in elections on school tax rates and bond issues. This type of participation, on an informal basis, should be encouraged and enlarged. However, it is essential that the more complex and more constructive modes of participation be given greater attention so that a cross section of the population is represented in these efforts. The most effective participation includes the total spectrum of community life.

11. *Participation should be adapted to the community.* Communities differ materially in their ways of working together, in the values which they hold, and in the nature of the relationships among organizations and cultural and ethnic groups. The form and organizational pattern of lay participation should be dictated to a considerable extent by the size of the community, the nature of its population, the values it emphasizes, and the relationships among organizations and groups and their customary ways of working together. This is not, of course, to say that unusual community characteristics nullify the operational principles set forth in this chapter. These principles apply in all communities, but the detailed plans of participation are subject to adaptation to community differences.

12. *Participation must be learned.* We are not, in this country or any other, born with the knowledge of how to participate effectively in community projects. Particularly is this true with regard to the educational project. Public participation is developmental in nature. We learn by doing. Small tasks successfully accomplished by joint effort prepare us for coping with larger, more complex problems. Effective ways of working together are learned when people are placed in face-to-face situations, when they are willing to learn from each other, when they respect the facts, when they discard preconceived notions and prejudices, and when they are willing to work unselfishly for a consensus. Both lay people and professional educators have the obligation to learn to participate.

13. *Participation should culminate in action.* The major purpose of participation is to improve education. Incidental benefits are many, but the principal one toward which participation should be directed is the improvement of the school, its program, and as a result its effectiveness as a national, state, and community institution. Therefore, to study, analyze, interpret, and discuss educational plans, policies, problems, and programs is not enough. If the school is to change to meet changing needs, there must be action. This action should come largely through the legally constituted board of education acting on recommendations growing out of the study and discussion of participating individuals and groups of the school community.

the necessity for effective two-way communication

This major principle underlies the preceding three. Only by effective two-way communication can the school be a truly public enterprise, searching for truth and enlisting the active participation of lay citizens. Communication is basic to every organized human effort, and particularly is this true of the educational enterprise.

If the people in the community are to share in the educational enterprise, they must have adequate information about the school and be able to register their opinions with school officials. If they are to join in the exhilarating quest for truth, they must have available the tools of inquiry. If they are to participate intelligently in shaping the school to meet individual and social educational needs, they must have continuous access to the relevant facts and be able to discuss them with the professional schoolworkers.

If the school is to be aware of educational needs, sensitive to community aspirations, and responsive to the will of the people, it must be in close communication with the community. Communication should be continuous. Its channels must reach into all corners of the community.

One of the areas in which joint efforts by lay and professional people are most fruitful is that of long-range planning for school development. Such plans, to be valid, must be based upon an intimate knowledge of probable future educational needs. These needs are of several orders. First, there are curricular or program needs. What must the school provide in its curriculum or program to meet the developing cultural, political, economic, scientific, and technological demands of our times? Then there is population growth to be taken into consideration. What numbers will require education of one type or another? How many students must be housed? How much and what type of educational equipment will be needed? What plant facilities will be required? How can a sound financial program to support expansion be developed? What resources are available?

All of these and many other questions demand answers as a basis for long-range plans. If they are to be answered intelligently, the planners must have a great deal of information. Communication must be highly developed, capable of transmitting immense quantities of data in forms that are readily understood by laymen as well as educators. Sound planning requires effective communication.

In a like manner, successful solutions to school-community problems involving the joint efforts of lay and professional people require the collection, interpretation, and dissemination of a great deal of information. Evaluation of the school and its program can be adequate and accurate only if the information on which it is based is adequate and accurate.

Continued change in the school community is bound to raise new issues, create new problems, and engender fresh criticism. In such a situation, effective communication is an absolute necessity. We are constantly in danger of having uninformed individuals and groups seeking to grapple with unfamiliar problems equipped with a minimum of pertinent information. This often leads to impulsive action or a retreat into the past with the proposal of outmoded solutions for current problems.

The importance of communication flowing through communication channels as freely one way as the other has been pointed out earlier. The school must be in a position to receive information if it is to have a solid basis for change. The reactions and attitudes of the community often hold the key to the solution of school problems. These can reach the school only if genuine two-way communication exists in fact as well as in theory. Too many school people deceive themselves when they accept silence as assent. Too often the valves in the communication channels open in only one direction, permitting the outward flow of information, but closing on any return flow.

Operational principles

1. *Good communication is the basis of good school-community relations.* Communication makes common the knowledge which is essential to both lay and professional people if they are to understand common problems and issues. While the school and community are inseparable, it is communication which serves as the lubricant which permits them to work together with a minimum of friction. Without communication cooperation is impossible. Without communication there can be no joint efforts.

2. *The communication system should involve both lay and school people.* This principle logically follows if school-community communication is to be two-way in nature. At first glance this principle may appear obvious. However, few school communities have recognized its potentialities with regard to community agents. Many key people in the typical community can be enlisted in the school-community communication system if they are made aware of the values in the service they render. Much of the community data which impinges on the school can be secured in usable form on a current basis simply by including key lay people in the communication system.

3. *The process of communication should involve as many people as possible.* The greater the number of people, all other things being equal, involved in the communication process, the greater the acquisition of information. The teacher who participates in organized communication learns more about the school in which she teaches as well as about the community she serves. Similarly, the lay person who is involved in the communication process learns about educational needs of his community simply from transmitting the information to the school. The well-organized system of school-community communication actually can become more efficient and much more effective as it increases the number of participants.

4. *Communication should be designed to reach all.* Communication is too important to be left to chance. It should be carefully de-

signed so that every individual, every group, every organization, and every segment of the population is reached by the communication system. This requires a thorough knowledge of the community and carefully developed channels of communication not only between school and community but within both school and community. This involves a structure which takes into account community characteristics and available media.

5. *Communication should be honest and accurate.* There is no room for equivocation in communication between school and community. People should have full and accurate information in an honest effort to provide the facts. This principle will go a long way to reduce the number and spread of rumors about the school and its personnel. Rumors are born in an environment where information is less than honest, is partial or inaccurate. Suspicion, fear, and open hostility breed in an atmosphere of half-truths and withheld information.

6. *Communication should be continuous.* Continuity of communication provides the day-to-day contact which is necessary to achieve adequate coverage, timeliness, and freedom from misunderstanding. Many schools make the mistake of suspending communication during vacations, particularly during the summer. In reality these periods when the school is not in operation present opportunities to communicate about school-community problems, state and national as well as local educational issues, and long-range school plans and goals.

7. *Communication should be long-range and planned well ahead.* The school is a long-range institution. Its goals are long-range, and its progress in achieving these goals is a matter of decades. The communication process and program should be long-range in outlook. The present communication program should lay the foundation on which future programs may be built. Only by a consistent program of communication over a long period can a desirable school image be built.

additional reading

Conant, James B.: *The American High School Today,* pp. 1–9, McGraw-Hill Book Company, New York, 1959.

Graham, Grace: *The Public School in the American Community,* pp. 35–254, Harper & Row, Publishers, Incorporated, New York, 1963.

Hamlin, Herbert M.: *The Public and Its Education,* pp. 35–78, Interstate Printers and Publishers, Inc., Danville, Ill., 1955.

Knezevich, Stephen: *Administration of Public Education,* pp. 3–36, Harper & Row, Publishers, Incorporated, New York, 1962.

Melby, Ernest, and Morton Puner: *Freedom and Public Education,* Frederick A. Praeger, Inc., New York, 1953.

Miller, Van: *The Public Administration of American School Systems,* pp. 1–23, The Macmillan Company, New York, 1965.

Olsen, Edward G. (ed.): *The School and Community Reader,* pp. 9–57, The Macmillan Company, New York, 1963.

Taylor, Harold: *On Freedom and Education,* Abelard-Schuman, Limited, New York, 1954.

Woodring, Paul: *Let's Talk Sense about Our Schools,* pp. 1–48, 139–155, 180–205, McGraw-Hill Book Company, New York, 1953.

the school
and social
change

9 The local community of today is a rapidly changing community. The majority of the changes in the local community are the reflections of changes going on in the state, the nation, and society as a whole. Some of these changes are international in character. All are of direct interest, and many have their implications for educational administration, curriculum, the school physical plant, finance, and, of course, school-community relations. The social changes of recent years have swept across the nation from coast to coast. They have shattered old and traditional patterns of living and introduced new ones. Maladjustments of a serious nature have resulted. Opportunities of a challenging nature have also been created.

The implications of these broad major social changes for the school are extremely significant. They pose difficult problems and at the same time present new avenues of progress. The school as a social agency is by its nature and purpose in the midst of both problems and opportunities. It may attempt to build a surrounding wall to insulate it from the forces of change, but it cannot succeed in doing so. No wall can shut out the forces of change, and no attempt should be made to construct such a wall. Quite the contrary is true. The school must learn not only to live in a world of change but also to be an effective and responsible social agency adjusting to, interpreting, and assuming leadership in influencing the direction of change in the interest of all the people. Such responsibility extends beyond the confines of the local community because these changes are national and even worldwide in character. The school as an institution of the larger community must accept the challenge of social change and discharge its responsibility of leadership.

The purpose of this chapter is to analyze some of these major social changes and to indicate the effects they have on the school and in turn how the school can exploit the opportunities inherent in them for the good of all.

population growth and mobility

Population growth

As the country passed the midcentury mark and entered into the first decade of the second half of the twentieth century, a great upsurge in the population began to make itself apparent. Demographers who had predicted a crest in the birthrate in the late forties were surprised to see the trend line continue upward. The total population in the 1950–1960 decade rose from one hundred and fifty-one million to almost one hundred and eighty million. Urban growth accounted for practically all the increase as the rural population remained almost stationary.

The nonwhite population increased by 26.7 percent during the decade in contrast to an increase of 17.5 percent by the white population. Some nonwhite groups such as the Chinese increased over 50 percent in the decade. Largely due to the increased birthrate during and after the Second World War and in the late nineteenth century, the youngest and oldest age groups showed the greatest increases during the decade. The declining mortality rate and immigration trends contributed to the population increase. As a result, the 1960 population count shows a gain of almost 37 percent in the number of persons under eighteen years of age and an increase of 35 percent among those sixty-five and over, during the decade.

The metropolitan areas accounted for about 84 percent of the twenty-eight million increase in population over the 1950–1960 decade. It is also important to note the nature of population growth in the metropolitan areas. The population increase in the decade in these areas as a whole was over 26 percent, as opposed to a 7 percent increase in the remainder of the country. However, the central cities showed an increase of less than 11 percent while their suburbs showed population gains of almost 50 percent. Two-thirds of the population increase of the metropolitan areas occurred in the suburbs.

Almost 18 percent of the population of cities of two hundred and fifty thousand and over is nonwhite. On the other hand, only 5 percent of the suburban population is nonwhite. It should be noted that approximately 95 percent of the nonwhite population is Negro.

Marked trends made themselves felt in the population of occupational workers. While the number of people in the professional services increased 58 percent, those in agricultural work decreased by 37 percent during the decade. Workers in the manufacturing industries increased 21 percent, and, significantly, the number of public administrators, which includes school superintendents and principals, increased 27 percent.

Finally the 1960 census revealed that there were more people than ever before enrolled in schools and colleges of the nation. More than forty-four million people under thirty-five years of age are attending some type of formal school. If we add to these the number over thirty-five who are enrolled in adult evening classes, the figure exceeds fifty million or well over one-fourth of the nation.

Since 1960 the population of the United States has continued its growth at the accelerated rate of the 1950–1960 decade. Midway in the 1960–1970 decade the burgeoning college-age population was knocking at closed college doors—closed because all classrooms had been filled.

No end to the population growth is in sight.

Population mobility

Today's population in America is on the move. First of all there is the massive movement to the urban areas where industry offers employment to both men and women in large numbers. Then there is the movement of the middle class from the central cities of the metropolis to the suburbs where new homes are being built in ever-increasing numbers to house those who seek escape from the congested cities. Whole communities are built in suburbia in the space of a year or two.

There is ethnic mobility as represented by Negroes moving from the South, and Puerto Ricans, from their native land to the large cities of the north. They in most cases help fill the vacuum left by the middle-class movement to the suburbs.

For some years the agricultural areas of the country have been feeling the effects of technology. While at one time in our agricultural history an 80-acre farm was about as large as a farm family could cultivate, the efficient farm of today is at least five times as large. Machines have replaced farm labor, and millions born and reared on the farm have been forced to move to the city to earn a livelihood. Many of these people avoid the large cities by finding employment in the smaller urban communities of ten to forty thousand people, which dot the landscape of the plains and prairies of the country.

Migrant farm workers who harvest crops of grapes, lettuce, sweet corn, tomatoes, beets, asparagus, and other vegetables illustrate seasonal mobility as they move northward with the ripening crops.

Finally there is a general mobility pervading the entire population as improved roads, more automobiles and trailers, and air transport service provide ready means of movement. More people winter in the South and spend their summers in the North than ever before. As industry decentralizes and expands, workers leave old homes and establish new ones near their work. Vacationers clog the highways during summer months.

Many forces contribute to the mobility of America's population. Most of these forces will persist and even grow stronger as time goes on. Certainly the rapid increase in automobile production and distribution and the establishment of broad networks of superhighways will provide even greater opportunity for people to seek new environments. Even the traditional desire to own and cherish a home is being dissipated by the wanderlust which is characteristic of our population. Apartment living has become popular in part because moving is easier when there is a minimum of domestic attachments.

The 1960 Federal census reports that almost three-quarters of the population in the twenty to twenty-nine age group had changed residence at least once during the preceding five years. Among children from five to fourteen years of age, more than half had moved at least once in the same period. Only one-half of the 1960 population over five years of age were living in the same house they occupied five years earlier.

In many large cities three-fourths of the population was born elsewhere and over one-half the population was born in another state. This reflects the in-migration of the skilled and unskilled occupational classes and the out-migration of the professional worker class.

Implications of population growth and mobility

The unprecedented growth and mobility of our population has significant implications for education in general and school-community relations in particular. First of all the sheer weight of numbers is posing serious problems for the school. Physical facilities are taxed beyond their desirable capacity; classes are larger than they should be for effective instruction; teachers with minimal training are employed; and little or no professional time is available for experimental and research work.

The mobility of the school population poses additional problems. Special programs must be instituted to take care of the children of migrant workers. These children are just as deserving of a good education as are the children from more stabilized homes. The introduction of sufficient flexibility in the school program to accommodate them and other pupils who, in the course of normal population movement, enter the school at various times during the school year is essential.

The extension of the educational program to provide for continuing education of the increasing proportion of the population which is in the older age group means a longer school day, more equipment, more teachers, and broader curricula. All these factors demand greater efforts by the school, which in turn requires that more money be spent on education.

The school can be successful in meeting these challenges only if it has the full support of the community it serves, as well as state and Federal financial support. The active participation of the community in the study of these problems is essential. They are in fact school-community problems rather than strictly school problems. Their solutions will be forged in the crucible of school-community discussion and decision. It is the responsibility of the school, through representative citizens groups, to provide the framework for deliberation and to develop and maintain an effective structure of communication between the school and every segment of the community. Failure to do this can only result in seriously handicapping the ability of the school to meet the challenge of educating a rapidly growing, mobile population.

urbanization

The great population movement of midcentury is the flight to the cities. The United States is rapidly becoming a nation of city dwellers. In the 1950–1960 decade many Midwestern and some Southern states which experienced substantial overall population growth contained vast agricultural areas which suffered steady losses of population. Today almost two-thirds of the total population of the United States is concentrated in the heavily populated metropolitan areas. The proportion is likely to be closer to three-fourths a decade hence. The movement in the metropolitan area is from the center of population to the suburbs. As people move outward more and more surrounding rural areas are assimilated into the sprawling metropolis while the population of the central city declines. In the last decade major cities such as New York and Chicago have steadily lost population to their fast-growing suburbs. Forces of change in economic and other fields are compelling. The structure of today's population is totally different from that of fifty years ago. This change in the population structure which has concentrated so many of our people in areas of dense population is of vital significance not only to the school but to the many social institutions which serve society.

The population areas of the country may be roughly divided into three categories: rural, suburban, and urban. Each has its advantages and disadvantages, its problems and opportunities. Although at one time the rural areas were predominant, the reverse is true today. This shift has, by the very force of numbers as well as movement, centered our major social problems in the metropolitan areas. On the positive side, it has opened new and broader avenues for economic, scientific, and political achievement.

On the other hand, rural communities must not only wrestle with their traditional problems but also endure the buffeting which follows in the wake of the churning movement to the city. Thus urbanization presents a national problem which affects all people wherever they live.

The nature of the metropolis

A statistical standard metropolitan area is defined by the Federal government as a population cluster containing one or more central cities with a total of at least fifty thousand people. The largest central city gives its name to the area. In fact the term "metropolis" means "mother city." Thus while Evanston and Oak Park, Illinois, are sizable cities in their own right, they are portions of the Chicago metropolitan area. Massive metropolitan areas such as New York and Chicago are also known as "standard consolidated areas."

Metropolitan areas are exceedingly complex economically, socially, and politically. There are very great differences in the economy of the various components of the metropolis. Some areas are devoted to manufacturing, some to merchandising, and others to the provision of professional services. Social characteristics of the various areas differ even more as one moves from the slums of the central city to the fashionable suburban areas.

The metropolis, like Topsy, just "growed." New words and phrases such as "urban sprawl," "scatteration," "mushrooming suburbs," "strait-jacketed core cities," and "suburban Balkanization" have been coined to describe the many complex features of the metropolis. They emphasize the unplanned, unregulated, and unequal development of the area. Needless to say, this type of disorderly development has been and is now attended with many problems of maladjustment and dislocation. Major problems may be classified as political, social, economic, and educational. The first three will be treated here briefly, while a succeeding section will be given over to the fourth.

The metropolitan area poses a number of painful political problems. When the nature of its development is considered, this is to be expected. There is no overall governmental structure to serve the area. Rather, these areas are governed for the most part by a governmental structure which is fragmented, inconsistent, uncoordinated, and overlapping. Under such conditions the typical citizen throws up his hands in disgust. With governmental responsibility so subdivided and fractionated, efforts by citizens are apt to be frustrating. There is little or no opportunity for a citizen to act constructively or even to act at all on the major problems confronting the whole metropolitan area or even a major portion of it. Cooperative government in such a situation is hard to come by although there are a few instances of progress in this direction in the South and in Canada, our neighbor to the north.

The political situation in the central city is often worse. Unscrupulous politicians seize the opportunity presented by the influx of people of the lowest socioeconomic levels which follows the flight to suburbia, to build huge political machines. Since such machines are maintained by excessive patronage, they soon grow corrupt. Sidewalk inspectors, blacksmith supervisors, cemetery consultants, and similar patronage workers with large salaries and no productive duties help to perpetuate the machine and increase the tax burden.

An incisive summary of the nature of metropolitan political problems is given by Robert Wood, a political scientist.

A single-minded fixation on the service concept of government, an insistence on the preservation of political autonomy and multiplicity, mean, first of all, that it is impossible to have a vision of what the metropolitan regions might become. When each jurisdiction goes on its separate way, urban sprawl continues, with its companions of spreading blight, cheap commercial developments along major highways, inadequate parks, congested schools, mediocre administration, smog, traffic jams, recurrent crises in mass transportation, and the hundred and one irritations of undirected growth. The "gray belt" . . . continues to expand, and the municipalities caught directly in its path are left to grapple with its consequences, one by one. In place of a coordinated attack on the less attractive byproducts of urbanization, each jurisdiction tries to avoid the conditions it regards as unpalatable, to protect its own, and to let its neighbors fend for themselves. When local government disclaims responsibility for the regional environment, the capacity to realize the potential of that environment is irrevocably lost.[1]

This situation is reflected in governmental services which are often grossly inefficient, unequal, and inadequate. Criticism of such governmental services as sanitation, control of air and water pollution, rubbish disposal, and police and fire protection is almost continuous. Complaints are lodged in one or more sections of the area every day by people who are dissatisfied with parking facilities, public welfare services, recreation facilities, airport operations, traffic control, zoning ordinances, and a host of other governmental services and regulations.

Transportation is becoming a more difficult problem as the metropolis sprawls farther and farther into the surrounding area. While the automobile has given the American people greater freedom of movement than any other people have ever had, it has created critical problems in areas of dense population. While it has made suburbia possible, it has made speed, comfort, and ease in urban travel almost impossible. A suburban dweller can fly from Indianapolis to New York quicker than he can get from the airport there to his home in suburban Scarsdale. Rapid transit and commuter trains are uneconomical and as a result are rapidly deteriorating and steadily and surely going into bankruptcy. Freeways and superhighways which have provided some help are rapidly becoming too expensive to build. Shoppers refuse to endure the hardships of fighting traffic, and as a result shopping centers are springing up in the outlying suburbs.

The problem of transportation of both people and goods is a matter of national concern. Congress has recognized the need for action on the national level to remedy a situation which, if not corrected, will most certainly lead to strangulation of whole cities.

The concentrations of the different types of economic productivity over the metropolitan area produce a very uneven pattern of assessed valuations. This is in turn reflected in a great divergence of governmental services ranging from broad and adequate to narrow and inadequate, to practically nonexistent. High taxes are paid in some localities for inadequate services, and low taxes for complete services in a neighbor-

[1] Robert C. Wood, "Metropolis against Itself," in the Area Development Committee's *Supplementary Paper,* no. 2, p. 41, Committee for Economic Development, New York, March, 1959.

ing community. Consolidation of governmental units is often blocked by those who are fortunate enough to live in areas of high valuations. As a result progress in this direction has been slow.

The social problems of the metropolitan areas are diverse, just as the population is diverse. Naturally not all or even most social problems are attributable exclusively to urban living. However, conditions created by the metropolitan milieu do contribute significantly to social problems. The vacuum created in the city by the movement of the middle class to the suburbs has been filled by the immigration of minority groups and members of majority groups who are in the lowest socioeconomic classes. They cluster in old residential areas of the city where large old homes are rented as apartments and house as many as a dozen families in homes which once accommodated a single family. Absentee landlords aim only to get as much money from the properties as possible without spending any significant amounts on repair or maintenance.

In these "pockets of poverty," or slum areas, dwell the unemployed, unskilled, unschooled, and uncared for of humanity. Here live families who have lost their breadwinners to disease, alcohol, narcotics, prison, and death. They suffer from lack of recreation, wholesome entertainment, clothes, food, and, last but not least, love and understanding. Such an environment tends to create and contribute to a long list of social problems including alcoholism, drug addiction, venereal disease, accidents, child desertion, juvenile delinquency, sex perversion, gang warfare, prostitution, and crimes of all descriptions. These congested areas have been aptly designated as the "breeding ground" of much that is undesirable in American life.

One of the most threatening phenomena growing out of the situation is the rise of criminal syndicates. They ally themselves with the political machine in power in the large city and proceed systematically to extract money from the poor, the gullible, the greedy, and all who are unfortunate enough to fall into their clutches. Not even the upright, respectable, well-heeled citizen is immune since this parasitical growth attaches itself to legitimate businesses and levies on them.

Today in many of our large cities and in some of their suburbs, organized crime, represented by the most notorious hoodlums and racketeers, not only mulcts society of millions of dollars but contributes heavily to the sorrow, degradation, and human despair of a sizable portion of our population. Organized crime in many metropolitan centers controls and promotes gambling, prostitution, "juice loans," and narcotic addiction. But this is not enough. The greedy members of the syndicate demand a tribute from legitimate business for "protection." The businessman who refuses is likely to have his storefront demolished, his trucks disabled, or his home bombed. Threats, intimidation, vandalism, bombing, and even physical torture are a way of life in organized crime. As if this were not bad enough, syndicated crime is infiltrating legitimate business through stock ownership and partnership arrangements.

This unholy alliance of crime and politics creates a social problem which threatens not only the people of the metropolis but the country as a whole. Congressional committees are tackling this problem with the hope of finding some solution in Federal laws. The U.S. Internal Revenue Service is attacking the problem through criminal prosecution of crime profiteers. Progress so far has not been encouraging. Action at the local level to separate crime and politics may present better chances for success.

The emphasis here on the social problems of the slum areas does not imply that there are no social problems in suburbia. Juvenile delinquency, broken homes, divorce, and alcoholism are problems of suburbia also. The major difference lies in the type of people who live in suburbia and the means at their disposal to deal with their problems. Serious as the social problems of suburbia are, those of the slums are more crucial.

James Conant in his book *Slums and Suburbs* says,

> I am convinced we are allowing social dynamite to accumulate in our large cities. I am not nearly so concerned about the plight of suburban parents whose offspring are having difficulty finding places in prestige colleges as I am about the plight of parents in the slums whose children either drop out or graduate from school without prospects of either further education or employment. In some slum neighborhoods I have no doubt that over a half of the boys between sixteen and twenty-one are out of school and out of work. Leaving aside human tragedies, I submit that a continuation of this situation is a menace to the social and political health of the large cities.[2]

Implications for education

Serious problems for education are inherent in the heavy concentration of population in the urban areas of the country. These problems are likely to become more acute as the trend toward urban living continues. A constructive program for attacking and solving these problems is imperative.

Probably the first task of the school is to redesign its administrative

[2] James Bryant Conant, *Slums and Suburbs: A Commentary on Schools in the Metropolitan Area*, p. 2, McGraw-Hill Book Company, New York, 1961.

structure to conform with the realities of urbanization. No longer will the traditional school-district structure suffice. A successful effort will involve a willingness on the part of some to sacrifice favored situations for the common good. Certainly the establishment of a metropolitan-area government even with limited powers will require that some municipalities give up to some extent advantages which they enjoy. Likewise an intermediate metropolitan-area school district will require that some local school districts relinquish some of their powers in the interests of the educational welfare of all.

Most authorities in the field of public administration are convinced that some effective form of metropolitan government is essential. It is possible that metropolitan-area government may replace county government, thus substituting natural population regions for artificial political units. There is also the possibility that metropolitan government will replace both county and city government and thus simplify state governmental structure.

The problem of school-district administrative structure is part and parcel of the larger problem. The uncontrolled growth of the suburbs is accentuating the difficulties. The inequalities of the property tax, based as it is on greatly divergent property values, breeds inequalities in the treatment of people as well as inequities among taxpayers. The same inequalities of financial resources among school districts are reflected not only in hardships on taxpayers but in the divergence of educational opportunity among people of the metropolitan area.

The problem of administrative structure is therefore a common problem which calls for a common effort for its solution. The school can and should assume leadership in attacking this problem.

In general a metropolitan-area governmental unit can, by virtue of its scope, be more effective than constituent municipalities in performing the following types of public service:

Traffic planning and engineering
Traffic control
Industrial-development planning
Control of air and water pollution
Development and maintenance of water and sewage systems
Maintenance of a civil defense program
Development and maintenance of park and other recreational facilities
Planning for urban renewal

Likewise a metropolitan-area intermediate school district can, in most instances, improve the educational situation by performing the following services:

Equalizing the financial support of schools in the area

Providing special pupil services on an area-wide basis

Developing a master plan for school construction in the area

Promoting policies and programs of pupil integration

Developing and maintaining pupil transportation systems

Conducting teacher recruitment programs for the area

An alternative to metropolitan-area governmental units and intermediate school districts is the federation. However, in practice the federation does not ordinarily provide the centralized power necessary for success in meeting the problems of urbanization.

A second alternative sometimes proposed is the consolidation of the suburban area into four or five regional units and the subdivision of the large central city into manageable units, at least for school purposes. While some advantages can rightfully be claimed for this plan, it fails to provide for the overall planning and development which is so important in the metropolitan area.

In the United States noteworthy progress in metropolitan government has been made in Miami, Florida, and Nashville, Tennessee. In Canada the city of Toronto is probably in the lead.

Political scientists and technical experts in government are generally convinced that little or no improvement in metropolitan government can be achieved without the understanding and support of interested and informed citizens organizations. The role of the school is to mobilize the human resources of the metropolitan area in the attack on the common problem of administrative structure. The school can help to involve all civic groups and other interested organizations in dialogue and discussion. It can aid in defining problems and clarifying goals. It can assist community forces in organizing to achieve the goal of effective metropolitan government.

The school can contribute further to the political development of the metropolitan area in academic ways. It can, in the curriculum, provide both youth and adults with accurate information about the area and its governmental problems. It can help to develop attitudes of unity and cooperation with regard to the metropolitan area by emphasizing the close interrelationship of local communities within it. Finally, it can present the problem of urban government as one of the great social challenges of the twentieth century to students both young and old.

If we are to cope successfully with the many other problems attendant on urbanization, fundamental changes must be made within the school itself. Some of these are described elsewhere in this book in connection with population mobility, scientific and technological advances, the socially disadvantaged, and the problems of integration. Suffice it to say at this point that urbanization calls for new programs, new tools of education, specialized personnel, expanded guidance programs, and a broader concept of educational responsibility.

Such substantial changes in the school cannot be accomplished by the professional people alone, no matter how clearly they may see their responsibility. An all-out effort by the total school community is necessary. The task is magnified in many urban school districts by the fact that they include widely divergent groups. Such districts are, in fact, multicommunity districts. The New York, Chicago, St. Louis, and Philadelphia school systems are illustrative of this type of urban district. In each we find neighborhoods and communities which range the complete spectrum of society from the wealthy luxury-apartment dwellers to the most poverty-stricken slum population. Add to this diversity the huge size of such school systems, and we have a situation which confounds even the most stouthearted school administrator.

The multicommunity school district, however, presents an opportunity for the school to mobilize the many diverse elements of the population in a common effort. Each element will have a unique contribution to make, and each will have a genuine concern in any educational effort directed toward a better life for all. The mechanics of mobilization and utilization of community resources in such an effort must be developed differently in each situation, but the essential elements are effective communication, broad participation, and close cooperation.

If the many social and economic problems of urban life are to be solved, a broad and inclusive program of cooperation among institutions and organizations of the community must be developed. Such an effort in a metropolitan area should involve school districts as well as many municipal governmental agencies, professional and labor groups, industrial complexes, business associations, and social welfare agencies. Some one school or group of schools can initiate action and gradually draw other institutions and agencies into the effort.

Probably the most promising instrument in the development of such a program of cooperative effort is the citizens advisory committee. A continuing, or permanent, committee selected and organized as suggested in Chapter 5 can become the focal point and coordinating agency of a system of citizens groups which will proliferate into all areas of municipal government, the professions, social welfare, business, and industry. The abilities, judgment, and skills of civic-minded citizenry can be brought to bear on the problems of the urban community. Such problems as those of securing good government, curbing crime, reducing juvenile delinquency, and providing adequate housing and recreational facilities in urban areas can be studied in depth, and action can be recommended to policy- and law-making bodies. Although organizations and social classes have special objectives, most are willing to pursue a comprehensive program of urban improvement if their own interests are included.

In multicommunity school districts the system of citizens committees here suggested will invariably generate an integrative process which will have a most wholesome effect on school-community relations in all areas of the educational effort.

The development of such a system of participation and communication in a number of school districts in the metropolitan area would naturally lead, with the stimulation of the school, to a multidistrict committee with representatives from the continuing advisory committee of each district forming the group. Such a committee would then be in position to mobilize action on a broad base and tackle metropolitan area problems which individual study and action committees could not hope to solve.

In a democracy the people possess the ultimate power. But in order to wield that power constructively and effectively, they must be organized on a broad front and provided the opportunity to define common goals and to plan the action necessary to achieve these goals. To provide leadership in this effort is the major social challenge of the school today.

scientific and technical revolution

Midcentury in America as in many other parts of the world is a period of scientific and technological revolution, or evolution, depending on the vantage point from which the observer assesses the situation. All phases of society have been affected. The impact on our economy is difficult to overestimate. While thousands of new jobs have been created, hundreds of thousands of people suffer technological unemployment. Automatic elevators have displaced more than forty thousand elevator operators in the city of New York alone. Automatic stokers have displaced more than eighty thousand railroad firemen. Complex mining machinery has been instrumental in reducing the mining work force by more than one hundred thousand in the decade of 1955–1965.

This phenomenon is part and parcel of the race for greater economic productivity. And the race is only in the beginning stages. Both government and private interests are spending huge sums of money on research and development. In 1964 the Federal government alone spent over 15 billion dollars on research and development, a sum almost ten times greater than that spent only a decade ago. The army of Federal scientists, engineers, and technicians is larger than the standing army of most countries of the world. Private industry is spending at the rate of 10 to 12 billion dollars a year on discovering new processes and new products for the American and world economy.

Although military research draws most heavily on the economy because of the defense nature of its goals and although industrial research follows not far behind, huge sums are also being spent in medical and educational research. Furthermore, beginning studies are being made in the area of social research as exemplified by studies of aging, juvenile delinquency, and crime.

The scientific exploits of the United States and Russia and other nations challenge the imagination. The secrets of the atom have been laid bare; power of incalculable magnitude has been harnessed; man-made satellites orbit the earth in increasing numbers; men walk in outer space beyond the pull of gravity; and exploration of the moon's surface by man is imminent. All this has been accomplished within the space of two decades. No one dares predict the scientific feats of the next twenty years.

Technological developments have kept pace in the form of automation and computerization. "Automation" may be defined as the performance by mechanical devices of both the sensory and the motory tasks characteristic of human labor. "Computerization" may be defined as the performance by mechanical means of tasks involving memory, analysis, classification, and decision making.

The devices of automation and computerization have transformed the world of business and industry and are rapidly making themselves felt in all phases of society. They can make analyses of the consumer market, keep inventories for the merchant, select workers for the personnel office, keep daily accounts for the banker, and read envelopes for the postman.

All this is just the beginning. The larger the circle of light, the larger the periphery of darkness. Each scientific discovery reveals greater areas of the unknown and opens doors to new discoveries. Each technological breakthrough is reflected in new machines and instruments which enable man to exercise greater and greater control over his physical environment. While innovations have a long way to go if they are to remove the limitations of human existence, each day finds us pressing toward what economist Daniel Bell calls "the compass of rationality itself."

The essence of science and technology is *change*—rapid, continuous, and revolutionary change. This change affects all the earth's peoples. We are just beginning to sense the extreme seriousness of its influence on our economic and social life. Unlike its effect on the military, which was dramatized so horribly in Japan in the Second World War, its effect in other areas has been slow to register on the consciousness of the nation. Its impact upon the various phases of human existence will probably be greater than can yet be realized. Certainly the impact on education will be massive. It is to be hoped that educational leadership will recognize that new frontiers in science and technology call for organized, purposeful innovations in the school.

Implications for education

Science and technology are placing and will place new and ever-increasing demands upon education. The educational program will have to be expanded to accommodate the new essentials of education for today's world. The nature of the secondary school program will most certainly undergo significant changes. For the great majority of youth it must become a general educational program, while the junior college, the technical institute, and the professional school supply the specialized training necessary for economic productivity in today's society.

Except in a few occupations the youth with only a high school education will be seriously handicapped. The dropout or "forceout" will be for all practical purposes unemployable. This means that the secondary school must adapt its program to accommodate the realities of the economic situation. It must provide those who now drop out a program which will make them employable in some skilled or semiskilled occupation when they finish high school, if that is to be the terminal point in their education. It must also provide a firm foundation in general education for those who will have post-secondary educational opportunities.

A second implication is that the public school must provide a broad and vital adult education program. The rapid changes in jobs and job-training requirements demand that adults have the opportunity to keep up with technological advances in their occupations and professions. Such a program must be offered at both the secondary and the junior college or vocational-technical institute level. It is no longer sufficient to educate for economic productivity; we must continue education of the working individual so that he can maintain economic productivity.

A third implication which stems from the first two mentioned is that education must have more, new, and better tools with which to do its job. The old shops, laboratories, and classrooms must be redesigned in the light of new knowledge of both how students learn and what they learn. School-building experts tell us that two-thirds of our high school science laboratories are out-of-date, three-fourths of the industrial arts shops are outmoded, and most of our classrooms do not reflect present knowledge of acoustics, ventilation, heating, lighting, and other conditions which affect the learning situation. Only a relatively few schools have electronics laboratories; fewer still are equipped with closed-circuit television. Teaching machines are still novelties in the majority of schools. Many schools are without the most rudimentary equipment necessary for introducing the student into the world of computers and automated machinery.

Instructors who have the knowledge and the skills necessary to use these tools will be needed. Some will be found in the teaching ranks; others will have to come from industry. If the current situation is to be remedied, we must spend huge sums on education. We as a nation are rich in material resources. We can afford to spend much more on education. In fact we cannot afford to fail to do so.

Implications for school-community relations

The fact that most people are not fully aware of the socioeconomic impact of science and technology poses certain problems in introducing changes in the curriculum which take this impact into account. People of the school community will not fully support curricular innovations unless they are convinced of their desirability. To be most effective the school must have both the financial and the moral support of the community.

This offers a real challenge to the school in its relation to its community. Its first responsibility is to secure a clear understanding of the problem and then, on the basis of the facts, adapt its program to meet student needs. The community should participate fully in gaining this knowledge and making these adjustments. The pattern of citizen involvement described in earlier chapters provides a means whereby citizens with special and expert knowledge may become active participants in assessing the effects of the new technology and useful assistants in developing the school program.

Most school communities of ten thousand or more people will have a number of businessmen, industrialists, and professional men who are not only willing but eager to cooperate with the school in its efforts to shape its curriculum in the light of new demands of the socioeconomic complex. By organizing citizens advisory committees and providing them with resource people and materials, the school can secure valuable aid in redefining its goals and redirecting its efforts.

This is not to say that lay people are to determine curriculum. Their function is auxiliary in nature but of vital significance. Their experience combined with that of school people can form the base for a critical evaluation of the goals and policies of the school program in light of the new technology and can provide appropriate direction to curriculum revision. The selection of appropriate courses and general curriculum content, the methods of instruction, and the techniques and materials used are matters for professional decision.

As has been pointed out earlier, the substantial changes indicated for the school curriculum and the attendant increase in the educational life span will cost large sums of money. Physical plant, equipment, and instructional costs will rise rapidly as time goes on. These costs must be met. In order to do so, the local community, the state, and the nation will have to recognize education for what it is, namely, an investment in the individual and in the society in which we live.

Communication is, of course, of extreme importance in this context. A school community which has established a structure of communication such as described earlier will be in a good position to publicize the deliberations and conclusions of the advisory group together with the facts upon which they are based. This will tend to raise the level of public understanding and help to ensure the community's moral and financial support.

the rise of organized groups

The growth of our population, its mobility, urbanization, and scientific and technological revolution, and still other socioeconomic changes have contributed heavily to the rise of organized groups. This development is one of the predictable phenomena of the mid-twentieth century. It is a natural concomitant of the growth and complexity of present-day society.

In early American culture the family was the basic organized group. Often the family group included not only father, mother, sons, and daughters but also uncles, aunts, nieces, nephews, grandfathers, grandmothers, and grandchildren. Under such circumstance the family, or the clan as it was sometimes referred to, was a very sizable group. In the small community such a group could, and often did, exercise considerable influence on local affairs. The family group was effective in the nineteenth century because most communities were relatively small, with the majority of their everyday concerns confined to the local community. There was ample opportunity for face-to-face discussions. Town-hall meetings and similar gatherings provided a forum for expressions of opinion and paved the way for political action. Most of the economy was based on agriculture, and the farmer cherished his independence and freedom of action. Economic and political interests were usually similar or complementary. The farmer, the shopkeeper, and the blacksmith earned their livelihood within the community and shared, in varying degrees, its economic fortunes.

Means of communication were slow, and people learned of national and international events long after they occurred. Only a minority of the population had access to books, magazines, and newspapers.

In such circumstances there was little incentive to organize groups representing economic, social, or political interests. Division, such as it was, followed sectional interests rather than class or special group interests.

The situation today is radically different. We live in a highly industrialized, specialized, and urbanized society with worldwide communication facilities. The economic and political interests of the state and the nation are shared in some measure by every community. The growth of huge corporations has made the local community sensitive to economic conditions thousands of miles away in another part of the country or on foreign shores. Specialization has created multiple divisions of labor. Each division has its unique interests along with common interests. Social processes have likewise tended to divide people into various interest groups. In the huge urban complex the voice of the individual as an individual is seldom heard above the clamor of the multitude. Only when he represents an organized group is he effective in determining public policy.

Today the organized group is the most effective means of shaping public policy. While there are many thousands of organizations which serve some felt need of their membership, many have little or no effect on shaping public policy. They may provide social and recreational outlets, offer educational opportunity, or just satisfy the human desire to belong. Seldom do such groups take an active interest in public affairs.

On the other hand, organized groups which are rooted in the economic and social structure and have been nourished and developed by common and often vital interests exert tremendous influence on public policy. Chief among such organizations are those representing occupational and professional interests. They include labor unions, associations of commerce, farm cooperatives, bar associations, and teachers organizations. Other organizations which also affect the contours of public policy are those which advance or protect the special interests of minority, racial, and ethnic groups. They include the National Association for the Advancement of Colored People, the American Civil Liberties Union, and the Anti-Defamation League of B'nai B'rith. Other organizations seek to promote a particular brand of patriotism or a political point of view. They include the American Legion, Daughters of the American Revolution, Pro-America, and Americans for Democratic Action. Church-affiliated groups, such as the Woman's Christian Temperance Union, also seek to influence public policy. The list is long, and the diversity in effectiveness of these organizations in shaping policy is wide. But in the aggregate their influence is difficult to overestimate and is destined to become even greater as time passes.

In a democracy such organizations are free to urge their points of view and their interests on the people as a whole or their legislative representatives. They have almost unlimited license to propagandize in attempting to secure public support for their objectives. They collect membership dues which are used for advertising and lobbying. Some contribute to one or both political parties in the hope of gaining legislative favor. Not infrequently special interest groups in their efforts to influence legislation exceed the bounds of propriety and good ethics by bestowing gifts and favors. A favorite stratagem is to sell to legislators at very low prices stock in a company which stands to gain by proposed legislation. Thus the legislator acquires a vested interest in legislation upon which he will be required to act. Only the most naïve will doubt the effect of such an interest on a certain type of legislator.

Although these organized groups perform other functions such as establishing and maintaining occupational, professional, and other standards among their memberships, we are particularly interested here in their principal function—promoting group interests. In this role they are known as pressure groups. They seek power so as to be able to shape public policy. The largest organizations are national with local branches or affiliations. It is typical that such groups often concentrate the full powers of the national organization on local issues in order to supplement and reinforce the efforts of the local affiliate.

Pressure groups work to influence public opinion at local, state, and national levels. In doing so, they seek to mold public policy in their favor as it is made at the local level by school boards and city councils, at the state level by the legislatures, and at the national level by the Congress of the United States. Sometimes these efforts are designed to secure special privileges for members; at other times the aim is to protect or maintain interests or privileges they already possess.

Regardless of the aim of the organization, it is almost always advanced in the context of the public weal. And in most cases members of the organization conceive their purposes as consistent with, if not actually supportive of, the common good, as indeed they are in many instances. Most of the nationally organized groups have developed a social philosophy and accept some measure of social responsibility.

Conflict often arises among pressure groups as they seek opposing objectives. For example, the American Association of Railroads has clashed bitterly on numerous occasions with the American Trucking Association. Both seek advantage in the transportation field. The Chamber of Commerce of the United States and the National Association of Manufacturers often have clashed with the American Federation of Labor and the Congress of Industrial Organizations.

Education is not without its pressure groups, which are headed by the National Education Association. This group was organized in 1857 and, with the exception of the Soviet Teachers Union, is the largest teachers organization in the world, having over six hundred thousand members. It is an outgrowth of state education associations which enroll over a million teachers. The NEA has thirty departments or affiliates including the American Association of School Administrators, the Elementary School Principals Association, and the Classroom Teachers Association.

Outside the profession there are a number of citizens organizations with membership open to all which have as their avowed purpose the promotion of better education. These groups include the National Congress of Parents and Teachers, the National Citizens Council, and the Council on Basic Education.

Organizations and the school

The relationships of the school to organized groups fall into three general categories. The first is that in which the organization attempts to persuade the school to support its aims or seeks to dictate or curb the course of action of the school so that it will conform with the goals of the pressure group. The second is the relationship in which the school as a social institution enlists the support of organized groups in the pursuit of its legitimate goals. The third and most unique type of relationship places the school in the position of an intellectual catalyst among pressure groups. While in our country, as in most, the government is the final arbitrator, the school as an institution representing all the people can provide an impartial forum where the relative merits of organizational goals may be discussed, explored, and evaluated in the context of the public welfare.

Let us now examine each type of relationship in the light of the nature, central purpose, and goals of the public school. While some educators have sought to insulate the school from pressure groups in order to preserve a measure of independence, such a course of action not only holds little hope of success but abdicates the responsibility of the school as a social institution. Furthermore such a negative attitude violates the concept of the school as a bold social enterprise in which all have a stake.

Organized groups are the means by which large segments of the American public express their needs, desires, and aspirations. As such, they have a vital interest in the public school and a legitimate concern about educational goals and objectives. They are part and parcel of the public which the school serves. Thus community participation in a large measure means participation of those whose interests are identified with organizational interests.

In connection with the first type of relationship, it cannot be denied that heavy and continuous pressures have been brought on the school by various groups. Some have sought to dictate the content of the curriculum and the method of teaching. Others have attempted to curtail financial support of the schools. Various kinds of efforts have been made, and not without some success, to place the school in the position of promoting the selfish interests or points of view of pressure groups. Too many organizations have on occasion sought to circumscribe the intellectual freedom of the school, where their particular interests were involved.

In extreme cases, picketing, sit-ins, marches, and other types of demonstrations against the school have been employed by pressure groups in efforts to achieve their demands. Pupils have been kept at home as a form of pressure on the school.

Obviously the school must resist any efforts to undermine its financial support, threaten its intellectual integrity, curb its freedom of inquiry, or substitute intimidation for reason. It must never be the advocate of special interests as opposed to the welfare of the public it serves.

However, to resist, to negate in such circumstances is not enough. The school must act positively and constructively in relation to such groups. It must move aggressively into the second type of relationship noted earlier; that is, it must enlist the support of organizations for education in general and the school in particular. Since the school represents all the people, it can legitimately seek the support of all interested groups, and all or almost all pressure groups are interested in education. Many support educational ventures of their own.

In general it can be said that the central purpose of the school, the search for truth, is consistent with, and supportive of, the legitimate goals and aspirations of socially responsible organizations. To enlist their support is therefore largely a matter of systematic, continuous two-way communication. Such support is helpful in influencing public opinion and legislative action at the local level but imperative at the state and national levels.

While educational organizations, such as the NEA, and others representing educational interests, such as the National Congress of Parents and Teachers, are effective in the state capitols and the halls of Congress, they are not sufficient. The efforts of organizations such as the AFL–CIO, the Chamber of Commerce of the United States, and the American Bar Association are essential. All have a vital stake in education in America, and in many cases support of these occupational and professional groups is a prerequisite to favorable action on proposed legislation. Their knowledge and experience in dealing with legislative bodies are a valuable asset when utilized in promoting legislation supportive of education.

The third type of relationship, which we have termed that of intellectual catalyst, complements the two types previously discussed. It requires organized, systematic participation of the community. As has been suggested earlier, a carefully chosen, fully representative citizens advisory committee is essential if this relationship is to be of maximum effectiveness. This committee, sponsored by the school, provided with human and material resources, and operating in close communication with the school community can provide the forum for discussion and the rationale for decision.

The school—having as its central purpose the search for truth and representing as it does all elements of the community—is ideally suited to perform this essential function in democratic life. In this way the school can help ensure that while many organizational goals are incorporated in the social design, none transcends that of the public good.

additional reading

Bettelheim, B., and M. Janowitz: *Social Change and Prejudice,* The Free Press of Glencoe, New York, 1964.

Bloomberg, Warner, Jr., and others: *Suburban Power Structures and Public Education,* Syracuse University Press, Syracuse, N.Y., 1963.

Brameld, Theodore: *Education for the Emerging Age,* Harper & Row, Publishers, Incorporated, New York, 1965.

Bredemeir, Harry C.: *Social Problems in America: Costs and Casualties in an Acquisitive Society,* John Wiley & Sons, Inc., New York, 1960.

Brightbill, Charles K.: *The Challenge of Leisure,* Prentice-Hall, Inc., Englewood Cliffs, N.J., 1960.

Chandler, B. J., and others (eds.): *Education in Urban Society,* Dodd, Mead & Company, Inc., New York, 1962.

Conant, James Bryant: *Slums and Suburbs,* McGraw-Hill Book Company, New York, 1961.

Dobriner, William M.: *Class in Suburbia,* Prentice-Hall, Inc., Englewood Cliffs, N.J., 1965.

Gordon, Mitchell: *Sick Cities,* Penguin Books, Inc., Baltimore, 1965.

Hodgkinson, Harold L.: *Education in Social and Cultural Perspectives,* Prentice-Hall, Inc., Englewood Cliffs, N.J., 1962.

Kimball, Solon T., and others: *Education and the New American,* pp. 163–215, Random House, Inc., New York, 1962.

Klineberg, O., and R. Christie: *Perspectives in Social Psychology,* Holt, Rinehart and Winston, Inc., New York, 1964.

Norfleet, Marvin B.: *Forced School Integration in the U.S.A.,* Carlton Press, Inc., New York, 1961.

Rodehaver, Myles W., and others: *The Sociology of the School,* pp. 67–83, Thomas Y. Crowell Company, New York, 1957.

Rodwin, Lloyd (ed.): *The Future Metropolis,* pp. 17–63, 103–142, 171–186, George Braziller, Inc., New York, 1961.

Silberman, Charles: *The Crisis in Black and White,* Random House, Inc., New York, 1965.

Stanley, W. O.: *Education and Social Integration,* pp. 1–38, Bureau of Publications, Teachers College of Columbia University, New York, 1953.

Thayer, V. T.: *The Role of the School in American Society,* Dodd, Mead & Company, Inc., New York, 1960.

Venn, Grant: *Man, Education, and Work,* American Council on Education, Washington, D.C., 1965.

Vidich, Arthur J., and Joseph Bensman: *Small Town in Mass Society,* Doubleday and Company, Inc., Garden City, N.Y., 1960.

West, James: *Plainville, U.S.A.,* Columbia University Press, New York, 1961.

basic issues in school-community relations

10

It has been said with considerable conviction that there are no greater issues in American democracy today than those being argued in the field of education. The most crucial as well as the most comprehensive issue in the field is that of the determination of the central purpose of the school. This issue involves the defining of the function of the school in our society and raises a large number of concomitant issues which are being fought out in local schools, in state legislatures, and in the highest courts of the land.

A second issue, likewise comprehensive, complex, and difficult to resolve, is the question of both intermediate and long-range goals or objectives which should be adopted by the school in order to achieve its central purpose and other purposes compatible with that central purpose. Few questions stimulate so many divergent answers. Even if

191

we could secure consensus on the issue of central purpose, we would still find major areas of disagreement on the validity of objectives and their consistency with the major purpose of the school.

A third issue which stirs up heated controversy is that of the relationship of the public school to the private school. As many private schools are sponsored and financed by church groups or organizations, the element of religion enters the controversy. Should the state aid the private school because it performs the educational function for certain children and thus relieves the state of expense? Should facilities, time, and public funds be shared by public and private schools? These are some of the questions which interlace the issue of the relationship of the public and private school.

A fourth basic issue is the role of the school with respect to the major social issues of our times. What is the responsibility of the school with regard to such burning social issues as integration, social equality, civil rights, opportunity for the socially disadvantaged, and the problem of extremism?

A fifth issue which will be dealt with in this chapter is, "How shall the public schools be financed?" This question, although somewhat mundane, calls for an answer which may well determine the very nature and scope of education. Shall we support education generously or half-heartedly? Shall the major source of support be the local community, the state, or the Federal government?

A discussion of these five basic issues in American education together with an application of the principles of school-community relations developed in earlier chapters will constitute the theme of this chapter.

what is the central purpose of the school?

Since time immemorial historians and graduation speakers have proclaimed their particular era new and different from preceding times. In a large measure such statements have been true. However, we are now in an era which is new in a terrible sense. For the first time in the long history of man, the means of self-annihilation, swift and devastating, are in his hands. Nor are these means confined to one nation, or even to one race. They are in the hands of enemies as well as friends. In a real sense all the world is at the mercy of those who hold this awesome power. We live in an era in which the powers of destruction are absolute. One fatal action can wreak irretrievable disaster.

We live today in a stalemate situation. Although those who may be regarded as our enemies hold within their hands the power to destroy us, they are reasonably sure that they in turn will be destroyed. There is intense rivalry in the pursuit of scientific knowledge. Behind the scenes scientists work feverishly to develop defensive mechanisms to ward off the potential destruction which waits in the wings, ready at a moment's notice to appropriate the world stage. Immense national resources are being poured into the effort to find some means of defense against the destructive power which has been developed. Such efforts in themselves represent an attempt to remedy a situation which scientific advances have created. In fact the only remedy is more knowledge. Knowledge gives power, and power is essential to survival in the world which we have created.

With the existing stalemate in the arms and counterarms race, the nations of the world are turning to economic development as an instrument of achievement. The undeveloped and underdeveloped countries of the world are stirring after ages of slumber. A very substantial portion of our national wealth is finding its way into these countries to aid their development and to ensure that not only economic but social development is along lines which preserve the freedom of man.

What are the implications for education? They are not only numerous; they are crucial. In a real sense higher education, built as it must be on elementary and secondary education, is the key to military, technological, economic, and political power. Education is one field, perhaps the only one, in which we can still gain a decisive advantage over other countries of the world. Education has become a major instrument of national policy.

An abundant supply of highly educated individuals is absolutely essential to technological, economic, and social development. Nations formed from colonial areas of the world supply ample evidence of the helplessness of uneducated people when in competition with more advanced nations in today's technological world.

A look at the educational scene reveals that since 1935 we have made remarkable progress in educating more people than ever before. Today four out of five of the youth of high school age attend high school. This is true despite a dropout rate which is indefensible. Thirty years ago only one of every eight members of the labor force had ever attended high school and only one in twelve was a high school graduate. College and university attendance has shown even greater advances. In 1935 only slightly over 3½ percent of youth of college age were in college; now the figure is close to 33 percent. At that time only 3 percent of the working force were college graduates; now the figure is 18 percent. Add to this the fact that today more adults than ever before are going back to school.

Adult education enrollments in the last ten years have grown more than college enrollments. Evening schools and afternoon classes provide the wherewithal for retraining, "retreading," refreshing, and for advanced work for skilled workers, technicians, teachers, and physicians.

This tremendous growth is both cause and effect. It has been made possible by the increased productive capacity which in turn is possible because of education which supplies the vision, knowledge, and abstract concepts necessary for increased productivity. Today the best index of a nation's productive capacity is the number, quality, and utilization of educated people.

This is the milieu in which we raise the question, "What is the central purpose of the public school?" Granted the school serves many purposes—too many, some authorities believe. Yet if an institution is to achieve maximum effectiveness, to fulfill its mission, to serve in the highest sense, it must commit itself to a central purpose which serves as a guide, a beacon of light shining in the distance and always plainly visible even over troubled waters.

Since early history the school has been the principal institution for planning the experiences of youth in a formal fashion in order to achieve a central purpose. Early schools typically had rather specific but limited purposes. For example, the Spartan school was dedicated to the purpose of producing physically fit warriors capable of defending the state against all enemies. While Socrates regarded good citizenship as the purpose of education and Aristotle sought virtue as its highest goal, both recognized the school as a social institution under control of the state.

By the very nature of the institution the school must have a central social purpose if it is to have a sense of direction. The development of the individual is seen in the context of broad social goals. The traditional central purpose of the school has been to preserve the contemporary culture and transmit it to the coming generation. However, if the school does no more than preserve the culture, it fails to exert constructive leadership or even participate in social change. This has led some to argue that the central purpose of the school is to develop a new and better social order. Such a purpose places a heavy responsibility on the public school, one which many groups and institutions would not willingly confer upon it. The parochial school with a central religious purpose is the first to object.

A few regressionists appear in each generation and insist the central purpose of the school is to preserve the virtues, customs, traditions, and social practices of the past. Such a point of view, based as it is on the concept of absolute, unchanging principles in a world of change, is of course unrealistic.

Most if not all proposals of a central social purpose hitherto advanced may be classified under one of the above categories.

The search for truth as a central purpose

The authors have suggested that the American public school should have as its central purpose the search for truth and the responsibility to teach men to live by it. As a concept this purpose is not new. In fact it is as old as history itself. Many men, scientists, medical researchers, political scientists, and educators have devoted their lives to the search for truth. Even the early caveman searched in a blind and perhaps disorganized, haphazard way for truth. His discovery of fire provided a means of protection from wild animals as well as a source of comfort in inclement weather. The development of the net allowed him to obtain increased supplies of food. Later the development of the axle and wheel gave man a tremendous advantage over other animals in transportation. These and many other discoveries were the result of searching for pragmatic truth, unscientific as the search may have been.

Today in view of the international situation, the stalemate in the military field, the abandonment of colonialism, and the rush for economic development on a worldwide basis, the search for truth has become a universal mandate. Even in the Communist countries where social dogma has been sacred, doctrine has been skillfully pushed aside when it interferes with scientific exploration. All the world is at one level or another searching for scientific, economic, and social truth. Mathematics has become a universal language; scientific principles are accepted as universal laws. In short the rational system dominates all cultures today.

Needless to say, in the world, in the nation, and even in the local community truth as we know it is not the absolute which some would have us believe. The search for truth suggests a constant redefinition of goals in the light of changing conditions and advances on the frontiers of knowledge. All values exist only in relation to other values. What was true in the context of our scientific knowledge with regard to the molecule twenty years ago is false today. The social values which we ascribed to many customs of thirty years ago have been superseded by new values. Educational values such as transfer of training and, more recently, the theory of mental creativity and the mathematical concept of three dimensions have undergone radical change. Change is certain to persist as man pushes closer and closer to ultimate truth.

To propose, then, that the central purpose of the American public school should be the search for truth and the responsibility to teach men to live by it is not only compatible with the past and consistent with the present but also imperative for the future. Not only social and economic progress are in the balance; even survival may be at stake.

What institution is better equipped, more naturally suited, or more strategically situated than the school to assume leadership in the never-ending search? What other institution has the opportunity to work in a learning situation with the individual from early childhood through the total life span? The assumption of leadership in this vital task is a responsibility which the public school should accept as a challenge. Its role is vital; the rewards, tremendous.

What does the adoption of such a central theme mean to the individual? First and foremost, it means that if he is to participate in the quest for truth, he must develop the ability to think. The discovery of truth, even in its most infinitesimal elements, requires logical, consistent thought. In an autocratic society the pressure to conform restricts free thought. In a free society man can fully exert his powers to think. He can weigh values and arrive at his own conclusions. He can discuss and compare these conclusions with those of others, and all can profit by such an exchange. This is the process by which we arrive at truth. This is the process which the school must help to develop in every individual to the fullest extent of his capacity.

In developing the ability to think, the importance of abstractions is difficult to overestimate. If the individual is to go beyond sensory experience, he must be able to formulate and manipulate concepts which involve theoretical elements. He must be able to operate in an intellectual atmosphere in which old traditions are examined, accepted behavior challenged, and new patterns of thinking developed, tried, and evaluated.

In accepting the development of the ability to do abstract thinking as the major function of the school with regard to the individual, we do not negate the development of behavior, effective citizenship, economic productivity, vocational competence, ethical character, good homemaking, and worthy use of leisure time in the student as legitimate goals of the school. But their achievement will in a free society be largely a result of the student's ability to think clearly, logically, and effectively. Their achievement to no little extent reflects the ability to apply abstract thinking to concrete problems.

At the same time the processes of abstract thought have gone beyond individual, concrete needs to produce theories of biological evolution and relativity which are fundamental in the search for truth. Today's explorations in space have been made possible by the abstract thinking of thousands of scientists.

In summary, therefore, in proposing the search for truth and the responsibility to teach men to live by it as the paramount social purpose of the school and the development of the ability to do abstract thinking as a corollary concept, we shift emphasis from how to act, that is, behave, to how to perceive, that is, think. By such a shift we do not minimize the importance of behavior but rather suggest that the best behavior is achieved only as the result of the employment of well-developed thought processes. The most appropriate action is that which is preceded by thought.

This concept of the central purpose of the school presupposes a democratic society in which freedom of inquiry is not only permitted but encouraged. The untrammeled search for truth will in the long run preserve that which is good in our society and help to cast off and replace that which fails to measure up to the needs of changing times.

what should be the goals of the school?

In the context of its all-pervading central purpose, the school has many goals or objectives incidental to and consistent with its major purpose. The definition and description of these objectives is a matter of some disagreement. Critics of education have always been with us and have become especially vociferous with regard to educational objectives in recent years. These critics from within and without the profession of education differ not only on the central purpose of the school but also, and even more diversely, on educational goals or objectives. On the whole such debate is healthy and should serve to stimulate continuous evaluation of educational goals.

Of course there are certain objectives which are generally accepted by all or almost all critics. They include teaching pupils the mastery of the basic skills of reading, writing, communication, and perceiving. Few will quarrel with the goals of developing good citizenship, worthy use of leisure time, and vocational or prevocational abilities. Most will accept as legitimate goals the development of a sound mind in a sound body, an understanding of the basic elements of natural science, and an appreciation of cultural values.

Less of a consensus can probably be obtained for goals such as developing an understanding of and providing practice in desirable social relationships, developing moral character, and developing everyday skills such as are aimed at by driver-training, industrial arts, and cooking and sewing courses.

Even where there is general agreement on a given objective, there may be strong disagreement as to the value or emphasis which should be placed on that objective in relation to others. Some take the position that since the school is only one of a number of educational agencies it is entitled to be selective in its objectives, adopting only those it is particularly equipped to achieve. The fact that in many individual cases the home, the church, and other educational agencies are not doing the job is not, in their opinion, a valid reason for the school to assume such responsibility.

There is basic disagreement as to the extent of the educational function of the school. Some would limit it to the transmission of knowledge in the form of the traditional subjects of learning. Others insist that it includes the responsibility of dealing with social problems and moral issues.

Is education to be restricted to the classroom and laboratory, or should it recognize social and economic endeavors as its proper sphere? Is the juvenile court a classroom; are the slums laboratories?

Are increasing juvenile delinquency, increasing highway accidents, and increasing mental and emotional instability proper concerns of the school? Does the school have an obligation to take up the slack where other social institutions have failed in their stated purposes?

Another basic issue is the scope of the school program. Shall free public education extend from the nursery school through the university? Is it the obligation of the school to provide continuing education to adults throughout their lives? There are those who argue that free education should be limited to the elementary and high schools. Others describe the ideal society as that which provides free education to all who seek to learn.

If we are to increase economic productivity maximally, persevere in our search for truth on a broad front, and preserve our democratic form of government, we must be fully committed to the ideal of education for all. We cannot afford to limit educational opportunity.

For many years the question of whether education should produce the generalist or the specialist has been argued. Should the school stress the humanities or the sciences? These issues have tended to recede in the face of onrushing events. Most thoughtful people will agree that today's society demands a generalist who has a specialty, a humanist who is acquainted with science. The actual quantity of knowledge required in today's society demands both broad education and specialized learning.

This has meant the extension of the minimal educational program from the elementary school through the secondary school and now into the junior college. We have or will have to recognize education as a lifelong process.

Another issue currently attracting wide attention is the matter of quality education as opposed to quantity education. This question applies regardless of what may be considered the major purpose of the school. Is it better to educate a comparative few well or the masses less well? Does the striving for excellence mean that some must be shunted aside by the school?

The answer to these questions seems clearly indicated by the times in which we live. We must have both quality and quantity in education. These two concepts are not incompatible. We do not have to make a choice if we are willing to pay the price, and the price is not in money alone. It is also in imaginative school administration, creative teaching, and intelligent community participation in the educational process. The pursuit of excellence rules out no one. Excellence is a relative term. We can pursue excellence in the education of the mentally retarded as well as the gifted. Excellence can and should be pursued in driver training as well as in physics or mathematics.

There are those who argue strongly for a return to the traditional educational pattern or, as it is sometimes called, basic education. They deplore courses in driver training or family living in the high school. On the other hand there are those who give life adjustment top priority. Those who argue for the life-adjustment curriculum present evidence to show that the traditional curriculum is not meeting life needs. They point to the large dropout rate in high schools as evidence of the nonfunctional curricula. On the other hand the basic education proponents argue that to base the educational program on personal and social needs is anti-intellectual and downgrades education. They insist such a curriculum makes the school a haven for incompetency, laziness, and immaturity. Such a curriculum, they contend, will never encourage ambition, mental discipline, and academic excellence.

In the words of Sir Roger de Coverley, "Much may be said on both sides." With the great diversity of ability and interest among high school pupils, it is hardly reasonable to expect all to profit by college preparatory courses or classical education. The impact of social change should not go unnoticed in the high school curriculum. On the other hand the ability to do abstract thinking is of such vital importance that the curriculum must provide for its development in every individual to the level of his capacity. The school must prepare the student for real life; but life,

if it is to be personally rewarding and socially significant, will demand
much more than adjustment. It will require that each individual develop
his ability to think to its highest potential.

The issues presented here and many others are subject to debate and
resolution by the people. They will and should be debated as we continuously reevaluate and redefine the goals of the school. The freedom to
debate them is inherent in a democratic society.

The issue of academic freedom is vital to the achievement of major
educational goals as well as to the achievement of a central purpose.
While the battleground for this issue has been largely at the college level,
some of the most bitter engagements have taken place in the secondary
school. The decision in the Scopes trial in Tennessee is a classic example
of restriction of academic freedom at the secondary level. Even at the
elementary level we find instances of parents and local organizations
attempting to impose undue restrictions on the quest for knowledge and
truth.

Teaching about communism, human evolution, social justice, and sex
has raised the issue of academic freedom across the broad vistas of
America. There are those who would exclude controversial issues from
the classroom. Communism is a word which should be deleted from
textbooks in the opinion of some conservatives. The recurrence of book
burnings and library investigations are symptoms of a philosophy which
brooks no inquiry into the justice or merit of the established cultural patterns.

Needless to say, if the search for truth is the central purpose of the
school, then academic freedom is essential. The right to free inquiry is
vital in today's world, and those who would deny it are ignorant of, or
oblivious to, the lessons of history.

what should be the relationship between the
public and private school?

Although the majority of Americans attend or have attended the public
school, a substantial number have shown a preference for the private
school. Almost all such schools fall into two categories: first, schools
sponsored by the church, and second, schools which are operated primarily for profit. Schools in the first category enroll pupils from the
elementary through the college level. Schools operated for profit are for
the most part preparatory schools at the secondary level and vocational-
technical schools.

The public school has drawn the fire of both types of private schools.
In fact it was dissatisfaction with the public school which helped motivate

the establishment of the church-related private school. Today the public school faces criticism from both the religionist who believes that schools are too secular and the agnostic who believes they are too religious. There is great difference of opinion among religious groups as to what the attitude of the public school should be with regard to religion and its attendant beliefs, ceremonials, holidays, and rites.

There are those who contend that all children should be compelled to attend public schools through the elementary and secondary levels. They maintain that to permit children to be exposed to various dogma in parochial schools is to encourage antagonism among our future citizens. Those who argue for parochial schools rest their case largely on the constitutional guarantee of religious freedom. The latter point of view was upheld by the United States Supreme Court in 1925 in an Oregon case. Since that time there has been little effort to challenge the right of the church to establish and maintain schools at all levels.

Therefore the issue at present is not the existence of the nonpublic school but rather the relationship between it and the public school.

Perhaps the major issue in defining this relationship is the extent to which public money should be expended in indirect aid to private schools. On legal, moral, and philosophical grounds public money can only be expended for a public purpose. The public school is the formal educational agency of the state, established by the people and supported by them. To divert public money from it to any private educational institution, whatever its nature, is contrary to tenets of our democratic society.

However, indirect aid such as the supplying of textbooks to pupils, the provision of transportation to parochial schools at public expense, and the support of lunch programs in the nonpublic school by Federal or state funds has been upheld in the courts. The theory is that such aid is given to individuals rather than to the institution which they attend. Where does this theory lead us? Are school dormitories, classrooms, and laboratories for individuals? Can instructional costs be shared because the teacher in the nonpublic schools teaches individuals? Can public school teachers go to nonpublic schools to teach special classes because these classes are composed of individuals? When does a conferred benefit cease to be an individual benefit and become an institutional one? Obviously the child-benefit concept is difficult to apply even though its legality is recognized.

Shared time

The practice of "shared time" has become one of the focal points of disagreement. Although we have had shared time in some form since early colonial times, its possibilities and problems are now receiving greater attention than ever before. The U.S. Library of Congress defines shared time as "an arrangement for pupils enrolled in nonpublic elementary or secondary schools to attend public schools for instruction in certain subjects." Other terms applied to shared time are split time, dual registration, part-time enrollment, and educational cooperation. Where the emphasis is on the use of such units of the school plant as the gymnasium, the auditorium, or industrial shops, the practice is often referred to as sharing facilities.

Current practice in shared time varies from one class per day to one-half-day enrollment. The NEA reported in 1964 that in a study of 12,366 school districts enrolling 300 or more pupils, 280 reported that they were operating shared-time programs. The Midwestern states of Michigan, Ohio, Illinois, and Wisconsin along with Pennsylvania were the states reporting the most shared-time programs. The most common shared-time programs of the public school are those in which the value systems which the religious schools seek to inculcate are minimally involved. Such courses include physical education, vocational-technical training, English grammar, foreign languages, mathematics, physics, and chemistry.

Shared time is legal under most state laws, and it is generally agreed that under the proper circumstances shared time would be upheld by the United States Supreme Court. However, the attorneys general of Louisiana and Iowa have given opinions that shared time violates state law in their states.

Aside from the law, shared time presents many administrative problems for educators. A sample list includes:

> The problem of different pupil-grading systems
>
> The provision of additional facilities and teachers for shared-time programs
>
> The unbalancing of the school program
>
> The division of student loyalties
>
> Divided disciplinary responsibilities
>
> Shared-time student participation in extracurricular activities

The National Defense Act of 1958, which has not yet undergone a test of constitutionality in the United States Supreme Court, contains the statement that, "The Congress hereby finds and declares that the security of the Nation requires the fullest development of the mental resources and technical skills of its young men and women." This may be interpreted to mean that Congress views both public and private schools as agents of the Federal government. However, most recent aid-to-education laws specifically state that no funds will go directly to nonpublic schools.

Those who argue for the expansion of the shared-time concept to encompass our whole educational system make the following points:

1. It offers a constitutional solution to the problem of public aid to private schools.
2. It would permit the public schools to serve all children.
3. The financial burden of education would be eased for the total population.
4. It would provide a broader social experience for all children.
5. It would encourage greater cooperation of public and private schools in all areas of educational endeavor.
6. It would relieve the threat of sudden heavy increases in enrollment caused by parochial schools closing their doors.
7. It would improve educational opportunities for parochial pupils without depriving them of religious instruction.

Those who argue for separate facilities make the following points:

1. The administrative problems of shared time are so great as to render the practice infeasible on a large scale.
2. It is a subtle form of aid to religion since it would ease the financial burdens of parochial schools.
3. It would prevent both public and parochial schools from achieving a correlated curriculum.
4. It would cause a widespread dislocation of both public and parochial teachers.
5. In view of travel and curriculum, shared time would hardly be feasible at the elementary level.
6. It would tend to divide the student body of the public school into groups identified with different religions.
7. Widespread use of shared time would weaken and possibly ultimately destroy the public school system.

A point of view

A review of the principles of school-community relations suggested in earlier chapters provides the essential guidelines for a mutually beneficial relationship between the public and private school.

First of all, the public school is a public enterprise which is established to serve all the people. As a social institution among many social institutions, it has the obligation to cooperate with other social agencies, especially those of an educational nature, to the extent that such cooperation is consistent with the purpose of the school. Parochial and other private school pupils as well as their parents are citizens with rights and privileges equal to those of other citizens. It is one of their privileges to attend the public school.

On the other hand, if parents so desire they may send their children to a nonpublic school if the school meets the educational requirements established by the state. In so doing they lose no rights or privileges in connection with the public school. They can help shape its policies and program by their participation in public discussions, by expression of their views to school officials, and by their votes in elections of board of education members, on proposals to issue bonds to build schools, and on propositions to increase tax levies to operate the public schools.

The implications of the concept of the public school as a public enterprise with its central social purpose, to search for truth, and its corollary individual purpose, to develop the ability to think, are reasonably clear in regard to the relationship between public and nonpublic schools. The public school along with other institutions shares the responsibility of education. It should assume leadership in this endeavor and extend full legitimate cooperation to those agencies, including the private schools, which share the endeavor.

Assuming the courts are in agreement, the public school will share its facilities with the pupils of the private schools. These pupils will be welcomed as members of the community which the public school serves. With the exception of the part-time nature of their program, they should be on exactly the same status and have the same rights and privileges as regular full-time pupils. No distinction of any kind should be made in their classes and programs. Guidance and special services such as remedial reading and psychological testing should be available to them on the same basis as they are available to the regular student. In effect, for that part of their school time spent in the public school they become *public school pupils*.

The philosophical position of the public school is not to be changed in any way by the practice of shared time. The public school remains entirely public. It is administered as a public school. No set of values is to be imposed on it. No political or parochial point of view is to be espoused. No organizational bias or orientation is allowed to invade the school. In its central purpose, the search for truth, there must be no dogma that cannot be examined, no social practice that cannot be subject to critical appraisal, and no decree that cannot be questioned. The public school, no matter who attends it (and all are welcome to do so), must preserve and foster for the individual the right of free inquiry and the responsibility to seek truth and live by that truth as he sees it. This means he decides on his values, establishes the priorities among them, chooses his religion, selects his profession, and practices his citizenship in what he believes is the most desirable manner.

The administration of the public school does not change in its essential nature. All shared-time pupils are under the full and complete jurisdiction of the public school while in attendance there. They are subject to the same rules and regulations as other pupils. From the moment the shared-time pupil sets foot on the school grounds until the time he leaves, his conduct, his relationship to other pupils, and his relationship to his teachers all come within the direct purview of the public school. A properly conceived and carefully spelled-out program will enable the school to extend its services to nonpublic school pupils without in any way affecting its essential character as a public institution.

The development and maintenance of this shared-time program will require a great deal of cooperative planning by the administrators of both schools. Long-range agreements as to the nature and extent of shared time will have to be reached so that facilities, equipment, and instructional staff may be provided without major dislocations in any of these areas. This will involve serious administrative problems, and their solution will require the combined efforts of both administrations and the sympathetic understanding of the community. But the results should be well worth the effort in terms of better educational opportunities for children as well as improved school-community relations.

what is the role of the school in social issues?

It is the purpose of this section briefly to set forth a number of the major social issues which impinge directly on the public school and to suggest some possible courses of action based on the principles developed in earlier chapters.

Preceding any discussion of the role of the school in social issues, it is only fair to state the assumptions on which the discussion is based. They are, first, that the school is a social institution; therefore, it has a major social responsibility in our democracy. Second, the accepted goals of the school require from the individual a commitment to constructive membership in society and to the discovery and development of ways in which he can most effectively contribute to the welfare of that society. Third, the school is obligated to seek constantly, in a changing world, appropriate guidelines for social action as well as individual development. And finally, intelligent, effective, and beneficial participation in society is achieved only through free inquiry and mature thought.

Integration

One of the burning social issues of our times is that of segregation versus integration. Is complete integration either feasible or desirable? If social integration is to be achieved, how can it best be accomplished? What is the role of the school?

It is not a matter of chance that the public schools have been and still are the major battleground on which the issue of integration is fought. It is in the public school, where attendance is compulsory, that social equality is a minimum expectancy. The school integration issue was brought to a head by the United States Supreme Court decision of 1954 which overturned previous decisions approving the separate but equal status for Negro schools in the South and certain regions of the North, East, and West. The court declared that so-called "separate but equal" facilities were "inherently unequal."

The problem of social integration has many facets, but we are concerned here with its educational implications. What is the responsibility of the school? Before attempting an answer, let us look at the existing situation.

First of all, *de facto* segregation exists in practically all large cities and in many smaller cities as well as suburban communities throughout the land. Such segregation is largely incidental to the economic level on which the average Negro family lives. The Negro family must live where it can buy or rent housing. Since the advent of a Negro family usually is the signal for a reduction of property values, white owners seek to exclude Negroes. Thus the Negroes are forced into segregated areas even in cases where they are financially able to buy elsewhere.

Urban area school districts with a population of fifty thousand or more almost invariably are organized into a number of neighborhood attendance areas. Each such area has an elementary school which serves children of the neighborhood. This is a logical and desirable situation from the viewpoint of pupil convenience. It does, however, in effect, produce a segregated elementary school. The situation exists to a lesser degree in large city high schools. However, the ability of high school pupils to travel greater distances to and from school places the high school in a somewhat different situation. It is not usually segregated to the same extent as the elementary school.

Thus school segregation has followed as a natural consequence of residential segregation. The administrative structure established in the interest of efficiency and convenience has tended to freeze the urban school system into a segregated pattern.

What can and should the school do in this situation? If the school accepts its responsibility as a democratic institution, it will exercise leadership in the development of policies and programs leading toward the gradual and orderly integration of the people it serves. To do less is to abdicate its responsibility as a social agency dedicated to the ideals of a country committed to freedom, equality, and justice for all. To do less is to isolate, during their school years, some of our children from the larger society to which they must later adjust. If the school is a public enterprise, it has the obligation to provide the most beneficial educational experiences for all. Certainly this includes providing, to the extent possible, an educational environment consistent with the democratic climate in which pupils of all races eventually will live. In addition specific programs in intergroup relations can be incorporated in the program of the school. The problems of integration must be divorced from prejudice and considered on the cognitive level, and this the school is uniquely equipped to do. It must not fail by default.

To be sure, the task is not an easy or a quick one. The educational patterns of segregation, embedded as they are in the economic and cultural heritage of the past, are strong. Changes in attendance area boundaries will, in most cases, be easiest at the secondary level, but changes in elementary school boundaries are quite possible in the fringe areas where different ethnic groups meet geographically. While complete school integration may have to await remediation in other social and economic areas, the school has the opportunity to make very substantial gains. Such gains, however, cannot be made by edict. It will take citizen participation on a large scale. It will take organized, constructive participation of citizens of all races under the sponsorship of the school. Their deliberations, their conclusions, and the facts upon which their conclusions are based must be effectively communicated to all citizens. There must be a structure of communication between school and community which reaches every segment of the population. It means, in short, that the school must be prepared for its role of leadership. If it is not, it is doomed to failure. If it is prepared, if it is patient but persistent, it will succeed in an area in which it can render a unique and outstanding service to society.

Civil rights and social equality

The United States is undergoing a major upheaval as minority groups seek social equality in general, and civil rights in particular. The Negro population, especially, is aggressively reaching out for rights long denied it by various social stratagems and political maneuvers. Hundreds of thousands of man-hours are being spent in marches, sit-ins, picketing, and other types of demonstrations protesting social inequalities and political disenfranchisement. These demonstrations have enlisted people of all races and many who are members of majority groups.

As might be expected, some of these pressure tactics have gone beyond the rightful bounds of legitimate protest and have interfered with the rights and privileges of other citizens. Streets have been blocked with the living bodies of demonstrators and buildings rendered unusable because of sit-in protesters. A case in point is cited. In one of our large cities where the problem of civil rights was and is a very serious one, demonstrators sought to dictate the appointment of city and school officials and force the resignation of those whom they opposed. This is raw, unvarnished pressure directed at individuals rather than a policy or practice.

Does the school have a role? If so, what is it? The answer to the first question must be in the affirmative. The school as a social agency should not avoid or sidestep the issue. The fight for social justice and political equality is a battle of the classroom as well as of the street. The school is the place where ideas are generated, analyzed, weighed, and evaluated. The unique purpose of the school, its search for truth, carries with it the responsibility to teach men to live by it. As the servant of all the people, the school cannot deny fairness, justice, and equality of opportunity to all.

The simple fact is that with minor exceptions the public schools, along with other institutions including the parochial school, the church, and the family, have, for the most part, given tacit approval in past years to social and political practices which deny equality and civil rights to a substantial sector of our population. In those notable cases where disapproval was voiced, it fell on deaf ears. Traditional patterns of living were not easily changed. Social preferences enjoyed by the majority at the expense of a racial minority were overlooked.

But now the winds of change are blowing fiercely over the land. We have sown the wind and are reaping the whirlwind. There are anguished cries from both sides when violence erupts in the streets of our cities. There are pleas for truces, for cooling-off periods, for negotiation, and for compromise. Local, state, and national governments are all involved to some extent and in varying ways. Minority groups are organized, dedicated, and characterized by aggressive, zealous leadership.

Fortunately the conscience of America is awakening, and we can look forward to a period of social adjustment which it is to be hoped will lead in time to the equality which befits free men. What is the role of the school? Again, as in the case of integration, the role of the school is educational leadership. First of all, the school must be an institution in which social and political equality is the accepted way of life. The school should present a model of democracy where every pupil has opportunities equal to those of his fellows. To do less is to militate against the achievement of legitimate educational goals. To do less is to deny the school its democratic birthright.

Second, it is the responsibility of the school as an integral part of its search for truth to explore the status of social and political rights in our country, so that students may measure the present status in terms of the ideals to which a free people are committed. This task requires a careful objectivity which is persuasive only as truth is persuasive and convincing only as facts are convincing. If students are to learn to think critically, they must have the opportunity to examine social and political practices in all their ramifications in the light of the social values to which we in a democracy are committed.

Third, the concept of the community school involves a commitment to all the people the school serves. This includes a majority of the adult population who have no formal connection with the school but who as taxpayers are shareowners in the enterprise. These people as individuals, as members of organizations, and as representatives of the various social institutions of the community, largely shape community life which in turn has a powerful influence on the school. As James Conant has so aptly said, "The school and the community are inseparable."

The function of the school in this context is to raise the consideration of social problems to the cognitive level and to supply the structure through which calm and thoughtful discussion may take place and valid conclusions may be reached. In effect, to quote President Lyndon B. Johnson, the school says, "Let us reason together." To do this requires citizen participation on a broad scale. Such participation can be generated by a school-sponsored citizens committee which opens the area of social equality to public consideration by tackling the problem from the viewpoint of the school. How can the school provide equal opportunity when the community does not? How can the school teach social justice while the community practices social injustice? These and many other pointed questions cannot fail to stimulate discussion and, if appropriate communication channels of a two-way nature have been established, the results are very likely to be beneficial.

In summary, both its unique function and the times in which we live demand that the school be the center of controversy. Let us, therefore, be sure that the debate is on the cognitive level and that an adequate and effective structure for both communication and constructive participation is provided. In this way the school can fulfill its purpose as a bold social enterprise which leads rather than follows, which meets challenges rather than avoids them, and which serves society in the highest sense of the word.

The socially disadvantaged

That there is a substantial portion of the people of the United States who live in slums and mountain shacks, who have inadequate income, who are unemployed and unemployable, who are physically sick and mentally frustrated, and who have a depressingly low standard of living cannot be denied. The actual number of these socially disadvantaged people varies by definition, but by any definition the group is large. The process of urbanization, technological revolution, and population mobility, as discussed in the preceding chapter, have all contributed significantly to the creation and maintenance of their social disadvantage.

The socially disadvantaged, composing as they do somewhere between 10 and 20 percent of our people, present a serious moral, economic, health, and educational problem. Only recently has government fully recognized the seriousness of the problem and launched major efforts to ameliorate the conditions which are at the base of the problem. The obvious first step in such efforts is to provide employment so that incomes may be raised and thus the disadvantaged may provide better homes for, and give better care to, their children and generally raise their standards of living. Education quickly comes into the picture as one important means of developing employability, of improving health practices, and of raising living standards in general.

The moral question as to the responsibility of society to this group is one which must be answered in the affirmative. The argument revolves around the best methods, the most effective means to be used, the money needed, and the nature and extent of aid necessary. Economically the socially disadvantaged are on the debit side of the ledger. Their productivity is low, and their cost in public welfare and actual financial support in the form of unemployment benefits and direct public aid is great. They face serious health problems created by poor nutrition, inadequate medical care, and ignorance of proper health practices.

Educationally the effects of social disadvantage operate heavily on the child, particularly in the preschool and elementary school years. Linguistic development, the capacity to solve problems, social customs, and cultural interest are adversely affected. In many areas of low economic levels schools are not as well staffed and equipped as are their counterparts in the more privileged areas. In fact in some large city systems only beginning teachers and those who are castoffs from the other schools are found in the slum areas. In the Appalachian territory and other poor mountain areas, teachers are difficult to secure because of the low pay and poor living conditions. As a result, for the most part, only those who cannot qualify elsewhere teach in these schools. Fortunately some teachers with a strong commitment to the profession and society, as well as strong constitutions, provide some notable exceptions to the general rule.

Among the socially disadvantaged, the perception of past limitations as well as a low level of expectation for the future debilitates ambition and undermines self-confidence. As a result, many socially disadvantaged youths never reach high school; of those who do, few graduate, and almost none attend college.

As a public enterprise serving all the people, the school has a special responsibility in the case of the socially disadvantaged. To argue otherwise would be contrary to good educational practice as well as social commitment. If in the school we are to treat the socially disadvantaged just the same as we treat others, we will have taken the first steps toward educational frustration not only on the part of the pupil but also on the part of the school. If the teaching process is to be effective, favorable conditions for learning are essential. It is the responsibility of the school to see that, to the extent of its power, such conditions exist for all students. Granted that many of the things which must be done to improve the lot of the socially disadvantaged are not within the province of the school, it is responsible for making educational accommodation directed toward improving learning opportunities for them. Such effort applies rather generally to the physically handicapped, the mentally retarded, and the emotionally troubled. The socially disadvantaged present the same type of problem, often in a more complex form as these children frequently suffer one or more of the handicaps mentioned in addition to their social disadvantage. If these children are to learn and equip themselves to take their place in a democratic society, special provisions must be made for them. It is not the purpose of this volume to propose methods of doing this but rather to point out that it is the task of the school to take appropriate *educational* measures to ensure that these youths have the opportunity to become educated.

This does not mean that the school is obligated to assume the role of an employment service, a birth control clinic, or a welfare agency. What it does mean is that the school should provide adjusted educational programs to meet the special needs of the socially disadvantaged. Such programs at the elementary level include orientation classes for migrants, psychological testing, special guidance and counseling, special classes in remedial reading, applied arithmetic, and basic communication, nursery school programs, home visitation, and similar programs directed toward compensation for inadequacies in the cultural background of these children. The "Higher Horizons" project in New York and the Banneker School program in St. Louis are good examples of such programs. The school, in brief, must in the case of these children supplement its program to provide those learning experiences which ordinarily are provided by the home, the family, the church, and other social institutions.

At the secondary level many of the provisions for disadvantaged elementary students must be continued. Guidance, counseling, remedial programs, and home visitation are just as important at the secondary level. In addition the high school must offer to these youths learning experiences which are of significant value to them in dealing with matters which arise in their daily living. Education must be real, vital, and presently valuable. Such an emphasis might be argued as useful to all pupils. It is not our purpose to debate the premise since if we grant it, our point is still valid.

Since the formal education of many of the socially disadvantaged will terminate at the high school level, there must be a strong vocational curriculum provided. But such a secondary curriculum needs to be more than mere job training. It must include the emerging science of the home and family life, the insights which psychology and sociology give to domestic life, employment, marriage, child development, and getting along with others.

To meet the needs of the socially disadvantaged, the school must become a center of learning. It must provide educational services which extend far beyond the school day and the nine-month school year. The school libraries and study areas should be available during the summer and long after the school day is over. "Operation Headstart," which provides additional educational opportunities for the disadvantaged, is an encouraging development in this context. Guidance and counseling should extend beyond the point at which the youth leaves school, be it by dropping out or graduating. Close and full cooperation must be extended to the other social agencies which work with the socially disadvantaged. Such cooperation will prove especially rewarding in dealing with those who leave school early.

The problem of motivation is a crucial one, and it is particularly important at the high school level. When compulsory education laws allow the student to leave school at sixteen, the socially disadvantaged must be strongly motivated if they are to continue. Adequate counseling will prove helpful in this respect.

More and more colleges and universities have recognized the problem of educating the disadvantaged, and for those who have the proper motivation as well as the ability, new avenues are opening in higher education. Talent hunts among the socially disadvantaged by colleges are becoming more common. A number of institutions have inaugurated experimental programs for students from pockets of poverty who do not meet traditional admission standards. Systematic and fully organized tutorial programs for these youths have been established in some colleges.

The public school at all levels is beginning to awaken to its responsibility to the socially disadvantaged. This is a hopeful development entirely consistent with its role as a public educational enterprise.

Extremism

While primarily political in nature, extremism as it has developed in the United States has broad social overtones. It is represented on the right by the John Birch Society, the American Nazi Party, and similar ultraconservative groups and on the left by the Communist Party of the United States and various organizations which follow more or less closely the Communist line.

We live in troubled times. Profound maladjustments characterize our social and political life. These dislocations develop tensions and emotional stresses which often reinforce prejudices of long standing. Extremist organizations capitalize on this situation to recruit members for their organizations. Infiltration is a way of life for these organizations. They infiltrate students and teachers organizations, parent-teachers associations, and taxpayers groups. Thus they extend their influence far beyond the formal organization, membership in which, in most cases, is secret.

Realizing the key position of the school in the community, these organizations often attempt to use the school as a tool for the accomplishment of their purposes. Infiltration techniques are designed to place them in a position to influence school policy and to select and remove teachers, administrators, and other school personnel. Disagreement and conflict among individuals and groups are nurtured and turned to selfish ends. Prejudice is fanned into flame. Despite the fact that most of these organizations are national in character, they operate largely through connections in the local community. They can best be neutralized at the local level where concrete and specific refutation of accusations and allegations is possible.

Extremism in the pursuit of either vice or virtue breeds intolerance, ruthlessness, and a total disregard of the rights and privileges of others. For the extremist, the end sought justifies any means. Extremism either on the right or the left is a direct challenge to the democratic way of life.

What is the role of the school? The answer is found in its central purpose, in the search for truth and the teaching of men to live by it. Truth is not only the best defense against extremism; it is the most powerful force which can be employed on the offense. Let the facts be known! Present all the evidence! Provide the essential information to the people so that they may make their decision on the basis of fact, not fancy or fiction.

The technique of the extremist is the presentation of half-truths and rumors in such a fashion as to influence opinion in the direction he desires. Accusations are made by inference. Sly innuendoes, unsupported allegations, coincidence, and distortion are his weapons. He uses them with recklessness but in such a way as to stay just within the bounds of law so as to avoid slander and libel judgments. He hides behind the cloak of anonymity when expedient and seeks wide publicity when he is convinced his cause will be abetted by so doing.

The school, if it pursues its central purpose in the broadest sense, will develop an atmosphere in the community which will discourage extremism. Extremism cannot flourish in a school community which is diligent in its search for truth, which considers the relevant facts and bases its decision on them rather than prejudice and hearsay evidence. Therefore, in the final analysis, the threat of extremism is best met by the facts, openly arrived at, fully communicated, and rationally considered. Again, it is the function of the school to provide the structure through which this may be accomplished.

how should the school be financed?

School expenditures are increasing by leaps and bounds. Taxpayers in many instances are raising their voices in protest. Votes on educational tax increases are drawing fire from competing institutions. Private schools are demanding access to public funds.

The rapid rise in school costs can be attributed to four major factors.

1. There are more people to educate than ever before. This is due not only to the increase in population but also to the fact that practically everyone goes to school during some period of his life.
2. People stay in school longer. The average span of school attendance has doubled and even trebled in some areas of our nation in the last few decades.
3. The demands of society have broadened the curriculum tremendously. Today we are concerned with areas of knowledge which were virtually unknown forty or even twenty years ago.
4. Instructional, operating, building, maintenance, and other costs of education have risen rapidly in the last two decades. Inflation has contributed to the rising cost in dollars.

Yet today's educational expenditures are relatively small when compared to the financial demands which will accompany a highly educated society. Is it any wonder that the financing of public education has become a major issue?

How shall we provide the necessary financial support to ensure an educational program which is consistent with the age in which we live? Regardless of preferences, it seems clear that a combination of sources will be required to meet the need.

However, we must discard the widely held notion that education is a necessary operating expense and adopt the more realistic concept of education as a capital investment. Such a concept does not negate in any way the valid purposes of education. Economic productivity is one measure of the educated man, and in our society it is certainly not an exclusive one. However, the man who can think, the worthwhile citizen, the person who uses leisure time wisely, the moral and ethical man, the responsible family man is typically also the economically productive man.

To the economist of fifty years ago labor meant unskilled labor or handwork, required no special training, and could be measured simply in man-hours. Today the picture is far different. Unskilled labor is less and less productive while educated labor is more and more productive. Economists have now come to realize that the most important capital any economy possesses is that which workers carry in their heads.

To illustrate, imagine that we could with the help of an Aladdin's lamp create a physical plant comparable to that of the United States—factories, power plants, modern farm machinery, communication facilities—in the African Congo. At the same time let us take away the productive capacity of, say, Switzerland or Holland. What would be the results? We can safely predict that much of the physical plant in the Congo would deteriorate from misuse or lack of use while the skills and knowledge in the heads of the people of Switzerland and Holland would soon rebuild the physical plant necessary to regain high productivity. We have seen this happen in Western Europe following the devastation of the Second World War. The key to productivity is not facilities but human capital.

Purely on a financial basis, education as an investment pays handsomely. It has been estimated that the educational cost of producing a college graduate is approximately 25 thousand dollars. If we add to this the money which could have been earned during his high school and college years, say 20 thousand dollars, we have a figure of 45 thousand dollars which is over four times the average investment in plant and machinery per worker. A college degree together with the schooling which precedes it is estimated to add about 200 thousand dollars to a man's earning power over a period of thirty years. Few investments hold the opportunity for an average yield over the years which is as great.

Investing in education

If we accept the thesis that education is an investment (and it would appear difficult to refute it), then let us appraise the values which may be realized and plan our program of finance on that basis.

First, we have suggested some approximation of the economic value of an education to the individual in terms of dollars. This alone would seem to justify an adequate expenditure to allow an investment in every youth capable of achieving a college degree. Next let us look at its value to the nation. The international situation described earlier places a premium on national productivity. There is no question the nation has a tremendous stake in educating the citizen for greater productivity. As has been pointed out earlier in the chapter, the world productivity race may well be the contest which will determine which nations will survive and flourish.

Second, the value to science of large numbers of well-educated scientists entering the research laboratories of the nation each year is incalculable. The vast horizons of the scientific world stretching before us challenge our schools to produce more and better-trained scientific personnel. The age of atomic fission, electronic energy, and space exploration demands a superior scientific education. In science as in economic productivity we are in momentous competition with other nations, other races, and other cultures. We have been successfully challenged in scientific discoveries by the Russians—an unprecedented occurrence which a few years ago shook the complacency of the nation and brought anguished inquiries about the efficacy of our schools. The simple fact is that we cannot afford to allow any significant sector of the scientific front to go unmanned. We must produce scientists in greater numbers than ever before and they must be better trained if we are to achieve the success which ensures our freedom.

In the third place, the problems inherent in the highly complex society in which we live demand for their solution the best efforts of an informed, intelligent citizenry. Democracy can survive in today's world only if we can continuously and consistently raise the level of intelligence of our population. As in economics and science, the stakes are high; the values of education are difficult to overestimate.

Finally, although the list might be extended, we mention the moral and ethical values which accrue to the educated society if the school does its job well. While a sense of justice, fairness, honesty, truthfulness, courage, compassion, and personal integrity are not exclusive to the educated, those who have the privilege of a well-rounded education will have the necessary perspective to value these virtues not only as an adornment for the individual but as essential to the good society. In the context of the educated man these virtues are demonstrable truths by which he can live to the benefit of himself as well as society.

Therefore if we consider the return on investment which a good education provides and the numbers to be educated, we will double, treble, and even quadruple our investment in education in the next two decades. How can this be done?

It will take a tremendous effort, a cooperative endeavor in which local, state, and Federal governments must share. Likewise business, industry, and foundations can and should dramatically increase their financial support by providing increased numbers of scholarships, financing educational research, and making outright grants to schools. In addition to the standard forms of tax support the Federal and state governments provide, a great expansion of scholarship and student loan programs is indicated. Financial aid on a long-term, low-interest basis should be readily available to every high school graduate who qualifies for college or vocational-technical school.

Such a program can only be achieved if the public becomes cognizant of the critical importance of more and better education. It is the responsibility of the school to assume leadership in communicating the compelling facts to the people of the country. The school as a public enterprise has this responsibility. If it has organized its communication structure along lines suggested in earlier chapters, it will be in a position to exercise leadership in a bold venture of immense importance and unprecedented magnitude. Such a venture, if effectively carried out in every school community in the nation, would increase financial support at a rate never before visualized. While some critics might challenge the role of the school by insisting that such efforts were propaganda and self-promotion, the times brook no delay. The stakes are too high for the school to be deterred by its critics from performing its unique function as a public enterprise, seeking the truth and teaching men to live by it.

additional reading

Bartky, John A.: *Social Issues in Public Education,* Houghton Mifflin Company, Boston, 1963.

Bruner, Jerome S.: *The Process of Education,* Harvard University Press, Cambridge, Mass., 1960.

Clark, Burton R.: *Educating the Expert Society,* Chandler Publishing Company, San Francisco, 1962.

Downey, L. W.: *The Task of Public Education,* Chicago Midwest Administration Center, University of Chicago, 1957.

Drucker, Peter: *Landmarks of Tomorrow,* pp. 114–194, 257–270, Harper & Row, Publishers, Incorporated, New York, 1965.

Frankel, Charles: *The Democratic Prospect,* pp. 1–9, 30–48, 145–179, Harper & Row, Publishers, Incorporated, New York, 1962.

Gardner, John W.: *Excellence: Can We Be Equal and Excellent Too?,* Harper & Row, Publishers, Incorporated, 1962.

Henry, David D.: *What Priority for Education?,* The University of Illinois Press, Urbana, Ill., 1961.

Killian, James, and others: *Goals for Americans, Report of the Commission on National Goals,* Prentice-Hall, Inc., Englewood Cliffs, N.J., 1960.

Lindvall, C. M. (ed.): *Defining Educational Objectives,* The University of Pittsburgh Press, Pittsburgh, Pa., 1964.

Miles, Matthew P.: *Innovation in Education,* Bureau of Publications, Teachers College of Columbia University, 1964.

Norton, John K.: *Changing Demands on Education and Their Fiscal Implications,* National Committee for Support of the Public Schools, Washington, D.C., 1963.

Olsen, Edward G. (ed.): *The School and Community Reader: Education in Perspective,* pp. 5–90, The Macmillan Company, New York, 1963.

Rodehaver, Myles W., and others: *The Sociology of the School,* pp. 105–134, 183–255, Thomas Y. Crowell Company, New York, 1957.

Russel, James E.: *Change and Challenge in American Education,* Houghton Mifflin Company, Boston, 1965.

Stanley, William O.: *Education and Social Integration,* pp. 1–137, Bureau of Publications, Teachers College of Columbia University, New York, 1953.

Thelen, Herbert: *Education and the Human Quest,* Harper & Row, Publishers, Incorporated, New York, 1960.

Westlin, Alan, and others: *The Uses of Power,* pp. 324–375, Harcourt, Brace & World, Inc., New York, 1962.

appendix

CONSTITUTION OF THE
CITIZENS CONSULTING COMMITTEE
DECATUR SCHOOL DISTRICT NO. 61
DECATUR, ILLINOIS

ARTICLE I—NAME

This committee shall be called the *Citizens Consulting Committee.*

ARTICLE II—PURPOSE

A. *The purposes of the Citizens Consulting Committee of Decatur School District #61, hereinafter called the CCC, shall be:*

1. To serve in an advisory capacity to the Board of Education of the Decatur School District #61, hereinafter called the Board

2. To advise the Board in developing and revising official policies for the public schools of Decatur School District #61

3. To advise and work with employees of the Board in ways mutually satisfactory to the CCC and to the employees in implementing the policies approved by the Board

4. To interpret to the public the goals and needs of the school system, and to interpret to the Board the concerns of the public about school problems

5. To study continuously the needs for education of the people of the District and the effects of the educational programs currently in operation

6. To facilitate communication between the officials and staff of the school system and the people of the District

7. To accept, on first priority, policy study assignments from the Board for future report and recommendation, and to make independent policy studies resulting in recommendations to the Board

8. To work with the Board and school staff to develop mutually satisfactory policies and programs

B. *The CCC shall not recommend nor support candidates for membership on the Board; take action regarding the employment, dismissal, promotion, or transfer of an individual school employee; or encroach upon the professional prerogatives of the teaching staff.*

223

A. *The CCC shall consist of 21 members.*

B. *Qualifications for membership*

    1. Residency in School District #61.

    2. High general ability.

    3. Understanding of the importance of public education and sufficient interest in it that time and effort will be given to the work of the committee.

    4. Personal characteristics essential to success of the committee: personal integrity, responsibility, maturity of thought and action, ability to cooperate, a constructive attitude, open-mindedness, and tolerance of varying points of view.

    5. Members shall be selected to achieve broad geographical representation, reasonably equal representation of men and women, representation of parents of preschool children and in-school children, and representation of older residents.

    6. Members shall be selected to achieve diversity of opinions on school problems.

    7. Members shall not be official representatives of organizations, nor shall they be employees of District #61.

C. *Membership selection*

The members of the CCC shall be recommended to the Board by a selection committee. The Board of Education retains the right to disapprove individual nominations of the Selection Committee, but it will appoint no one who is not approved by the Selection Committee.

D. *Selection committee*

    1. *Membership*

    The Selection Committee shall have nine members, all of them lay citizens appointed by the Board for a term of three years. A representative of the Board, the Superintendent of Schools, and an elected representative of both the teaching staff and the nonprofessional staff shall sit with the Selection Committee as consultants.

    2. *Organization*

    The Board shall call the committee together for the purpose of explaining fully the functions of the Selection Committee. At this first meeting or its next meeting, the committee shall select its chairman.

3. *Duties*

In drafting a list of nominees for the CCC, the Selection Committee shall:

a. Consult with a large and representative part of the citizens of the district by whatever means it may devise in making up a list of persons to be considered for membership on the CCC.

b. Screen the persons under consideration to provide nominees who meet the requirements for membership stated in Article III, Section B above.

c. No one is to be recommended for membership or barred from membership in the CCC because he is an officer or representative of any organization or institution.

d. Preparation of nomination list: For the original CCC the Selection Committee shall prepare a list of twenty-one nominees and an alternate for each nominee. This list shall be submitted to the Board for the original CCC. Although the Selection Committee serves for three years and makes only one canvass of the community at the beginning of its term, it will be required to recommend persons to fill vacancies throughout the three years. Along with the list of nominees, the Selection Committee shall show geographical areas represented together with pertinent descriptive data about each.

e. Willingness to serve: The Selection Committee shall have explained the function and responsibility of CCC membership to prospective nominees and secured their willingness to serve before placing their names in nomination to the Board.

f. Notification of appointment: Formal notification of appointment to CCC shall be made officially by letter from the Board. A copy of this constitution and an invitation to attend a selected meeting shall be included.

g. Replacement of resignees: When a resignation of a CCC member occurs before expiration of a regular three-year term, replacement appointees shall serve for the balance of the unexpired term. Replacement appointees shall be selected by the Board from a previously approved nominee list. If no nominees remain available in the area of classification vacated, the Board shall request a new list of nominees from the Selection Committee.

h. Permanent nomination lists: The Selection Committee chairman shall preserve a master nomination list showing all nominations made, with suitable notations on disposition of all names submitted for consideration. He shall transfer this master list to his successor.

E. *Term of members*

1. The term of members of the CCC shall be three years, except that the original committee members shall determine by lot the one-third that shall serve one-year, two-year, and three-year terms.
2. When a vacancy occurs, the newly appointed member shall serve during the unexpired term of the member he replaces.
3. Members who have served one term are ineligible for reappointment until two years have elapsed following expiration of their terms. This provision shall not be considered applicable in the case of a member whose expiring term as a replacement appointee was of one year duration or less.

F. *Termination of membership*

1. If any CCC member is absent from three consecutive regular CCC meetings, or if a member is absent from over one-half the CCC meetings in any one Committee year, such member shall be deemed to have insufficient interest to continue as a CCC member. Such absence shall be certified in writing by the Secretary of the Executive Committee.
2. The Executive Committee may then recommend to the CCC that because of special temporary circumstances no action be taken for dismissal of the member, or that action be deferred for a specific period. Or the Executive Committee may direct the Secretary to notify the member that he has been dropped from CCC membership. In such event, the Board, the Superintendent, and the CCC membership shall be so notified.
3. If a member is dropped, the replacement shall be named in accordance with the procedure set forth in Article III, Section D3, Paragraph g.

G. *Nonmember consultants*

The CCC will make use of consultants from within or without the school district for service to the CCC or any study committees as may be needed.

ARTICLE IV—OFFICERS

A. *Election*

Officers of the CCC shall consist of a Chairman, a Vice-Chairman and a Secretary. Nominations shall be made at the April CCC meeting by means of a slate of nominees presented by the Nominating Committee and nominations from the floor. Officers shall be elected by the members of the CCC for a one-year term, beginning June 1. Election shall be held at the May CCC meeting. Together these officers shall constitute the Executive Committee.

B. *Duties of officers*

1. *The Chairman* shall preside at all meetings of the CCC and of the Executive Committee and serve as ex officio member of all standing and special committees. The Chairman may call special meetings of the CCC and must do so at the request of the Executive Committee or the written request of five CCC members.

2. *The Vice-Chairman* shall preside at meetings in the absence of the Chairman.

3. *The Secretary* shall record minutes of all CCC and Executive Committee meetings and mail copies of minutes of all CCC meetings to all CCC members, members of the Board, and the Superintendent. The Secretary shall notify CCC members, members of the Board, and the Superintendent of regular CCC meetings at least five days in advance of such meetings. He shall notify the Chairman of excessive absences as defined in Article III, Section F, 1. He shall maintain a roster of present and past CCC members showing area representation and term of office. He shall maintain a listing of monies received and disbursed and advise the CCC of financial obligations incurred. The Secretary shall not incur indebtedness in excess of amounts specified in the By-Laws.

ARTICLE V—COMMITTEES

A. *Executive committee*

The Chairman, Vice-Chairman, and Secretary shall constitute the Executive Committee. The Executive Committee shall meet at the call of the Chairman or any two Executive Committee members. It shall assist the Chairman in appointments when so requested, suggest programs of work and study to the CCC, plan the agenda of CCC meetings, and implement CCC work between meetings. Minutes of Executive Committee meetings shall be submitted for approval by CCC membership at the regular CCC meeting next following and shall be included in the minutes of the CCC meeting.

B. *Nominating committee*

This committee shall consist of three members who shall be appointed by the Chairman at or before the regular March meeting each year. It shall present a slate of officer nominees at the April meeting of the CCC. The Nominating Committee shall supervise the election of officers provided for in Article IV.

C. *Special committees*

Committees for special purposes will, by formal motion at any CCC meeting, be authorized as needed and appointed as directed. These committees may include members and nonmembers.

D. *Committee procedure*

When a problem has been selected and assigned to a CCC committee for study, the committee shall ask the whole CCC for guidance in developing its work, and shall secure CCC approval for formal contacts with groups inside or outside the Decatur #61 school system. While actual work is the responsibility of the committee, the responsibility for the overall direction a study takes belongs to all CCC members. When the study of a committee appears complete and recommendations to the Board appear indicated, the committee chairman shall send copies of the report detailing the study and recommendations to all CCC members at least five days before the CCC meeting at which it is to be presented for approval. After CCC approval, the CCC Chairman shall arrange with the President of the Board for allocation of time on the agenda of a suitable Board meeting, at which time the CCC will present its report. The CCC Executive Committee and other interested CCC members should be present and may participate in the discussion. A copy of the committee report shall be given the CCC Secretary for the permanent CCC file.

ARTICLE VI–BOARD AND CCC COMMUNICATIONS

A. The agenda of every CCC Meeting shall provide for reports, suggestions, and requests from the Board. The CCC shall request a reciprocal agenda arrangement at Board meetings. A representative reporting from one body to the other shall state whether he speaks on any matter as an individual, a committee representative, or as a spokesman for the Board or the CCC.

B. Recommendations to the Board shall be first approved by action at a CCC meeting, and presented in written form.

C. Requests for special conferences between the Board and the CCC shall be approved by action at a CCC meeting and presented to the Board in written form. This letter shall outline the problem area for discussion and request an appointment.

D. Joint meetings of the Board and the CCC or its committees may be requested by either body, and such meetings shall be held at a time satisfactory to both. The agenda of such meetings shall be proposed by the initiating body.

ARTICLE VII—MEETINGS

A. The CCC shall meet monthly. The date of any regular meeting may be changed, or a meeting omitted, upon majority vote of those present at a CCC meeting. Special meetings shall be at the call of the CCC Chairman. See Article IV, Section B, 1.

B. A quorum shall comprise a majority of the members of the CCC. When a quorum exists, a majority of those present may act.

C. All meetings shall be conducted according to general parliamentary procedure as outlined in Robert's *Rules of Order.*

D. Meetings shall be open to nonmembers by CCC invitation only. The CCC may designate certain meetings to be open to the public.

ARTICLE VIII—PUBLICITY

A. Publicity regarding the work of the CCC or its affiliated committees will be released only after approval by the CCC Executive Committee and the Board of Education or its authorized agent.

B. Recommendations of the CCC to the Board may be released by the Board for public discussion either before or after action is taken on them by the Board.

C. The Board may designate the CCC or its affiliated committees to assist in publicizing and promoting the district policies and proposals approved by both the Board and the CCC.

ARTICLE IX—AMENDMENTS

A. Amendments to this constitution may be proposed at any regular CCC meeting. A written notice of the proposed change and the date of the next regular meeting at which the proposed amendment will be discussed shall be sent to each CCC member, the Board members, and the Superintendent at least two weeks prior to the date of meeting. A favorable vote by a majority of the total membership shall be required to submit the recommendation for change to the Superintendent who will convey said recommendations to the Board at its next regular meeting. Board action on the request shall be conveyed to the CCC in writing by the Secretary of the Board immediately following the meeting in which action is taken.

B. The By-Laws may be amended at any regular meeting by majority vote of the total membership.

BY-LAWS

1. The time of meeting shall be _____ P.M. on the _____ of each month, and the place of meeting shall be _____ _____.

2. The CCC shall request access, through appropriate administrative channels, to pertinent facts and information available in the Superintendent's office or other offices in the school system to assist it in study and evaluation of problems of CCC concern.

3. Such clerical and duplicating services as may be needed by the CCC shall be requested, within reasonable limits, of the Superintendent's office.

4. No indebtedness shall be incurred in the name of the CCC without approval of the Executive Committee, except that the Secretary may incur indebtedness up to three dollars ($3.00) without prior approval.

5. *Program*
   Proposals from the members will be considered by the Executive Committee which will formulate a proposed annual program to be presented to the CCC between March and May of each year for its action.

6. The regular meeting in May shall devote time to the evaluation of the work of the CCC and its affiliated committees during the past year.

7. Each meeting will begin at the announced time and will continue no more than two hours unless by unanimous consent of those present.

Your Voting Precinct _____

CITIZEN QUESTIONNAIRE
(This form not to be signed)

PART I - BACKGROUND INFORMATION
(Mark X for Choice)

1. Parental Status
    ____ (1) Parent of child in Public School
    ____ (2) Parent of child in Private School
    ____ (3) No children in school

2. Schooling
    ____ (4) In Kankakee Public Schools
    ____ (5) Elsewhere

3. Occupation (if housewife give husband's occupation)
    ____ (6) Unskilled or semi-skilled
    ____ (7) Skilled
    ____ (8) Business
    ____ (9) Professional

4. Age
    ____ (10) Under 35
    ____ (11) Between 35 and 65
    ____ (12) Over 65

5. Sex
    ____ (13) Male
    ____ (14) Female

6. Property owner in School Dist. 111
    ____ (15) Yes
    ____ (16) No

PART II - YOUR OPINIONS

This is an attempt to find out what the people in Kankakee think about their public schools. All replies will be treated confidentially and no names will be used. (Mark X for choice)

1. What do you think of the educational program? Would you rate it:

	Grade School	Junior High	Senior High
Excellent	____ (1)	____ (5)	____ (9)
Fair	____ (2)	____ (6)	____ (10)
Poor	____ (3)	____ (7)	____ (11)
Don't know	____ (4)	____ (8)	____ (12)

2. What do you think of the administrative staff of the Kankakee school system? Would you rate it:
    ____ (1) Excellent   ____ (2) Fair   ____ (3) Poor

3. Do you believe the administrative staff to be:
    ____ (1) Understaffed   ____ (2) Overstaffed   ____ (3) About right

4. Do you believe that the teachers of the Kankakee school system, on the whole, are well qualified?
    ____ (1) Yes   ____ (2) No

5. Do you think that Kankakee High School loses too many pupils before they graduate?
    ____ (1) Yes   ____ (2) No   ____ (3) Don't know

6. Are fundamentals (reading, writing, spelling, etc.) adequately learned in the elementary schools?

     ____ (1) Yes   ____ (2) No   ____ (3) Don't know

7. Are fundamentals being learned adequately in the junior high schools?

     ____ (1) Yes   ____ (2) No   ____ (3) Don't know

8. Are fundamentals being learned adequately in the senior high school?

     ____ (1) Yes   ____ (2) No   ____ (3) Don't know

9. Are you satisfied with the Kankakee school system?

     ____ (1) Very well satisfied   ____ (4) Dissatisfied
     ____ (2) Satisfied   ____ (5) Very much dissatisfied
     ____ (3) About half and half   ____ (6) No opinion

10. Do you believe the present double shift system in the high school is good for the students?

     ____ (1) Yes   ____ (2) No

11. Do you believe the buildings of the Kankakee school system are adequate in respect to:

	Adequate Size	Adequate Quality	Adequate Facilities
Grade Schools	____ (1) Yes ____ (2) No	____ (3) Yes ____ (4) No	____ (5) Yes ____ (6) No
Junior High School	____ (7) Yes ____ (8) No	____ (9) Yes ____ (10) No	____ (11) Yes ____ (12) No
Senior High School	____ (13) Yes ____ (14) No	____ (15) Yes ____ (16) No	____ (17) Yes ____ (18) No

12. If you believe additional school buildings are needed check those you believe most badly needed.

     ____ (1) Grade School   ____ (2) Junior High School   ____ (3) Senior High School

13. If you believe additional high school facilities are necessary should they be:

     (a) By adding to the present structure   ____ (1) Yes   ____ (2) No
     (b) By building a second unit in another area   ____ (3) Yes   ____ (4) No
     (c) If your answer is "yes" to (b), should it be located in the
         ____ (5) East   ____ (6) West

14. Do you believe that the Kankakee school system has a problem with overcrowded school rooms?

     ____ (1) Yes   ____ (2) No   ____ (3) Don't know

15. How do you rate the judgment of the Board of Education on running the schools?

     ____ (1) Excellent   ____ (2) Good   ____ (3) Fair   ____ (4) Poor

16. Should the Kankakee school system provide:

    (a) Adult education after regular school hours?   ____ (1) Yes   ____ (2) No

    (b) Adequate academic program for college preparation?   ____ (3) Yes   ____ (4) No

    (c) Vocational program for non-college preparation?   ____ (5) Yes   ____ (6) No

    (d) Creative arts and crafts (painting, drawing, drama, poetry, designing, etc.)?   ____ (7) Yes   ____ (8) No

    (e) Music: Band and Chorus

         Grade School   ____ (9) Yes   ____ (10) No

         Junior High   ____ (11) Yes   ____ (12) No

         Senior High   ____ (13) Yes   ____ (14) No

    (f) Kindergarten program   ____ (15) Yes   ____ (16) No

    (g) Interscholastic sports

         Grade School   ____ (17) Yes   ____ (18) No

         Junior High   ____ (19) Yes   ____ (20) No

         Senior High   ____ (21) Yes   ____ (22) No

17. Should the Kankakee school system provide:

    (a) Specialized instruction for students with mental, physical, or social handicaps?   ____ (1) Yes   ____ (2) No

    (b) Specialized instruction for the gifted students?   ____ (3) Yes   ____ (4) No

    (c) A school lunch program?   ____ (5) Yes   ____ (6) No

    (d) Student driver program?   ____ (7) Yes   ____ (8) No

18. Do you believe there is adequate cooperation and understanding between the Board of Education and school personnel?

     ____ (1) Yes   ____ (2) No   ____ (3) No opinion

19. Do you consider your responsibility to the school system as a continuing one whether or not you have children in school?

     ____ (1) Yes   ____ (2) No

20. If one or the other must be done, should taxes be increased or should school services be cut?

     ____ (1) Strongly feel taxes should be increased   ____ (4) Inclined to feel school services should be cut

     ____ (2) Inclined to feel taxes should be increased

     ____ (3) Not sure   ____ (5) Strongly feel school services should be cut

     ____ (6) No opinion

21. What, if anything, do you think is wrong with the Kankakee schools?

index